D1601278

Cognitive and social action

Rosaria Conte &
Cristiano Castelfranchi
Institute of Psychology,
Italian National Research Council

UCL
PRESS

First published in 1995 by UCL Press

UCL Press Limited
University College London
Gower Street
London WC1E 6BT

The name of University College London (UCL) is a registered trade mark
used by UCL Press with the consent of the owner.

British Library Cataloguing in Publication Data.
A catalogue record for this book is available from the British Library

Library of Congress Cataloging-in-Publication Data are available

ISBN: 1-85728-186-1 HB

Typeset in Sabon.
Printed and bound by
Biddles Ltd., Guildford and King's Lynn, England.

Contents

CONTENTS

Preface

What is the book about?

In this book we aim to explore the role of the external (social) environment in the regulation of cognitive autonomous agents' behaviours. In particular, the following issues are examined:
- how objective conditions and relations regulate social action, i.e., how they determine the agents' knowledge and motivations to act (their beliefs and goals);
- how an autonomous agent becomes an instrument for external forces (an instrument for other agents' needs and requests, as well as for social conventions, norms, laws, etc.).

In other words, when, why and how do external demands *on* one given agent become goals of that agent?

We endeavour to show that cognition is a fundamental medium between individual action and external (social) forces, cognitive medium meaning the mental interpretation and processing of these external forces.

Why read it?

The field of cognitive science has developed as a consequence of the impact of cybernetics and artificial intelligence (AI) on the *human* sciences (linguistics, psychology, logics and philosophy). Computational models and methodologies influence the *social* sciences (sociology, economics, political science, etc.) in many ways. What new disciplinary synthesis will arise from this contamination?

In this book, we claim that a *cross*-fertilization is both possible and desirable. AI can provide the social sciences with conceptual and experimental tools, namely the capacity to model, and make up in parallel, reactive and cognitive systems, and the means to observe their interactions and emerging effects. Therefore, AI is essential for solving the *vexata quaestio* of the relationships between psychology, on the one hand, and economics, sociology and political science on the other. More generally, AI is required in the treatment of the well-known problem of the micro–macro link. Only by representing (either formally or experimentally) agents' internal mechanisms, interactions and global functions can we have a chance to solve this problem in a non-speculative way.

On the other hand, in order for AI to provide a significant contribution, and deal with issues of social theory in a non-naïve way, it must be able to handle social science's typical puzzles and relevant data, and closely approach existing theories.

Who should read it?

- All interested in computer science and its applications, particularly to theories of action and agent architecture, multi-agent systems and distributed AI, computer supported co-operative work (CSCW), etc.
- Cognitive scientists, philosophers and psychologists.
- Social scientists, especially sociologists and theorists of rationality, game-theorists and social simulators.

How should you read it?

For a book on AI, this has too many formal motions and too much theoretical discussion. For a social science text, it is too obsessed with conceptual definition and the challenge of formalization. Its philosophical content lacks references to relevant theoretical debate. However, to transcend the boundaries of all these disciplines, a level of compromise and a relaxation of traditional (subject specific) style have been adopted. In reading the text, it is possible to bypass the formulae (although you are invited to help us to improve them). You could also skim over the discussions and arguments.

We know that there are other hypotheses, but we believe that all hypotheses and proposals cannot simply be tested within the confines of the individual disciplines, and their own standards and criteria. We will feel that we have come some way towards our objective if, on reading this book, psychologists and sociologists start to reformulate some of their own eternal questions in an operational way, or if AI scientists persuade themselves that in order to deal with autonomous (social) agenthood, they should turn to the instruments used by cognitive and social scientists.

Foreword

Those born of more than one cultural or intellectual tradition encounter special opportunities, but face special problems. They have access to a richness of ideas and techniques, but are not quite at home with any of them. They can often see connections, contradictions and opportunities that others miss, but their insights are not easily accepted by those embedded in just one tradition. And so those of mixed ancestry must struggle to be heard and to be permitted to follow their own way.

So it is with this book. Rosaria Conte and Cristiano Castelfranchi are working where ideas from social science, psychology, cognitive science and artificial intelligence meet. They are interested in social cognition and social action, and in the complex linkage between environmental structuring and the micro and the macro phenomena (including phenomena of "emergence") of society. More generally, they are striving to bring rigorous order, insight and development to the study of societies and of action within society – a study domain in which dispute and polemic have always been endemic, and which of late has frequently seen an explicit rejection of science method. Conte and Castelfranchi have built an international reputation by deploying to these ends the new intellectual and technical repertoire of Distributed Artificial Intelligence which has emerged over the past decade.

This is a timely and exciting, but difficult and controversial endeavour. Distributed AI studies the properties of systems and communities of formal or computational agents. In its gift is the ability to explore in precise, repeatable terms the relationship between cognition within agents, and the behaviour of agent communities in particular environmental settings. Realistic models may be created and their implications found by exploiting the computer's ability to handle otherwise intractable amounts of detail. But it has to be said that many, even most, social scientists will find the technical content of such work alien, even ideologically alien, and difficult to assimilate. I encourage such readers of this book to make the effort needed to master it, and to reject the temptation of an easy dismissal on ideological or methodological grounds.

AI specialists will have no similar difficulties. The potential linkage between Distributed AI and social science (analogous to that between AI and psychology) will be apparent to them. The danger, rather, is the naivety of those who believe too easily that their everyday view of society corresponds to reality, or the intellectual elitism of those who insist on formal sophistication even when it is not needed. And even within DAI there are clashes of culture, for there exist two sometimes discordant subtraditions: the formalist and the experimental. These subtraditions Conte and Castelfranchi work to integrate (starting from a more formalist position) and that is one of their achievements.

Distributed AI based formalisations and simulations of society have the potential to open a new and productive dimension to the social sciences. This is more than merely a reworking of general systems theory or mathematical sociology. It is the opportunity to add the previously missing ingredient to precise models – the details of cognition and the internal representations it uses. Conte and Castelfranchi are creatively, skilfully and with determination working to realise this potential. This book reports the end of a fascinating and important beginning.

PROFESSOR JIM DORAN   University of Essex

Acknowledgements

We are grateful to our colleagues Amedeo Cesta and Maria Miceli for their helpful suggestions and kind encouragement. Many ideas presented in this book have been discussed together, and several hypotheses in some way or another refer to a common research program.

We would also like to thank Phil Cohen for his precious comments; Gianni Amati, for his priceless and expert help about the formal aspects of the work; Nigel Gilbert, who encouraged this enterprise; Domenico Parisi, for supporting our research program; Ian McGilvray for his patient and understanding language revision; and all the anonymous reviewers of UCL Press, for their useful comments.

ROSARIA CONTE & CRISTIANO CASTELFRANCHI

Introduction

Socially bounded autonomy

This book deals with a paradox concerning social agenthood, namely the paradox of bounded autonomy. On one hand, the social world provides inputs to the agents' goals. On the other, social agents are autonomous, that is, endowed with the capacity to generate and pursue their own goals. How is it possible that an autonomous agent's goals be inputted from the outside? This is the dilemma we will deal with.

We intend to deal with this dilemma by proposing an integrated approach. By this we mean an approach to social action where the **cognitive modelling** is intimately combined with an account of the non-cognitive or **extracognitive causes**.

By *cognitive modelling* we mean an explicit account of the cognitive, that is, symbolic representations and the operations performed upon them, involved in mental activities including understanding, problem-solving, (social) reasoning and planning, communicating, interacting, and many forms of learning.

The *extracognitive causes* include the objective, structural relationships between agents located in a **common world,** and the functional mechanisms underlying, for example, the spread of conventions or the formation of elementary forms of co-operation.

Finally, an **agent** is defined as a **goal-governed system.** By this, we mean an entity, not necessarily autonomous, that has the capacity to act upon the external world in order to reduce the discrepancy between the world itself and some regulatory state that is somehow represented within the entity. Such a representation does not need to be a cognitive representation. Agents are not necessarily cognitive systems (see Fig. 1). There are as many different kinds of agents as there are kinds of goals. Agents vary as a function of the type and level of **goal** achieved. However, when speaking of agents, we shall be referring to cognitive systems, unless otherwise specified.

We will propose a model of **social action** as a multi-level phenomenon emerging from the interaction among cognitive agents, a **cognitive agent** being defined as an agent endowed with cognitive representations of goals and

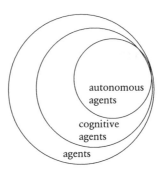

Figure 1 Types of agents.

the capacity to pursue them. The stress here is on both emergence and cognition. These two concepts are sometimes considered to be incompatible, and the theories based upon them to be complementary (cf. the controversy between conventional Artificial Intelligence (AI), aimed at building cognition into the systems, on one hand, and neural nets and Artificial Life (AL) studies, used to observe the **emergent properties** of **subcognitive systems**, on the other). On the contrary, and in line with the scientists dealing with the study of social and political networks (cf. Knoke 1990), we strongly maintain that (social) action never occurs *in vacuo*, but in a complex network of pre-existing conditions and relations. Consequently, our main claim is that cognitive social action is derived from, and can be predicted on the grounds of, pre-existing conditions and relations. AL would provide a strong methodological potential for exploring the emergence of social and cultural processes. Unfortunately, however, AL studies usually deal with subcognitive agents, and to explore the emergent effects of interaction among cognitive agents is at present beyond the scope of this area of investigation.

Indeed, an adequate theory of social action *ought* to allow a step-by-step reconstruction of the process by means of which intelligent agents decide to take a given course of action. A cognitive scientist is but a sort of unknown spelaeologist unearthing layer after layer of the complex roots and reasons of agenthood. However, let us warn against a possible misunderstanding caused by the spelaeological metaphor: to dig out the objective history of agenthood does not mean to bring to light only its most remote causes, such as its biological foundations. This is one fundamental and interesting direction of study which should always be taken into account while investigating the behaviour of complex systems, but there is another direction that is essential, especially for modelling social agents: to explore the footprints that a **multi agent system** (MAS)(social system or macro-system) leaves not only on the behaviour of its component members[1], but also in their **minds**; to examine how a social system is embedded or incorporated into the behaviour of its members; to reconstruct how the social system works through its members. But what is meant by saying that a social system works through its members?

Before addressing this question, let us say that a social system is viewed here as an aggregate of agents that produce some effects in the world, acting *as if* their action were goal-governed.

The idea that a social system and, more generally, the social environment are incorporated into the characteristics of the agents involved, is not a new one. Let us examine, in very broad terms, three main formulations of this idea:

(a) The *building through interaction* formulation, very popular in the 1960s, according to which the social systems are viewed as macro-uniformities produced by a mass of interpreted interactions (Berger & Luckmann 1966, Blumer 1969). Rules and norms are not imposed on the agents from the outside, but are negotiated by the interacting agents (Garfinkel 1967). Any social interaction, therefore, "effects a form of social organization" (Schegloff 1987: 207).

(b) The theory of the *social shaping of the mind*, implying that cognitive structures and processes are shaped by objective social and material conditions. This view, introduced in the 1930s by the Soviet school of psychology (Vygotsky, Leontiev, Luria, etc.), has strongly influenced cognitive, developmental and social psychologists. From the 1970s, a large number of studies have been conducted (cf. Cole et al. 1971, Scribner 1975, Cole et al. 1978; cf. Riegel & Meacham 1975) into the impact of literacy and the school education system on cognitive development. Gradually, this view has led to a somewhat generic assumption of learning and cognition as necessarily social processes (Suchman 1987, Resnick et al. 1990).

(c) The hypothesis of the *mental implementation of the social systems*, which is closer to formulation (b), at least in its earlier version, than it is to formulation (a); it extends and enriches the theory of shaping, and claims that the social system not only shapes cognition by virtue of some sort of side-effect, but also influences directly, and sometimes even explicitly, the behaviour of its members by modifying their cognition. More explicitly, it is claimed that a social system achieves a purpose by means of its members' actions, and therefore through their minds. By an agent's mind, we do not necessarily mean a cognitive apparatus, in the sense previously defined, but any regulatory mechanism which allows the agent to achieve its goals however represented.

We believe the latter hypothesis is crucial for an adequate theory of the **micro–macro link**, that is, a theory of the connections between the macro-social systems and their members. Indeed, our main questions are as follows:

(a) how can a social system regulate the behaviours of its members? How can these behaviours adapt to the macro-system goals?

(b) Does answering (a) imply that the minds of the micro-systems are able to represent explicitly the macro-system's goals? Or, do micro-systems' goals and plans happily coincide with the macro-system's? Our answer to both these questions is: not necessarily!

(c) What is the relationship between the macro-system's goals and the goals represented inside the agents, that directly and actually regulate their actions?

We will briefly examine the main solutions that have been proposed to such questions, and then clarify how we intend to approach the micro–macro link problem, and what type of contribution to a solution of this problem the work presented in this book is intended to provide.

The problem of the micro–macro link

The micro–macro link problem, a classical problem of the social sciences, was raised again during the 1980s (e.g. by Alexander et al. 1987). Despite this renewal of interest, we are still far from a satisfactory solution.

As Manicas (1987) states, the recent debate on the philosophy of the social sciences shows a strong polarization between a subjectivist and an objectivist view of the relation between agents and the **social structures**[2]. Owing to the objectivist view, the social scientific explanation has often been reduced to the methods and aims of "social research", and therefore to a statistical investigation aimed at quantifying, rather than explaining, the social facts. While this view has depicted social reality as a desert, a world without agents, the subjectivist view has been plagued with the ghost of philosophical idealism.

An overview of this polarization and of the existing models relating the micro- and macro- levels is beyond the scope of this introduction. There are several insightful and comparatively complete presentations of these models (apart from Manicas, a couple of very good examples are offered by Giesen (1987), and Muench and Smelser (1987)). What we propose is an unbalanced analysis guided by specific research aims. Notably, we will endeavour to show the inadequate treatment of cognition in current solutions to the problem of the micro–macro link.

The hypercognitive solution

Although we think cognition is essential for an understanding of the micro–macro link, we believe it is not sufficient. In our view, the role of cognition has sometimes been overestimated owing precisely to a fallacious view of cognition. In what Manicas calls the subjectivist view, we envisage a *hyper-cognitive view* of the relation between micro and macro. In Chapter 1 we will show that this view of social agents is also shared within the social studies conducted in AI.

Undoubtedly, a necessary *agent revolution* has been accomplished by some thinkers (phenomenologists, such as Schutz, ethnomethodologists such as

Garfinkel, Schegloff and Cicourel, critical thinkers, such as Habermas and Ricoeur, and hermeneutic philosophers, such as Gadamer, and so forth). These authors have the great merit of having restored the social world to the agents. However, many of these authors view the social agent as fundamentally involved in the understanding and interpreting of the macro-social structures, up to the point that the social structure itself is believed to be accessible only through the mental representations of the agents. The following misunderstandings occur:

(a) the *process of construction* of social reality on the part of the social agent has been equated to the process of understanding it. We now believe this equation to be unclear and generic. What aspects of the constructed object are known? Are all the effects introduced by this construction necessarily predicted by the agents?

(b) Moreover, *what type of understanding and knowledge* is being considered? This is, perhaps, the most important question. Undoubtedly, some sort of *procedural* knowledge is necessarily possessed by the agents. This knowledge includes some fundamental rules and routines that allow the agents to interact adaptively with their (social) environment. However, this does not imply that the agents have an *explicit* representation of such knowledge. Consequently, why should they be considered as the primary, indeed the only, source of information about the social structures?

Be it underestimated, as in quantitative social research, or overestimated, as in the subjectivist approach, the implicit or explicit characterization of cognition that is found in social scientific literature is essentially inadequate. Cognition is seen as a theory, a reconstruction, an *interpretation* of a given piece of reality rather than as a necessary ingredient for *acting* upon it. Members of the social systems are *observers* who categorize and interpret the (social) world, rather than *agents* who explore it in order to take advantage of or adjust themselves to it. Social cognition is equated to social theory, and the social agent is likened to the social scientist.

The rational solution

Theorists and philosophers of rationality and game theorists did not have to go through the agent revolution. They did not need to be reminded of the central role of the individual agent. Theories of rationality are based upon a methodological individualistic assumption, according to which phenomena at the macro-level can probably be accounted for by properties and features at the micro-level (Watkins 1952). Based on this assumption, theorists of rationality and game theorists have attempted (not always successfully) to explain all sorts of macro-phenomena, such as political action, norms, etc. as emergent properties of rational individual choices.

However, the treatment of cognition proposed by the theory of rationality is no more adequate than that proposed by the hypercognitive solution. To re-phrase Elster's notion of *subversion of rationality* (1985), we could say that the theory of rationality has produced a substantial *subversion of cognition*.

In fact, according to the theory of rationality, autonomous, self-interested decision-making is explained in terms of the **rational choice principle**, that is, in terms of the maximum expected utility. Given two options, a rational agent is expected to choose the one which ensures the maximum outcome compared with the relative probability of occurrence. This fundamental mechanism is essential for explaining decision-making processes, but it is neither the only, nor the primary motor of deciding systems. Agents are *not* moved to action by the principle of maximum utility, although their actions are controlled by this principle. Actions are motivated by needs, desires, etc. In a word, they are directed towards realizing specific *goals*.

Conversely, in the theory of rationality, *the agent's goals are ignored*. In AI and cognitive science, the agent is a *planning* system, and goals are essential for explaining why and how actions are planned. But in the theory of rationality, agents are not seen as planning systems and their actions are explained directly in terms of the rational choice principle (Binmore 1987, Luce & Raiffa 1989, Rasmusen 1990). In particular, in game theory, which can be defined as a theory of rationality applied to situations involving more than one agent, the agents' social goals, the agents' reasons for actively engaging in social actions, are ignored. Therefore, while macro-social phenomena are allowed to emerge from the agents' choices, the mental mechanisms of micro-interactions are taken for granted. They always pre-exist and explain the macro-social level, but are never shown to be produced or influenced by it. Essentially, the mental mechanisms are considered irrelevant by game theorists for explaining rational social choice. Let us make a short digression to examine more concretely the model of agent implicit in game theory.

Given perfectly rational agents, game theory can predict the point where no agent unilaterally "wishes" to change his choice. Consider the famous story of the prisoners' dilemma. Two fellows, responsible for a given common crime, are taken to jail. Each of them, separately, is given the chance to confess his crime. They both know that if neither confesses both will get off fairly lightly. Alternatively, if they both confess, each will be sentenced to a more severe punishment. But if one keeps silent while the other confesses, the former will be set free, while the latter will receive the maximum punishment. The classical pay-off matrix of the prisoners' dilemma (PD) game is shown in Table 1 (reproduced from Ullman-Margalit 1977:18), where D stands for Defeat (confess) and C for Co-operation (not confess). The most rational choice for each player is to play Defeat when the opponent has played Co-operation. Moreover, the action D always dominates the action C for both players. This can be easily shown in mathematical terms: for each player, playing D *dominates* (that is, gives a better outcome than) playing C

Table 1   The Prisoners' Dilemma.

		Player 2 C		Player 2 D	
Player 1	C	1	1	−2	2
	D	2	−2	−1	−1

not only when the opponent plays D (−1 > −2) but also when the opponent plays C as well (2 > 1). The DD situation (bottom right cell) is an equilibrium in the sense that if any player unilaterally deviates from that choice, he will be worse off. The consequent obvious question is how a co-operative answer can be made possible.

Now, this scenario shows a fundamental gap in the game theoretic account of social action. Although very elegant, the prisoners' dilemma structure is irrelevant precisely as far as its specific aim, i.e. to explain the *social* choice, is concerned. It is irrelevant not because it is unnatural, or not primarily for this reason, but because its unnatural structure allows for a rather peculiar type of social action rather than a most *general*, ideal type. Let us define the game theoretic social action as a choice between alternative courses of action the convenience of which for a rational agent depends on the choices actually made by the other agents involved in the same situation. As Axelrod (1984) says, there is no *a priori* best strategy, since the success of a strategy depends upon what the other players do after its application. A game theoretic social action is by definition a *strategic action*, or more precisely an individual action accompanied by a *strategic belief*. It helps avoid **negative interference** and optimize co-ordination in all those situations in which an agent ought to anticipate the others' doings. A typical game theoretic situation is found in car traffic, where each driver ought to predict the behaviour of the other drivers and regulate his own accordingly. The game-theoretic structure does not account for social action aimed at modifying the behaviour and mental states of other agents. This type of social action is at least as important as the game-theoretic one. It plays a fundamental role in social life. Without it, it is impossible to account for the most elementary forms of interaction. Indeed, even in traffic we do not limit ourselves to monitoring other drivers and their intentions. We try to influence them by blowing our horn, flashing our lights, speeding up in order not to be passed, and calling other drivers names. More interestingly, we often try to guess what the other car is going to do in order to prevent or take advantage of its move rather than simply adjust ourselves to it.

Concisely, the game-theoretic agent is not governed by any truly *social* goal[3], but only by a rational principle of choice supported by social, namely strategic, beliefs.

To get back to the micro–macro link problem, the rational solution explains how macro-social behaviours emerge from micro-social behaviours, i.e. from rational action. Two orders of questions are left unexplained:

(a) *Why do agents engage in social action in its most general form?* What are the internal mechanisms regulating it?

(b) How are micro-interactions influenced by the macro-social phenomena? Moreover, *is the agents' minds modified under the influence of the macro-social level*, and if so, *how* does this happen?

In sum, neither the hypercognitive view nor the rational view seems to account for *how* the two-way link is realized, how society directs the agents' behaviours through their minds, by acting upon their minds. In other words, neither theory accounts for the mediatory role played by the agents' cognition.

The dialectic solution

Undoubtedly, a fundamental step forward in the attempt to construct a model of the two-way link between micro-level and macro-level is represented by the *theory of structuration* (Giddens 1984). This theory points to a fundamental, substantive *circularity* between society, on one hand, and the social action, on the other. The societal properties – resources, habits and institutions – are embedded in social action, and structure it. Social action, on the other hand, reproduces the structuring properties of society, thus contributing to the reproduction of society. As Gilbert (in press) observes, this "*dense* and possibly *opaque* statement of the theory" needs explanation (our italics).

Again, this is not the place for an attempt to clarify Giddens' claims. Rather, we shall endeavour to provide some contribution in the direction suggested by Giddens. In particular, we shall claim and, hopefully, demonstrate that *cognition is the medium of the theory of structuration*. Of course, in this context cognition is to be understood as distinct from, and weaker than, awareness: a cognitive representation is not necessarily conscious. Cognitive agents are not always aware of their cognitive representations and processes. Holding such a general view of cognition, we dare say that the two-way link between the structuring properties of society and social action is allowed precisely by the cognitive endowment of the social agents.

Cognition as a medium between micro and macro

Giddens indicates the notion of structuration as being the only possible direction of development of the theory of the micro–macro link. However, while convincingly advocating a two-way account of this issue, he does not, could not perhaps, provide a model of *how* this two-way link is realized. He could not provide it precisely because his is not a cognitive theory!

We believe that the micro–macro link is not a *two-fold* issue: it is not simply a matter of relating macro-structures and micro-interactions, society and action, as many social scientists, including Giddens, seem to think. In our conception, it is a *three-faceted* issue, including (a) external forces and structures, (b) agents' cognition, and (c) their actions. Cognition plays a fundamental linking role between the external forces and the agents' behaviours. Let us be more explicit.

(a) Unlike scientists of rationality, we believe that cognition reflects and *embodies* in various ways objective pre-conditions, societal prescriptions and institutions, and reinforcing effects. *Cognition is undoubtedly structured by society*. The question is, how is this possible?

(b) Unlike what is implied by the hypercognitive solution, however, *not all social structuring properties are explicitly represented in the agents' minds*. Some (functional effects) are not represented at all. In any case, what sort of representation is implied and what is it implied for? What use are the different representations?

(c) *Macro-social phenomena may emerge*, unintentionally, from *micro-interactions*. However, there are three considerations:

– Emergence is not the only possible explanation of the origins of macro-phenomena. Often, macro-phenomena are deliberately set up and, of course, the question becomes how and why is this possible?

– Macro-social phenomena not only directly emerge from behaviours, they also derive from the agents' cognitive representations and states. For example, while conventions directly emerge from behaviours, other types of norms necessarily presuppose some specific cognitive objects, which we call normative beliefs and goals (see Ch. 6).

– The direction of emergence is not necessarily from micro to macro. Macro-phenomena may unintentionally feed back into micro-phenomena, as happens with the functional effects of actions.

As initially stated, we consider those aspects addressed by functional-structuralists that we have called extracognitive causes of social actions (i.e. the objective pre-conditions of social actions and their effects, including functional effects) to be of vital importance. We consider of primary interest the study of the macro-social forces, which direct and regulate the agents' behaviours. Unfortunately, ever since the decline of functional-structuralism, social scientists have been burdened with a mistaken feeling of guilt, much as happens to many people nowadays. A number of social scientists are now *repentant* structuralists. This is understandable, since any statement concerning the aims of social systems and institutions can be charged with reification. Nonetheless, we maintain that only by subscribing to a view of social systems as systems that somehow guide the behaviours of their members can a theory of micro–macro be handled adequately.

What is needed is a theory of

(a) how the macro-social system is implemented in the agents, and how it

works through their minds. That is, a theory of:
- *cognitive shaping*, or in other words, the reasons and processes by means of which the agents acquire beliefs and goals from external social sources;
- *behavioural shaping*, especially the functional mechanisms of reinforcement;

(b) how macro-social phenomena may be derived from micro-interactions.

In this book, we will endeavour to provide some contributions to point (a), that is, to modelling some aspects of cognitive shaping, and in particular, how agents acquire beliefs and goals:
- from objective pre-conditions;
- from one another;
- from the macro-social system (e.g. normative beliefs and goals).

Some very preliminary and partial contributions also include:
- a reconsideration of the notion of social function;
- some working hypotheses for a model of how collective entities can be derived from relations among the agents;
- some general, unifying concepts (such as goal, agent, etc.) and hints for their application at different levels of abstraction.

Distributed Artificial Intelligence (DAI) for the social sciences

Our point of view is that of cognitive scientists interacting with artificial intelligence (AI) and more generally with computer science. For the latter, we are mainly concerned with the computer-based simulation of social processes and phenomena, whereas for AI we are especially interested in the subfields of DAI, that is, in the research and design of systems whose performance is distributed over a number of units interacting with one another and with a central unit, if any. We are also involved in research on so-called multi-agent systems (MAS), where a number of separate programs are modelled as *agents* moving and acting in a common environment. Furthermore, we share to some extent the application of the logics of action to the modelling of communication and interaction that is now common in AI. Finally, we are interested in various applicative, AI-based domains, such as human–computer interaction (HCI), computer-supported co-operative work (CSCW), and so on.

Our criteria of analysis are suggested by specific research aims and conditioned by a definite methodological option. We aim to provide explicit, formal models of social action that could be translated into computational models. Therefore, one of the main objectives of this book is to get cognitive science and AI to interact with the social sciences.

So far, the co-operation between the social sciences and AI has been essentially one-way, from the former to the latter. In AI social studies, the outstanding topics (negotiation, commitment, co-operation, co-ordination, etc.) as well as some general theories (game theory and, more generally, decision theory) come from sociology, economics, and political science. The very characterization of the social agent, the most recurrent social agent model, draws upon one or other of the ideas circulating within the social sciences. (Think of the model of rationality, on one hand, and the hypercognitive view, on the other. The former is largely shared by DAI scientists, and the latter has an extensive influence on the logics of action, as will be shown in Chapter 1.)

Conversely, the way back from AI to the social sciences has not produced impressive effects. The main result is technological and applicative. The spread of AI technologies has drawn the attention of a number of social scientists who, in the last decade or so, have been investigating the micro- and macro-social consequences of this massive technological revolution. This investigation, however, had only a minor impact on the methodological and theoretical aspects of the social sciences.

We question precisely whether DAI, and more generally AI social studies, could somehow contribute to an approach to some of the problems that the social sciences are now facing. Our working hypothesis is that AI can provide a methodological contribution which, indeed, may have an additional theoretical import; the agent modelling and make-up for implementing useful systems in various domains of application. More precisely, AI and computer science may provide:

- *concepts and theoretical instruments* (see, for example, the notion of planning, goals, problem-solving, etc.; theories of knowledge representation; and so forth)
- *a methodological, namely experimental, apparatus* (applications of models to the construction of artificial systems; computer simulations for testing hypotheses; different types of formal languages, etc.)

However simplified for reasons of computational feasibility, AI-based agent modelling implies the designing of a (social) mind; of a more or less complex regulatory apparatus that mediates between the performance of the system and the requests and expectations of the user/designer. Therefore, AI represents an occasion and provides the external, applicative, motivation for designing and realizing one (or more) minds and observing their functionalities. No other discipline, psychology included, has ever focused upon such an objective.

Prescriptive vs. descriptive

Sometimes, AI is used for cheating. It is an ambiguous discipline: it is hard to say to what extent it is (or aims to be) a *science* and to what extent it is pure *technology* (engineering). According to the circumstances, AI scientists choose the most convenient self-presentation, the best façade.

The poor person intending to discuss (D)AI models from a cognitive and/or social science perspective finds himself in an awkward position: if he objects that the models proposed are too idealized and do not account for many interesting empirical situations (explained within other disciplines), he will be told that his arguments are "irrelevant". AI scientists answer or dodge this kind of objection by claiming that they do not intend to describe "natural facts": their discipline is not descriptive. However, if (D)AI scientists maintain a *prescriptive*, rather than *descriptive,* purpose, they will certainly find an audience in such disciplines as operational research, economics, decision theory, and game theory, but they will tell us little about how and why human agents and groups work. Their contribution to cognitive and social science will be radically limited. Indeed, artificial agents can and should be designed to be rational, but they should also be integrated into human organizations, and be capable of interacting with their human partners in an adaptive and understandable way. Is this possible without an understanding of the effective human interactions, without some representation and reasoning about the human co-operative work?

Presentation of the volume

This book is a concrete representation of the micro–macro link problem. It should have been written *twice*; the first version ought to have addressed the way up, from the objective conditions of social action to its effects, and the second version ought to examine the way back, from effects to social action again. But since a book can be written only *once*, we decided to set an arbitrary beginning and an end to what in fact is a circle. Some moving back and forth could not be avoided and this has probably caused some repetition, for which we apologise. The effort to show concretely how the two-way direction of causation works in social action is meant to be one of the main contributions of this book.

The book includes four parts and a concluding chapter. In each part, a different type of external input to one agent's goals will be examined.

In the first part, inert **objective pre-conditions** of social action will be defined and discussed (Ch. 1). Furthermore, different types of social actions will be shown to be predicted on the grounds of those pre-conditions (Ch. 2).

In the second part, further input to one agent's goals will be identified in the other agents' requests, and more generally in their goals (Ch. 3). Further input, consistent with the preceding one, is represented by the other agents' interests, that is, objective states facilitating their achievements (Ch. 4). The major question that will be addressed is: On what conditions and why do autonomous agents comply with others' requests and adopt their goals?

In the third part, a special type of external input to one agent's goals will be addressed, namely the normative prescriptions. A two-sided notion of normative prescriptions will be proposed (Ch. 5) to consist of one external or social side, and the other internal or mental. A model of the mental side of norms will be presented (Ch. 6), and aspects of the **normative decision-making**, namely some factors leading to obedience or transgression, will be accounted for (Ch. 7).

In the final part of the book, a further external input will be identified in the functional effects of social action that close the micro–macro circle. Functional effects are emergent effects of action that select the action itself by reproducing it. This part will be introduced by a general chapter that proposes and discusses the unifying notion of **external goals** (Ch. 8), which can be applied at different levels of abstraction and identify the similarities between providing inputs to the goals of other agents, on one hand, and selecting or shaping the features of entities, be they goal-governed or inert (as physical objects) on the other. The notion of social **finality** as a mechanism which provides a feedback to social action from its effects will be reconsidered (Ch. 9). Some working hypotheses about the formation of a **collective agent**, and the definition of a **collective mind** will be put forward (Ch. 10).

In the concluding chapter (Ch. 11), some potentialities of the work presented in the book for computer-based research and applications will be examined. In particular, already implemented systems based on one or other aspect of our theoretical work will be presented; possible applications in several AI subfields (such as DAI, MAS research and design, CSCW, AI collaborative design, etc.). Finally, current and future applications of our work in the field of **social simulation**, that is, the computer-based simulation of social processes and phenomena, are explored.

The formal expression

We will briefly present the formalism that will be used throughout the book, and discuss its limits and deficiencies, and the role it is designed to play within our approach.

About the term "formal"

The present work includes the use of a formalism derived from Cohen and Levesque's (1990b) language.

However, here the term **formal** is meant in a more general sense than is implied by the use of a mathematical or logic-based language. By this term, we mean something very similar to what is meant by Ullman-Margalit (1977: 6–7), that is to say, as referring to the *abstract* and *structural* aspects of the situations of study. As a consequence, concrete, idiosyncratic aspects of the phenomena will be ignored.

Furthermore, by "formal" we mean explicit, consistent, controllable and unequivocal, or almost unequivocal, ways of expressing thoughts.

Read or jump the formulae: which is more convenient?

This book has been written in such a way that the reader who is unfamiliar with this or any other type of formalism, or is unwilling to make the effort to become familiar with it, can imperfectly follow the reasoning. Formulae are always justified and translated into verbal expressions.

However, we believe that those readers who, being unhappy with logic-based formalization as social thinkers often are, tend to ignore it, give up a fundamental function of control over the scientific production. The longer the social scientists indulge in informal argument, the longer other disciplines, decision theory and AI for example, will be allowed to re-discover social issues, re-formulate social theories, and so on, without receiving any control from social science. As a consequence, important phenomena may be ignored or oversimplified, and biases and fallacies will be presented as necessary constraints to reduce the problems' degrees of freedom. This is precisely what has happened with the market-like model of co-operation, which enjoyed huge popularity in DAI's early studies.

Social theory can no longer afford informal argument. Whether we like it or not, social issues are increasingly relevant to technological applications. Why leave the ground laid open to everybody but the social thinker?

In the following, we will discuss general issues concerning logic-based formalization. In the Appendix (pp. 185–90), we provide more specific information, as well as definitions, assumptions and rules, which may interest the reader and that are necessary in order to understand the formulae contained in the rest of the book.

Our formalism

In agreement with a general view of logic, especially that prevailing in some AI subfields, such as MAS research and models of rational interaction and communication, we believe logical instruments to be necessary to express unequivocally certain notions and to infer true consequences from true premises. However, our reliance on logical formalism is a cautious one, since we are also aware that this formalism sometimes disrupts implicit knowledge and theories, forcing them into strict expressions that do not do justice to the underlying insights. In other words, formalism sometimes precedes and prevents full theorizing, even without the theorist being aware of it. When this happens, and anyone who is familiar with the working out of formal models must acknowledge that *it does happen*, fortunate insights may be wasted. On the other hand, without any control over formalism, vague definitions, obscure concepts and trivial thoughts may easily be passed off as insightful contributions.

In our work, logical tools have so far not been used for proper theorem-proving. In particular, the deductions presented in the book have *not* been proved. Although reasonable and apparently sound, they are still hypothetical. In any case, we challenge the idea that (logical) formalism is fundamentally aimed at theorem-proving. The latter is certainly an important aspect of the scientific explanation. But, in our view, it is neither the only nor the most important task. A primary objective ought to be to provide good concepts, clear notions, and heuristic categories of description. Logical instruments are essential for concepts and categories of description to be defined in a rigorous, explicit, concise and controllable way.

Such theorizing and describing is aimed at producing computational models, and therefore at designing and constructing systems performing tasks in accordance with theoretical expectations.

As the reader will soon realize, however, the formalism – essentially a first-order language with operators for beliefs, goals, obligations and sequences of actions by means of which we will express most notions and deductions – does not allow a direct computationalization of the model. This should not be considered as a limitation of the work, however, for two main reasons:

(a) the *translation of the formal and pre-formal models presented here into computational models proved feasible*, as is shown in Chapter 11, where some computational models and some implemented systems are presented schematically;

(b) moreover, *the formal or pre-formal tools employed here proved useful in the modelling of social action*; they seem to help elucidate a number of theoretical issues that are computationally premature but may have potential for improving the performance of systems.

An example will probably help clarify this issue. Consider the DAI systems for co-ordination and problem-solving based upon contract-nets, that is, communication modules where any contractor unit which needs co-operation can send out requests, and bidders, if any, will send back messages of acceptance. The problem is how to deal with the communication overhead that characterizes these systems. Now, an explicit model of the structural relationships holding among the members of a MAS allows the interdependencies and the mutual utilities of these members to be predicted, and hence to channel the agents' search for help (Miceli & Cesta 1993, Sichman et al. 1994b) at the same time avoiding unnecessary communication overhead. What is only one of the possible side-effects of structural relationships in natural systems becomes a primary objective in artificial ones. Generally speaking, natural systems are *multi-purpose* entities trying to gain as much as they can from the external conditions. The study of natural facts and systems provides insightful ideas for the implementation of artificial systems provided it is not governed by the aims of applicative problem-solving and system optimization, but is rather applied to such aims.

PART ONE

From structural pre-conditions to micro-level action

CHAPTER ONE
Precognitive bases of social interaction

The cognitive cart and the social horse

A fundamental misconception has pervaded the social sciences, and is also reflected in the social studies carried on in AI. It is a static, non-emergent view of micro-interactions. Social needs and capabilities are taken for granted, either because they are inherent in the structure of the situation investigated (think of game theory), or because they are built into the agents (think, again, of the strategic beliefs found in game theory and, more generally, in the theory of rationality). This statement may appear unwarranted given the impressive number of game-theoretic studies about the *emergence of co-operation*. However, co-operation and other positive social phenomena are considered as emergent macro-effects of micro-interactions, the latter being essentially taken for granted.

An analogous consideration should be made with regard to the social studies conducted within the field of AI. Over the last decade, AI has certainly taken on a significant role within cognitive science and has usefully contributed to a general theory of intelligence and of cognitive processes. Unfortunately, this is not true of social studies in AI. Indeed, none of HCI, MAS research, and CSCW are good candidates for working out a general theory of the bases and reasons for social relations and interactions.

In the following, we will examine some reasons underlying this evaluation, which seem to apply both to the theory of rationality and to social AI.

Pre-established social architectures vs. emergent sociality

One of the major concerns of game theorists is with the development of conventions as useful social solutions to problems of co-ordination (see also Ch. 5 for treatment of this aspect of game theory). AI social studies have inherited the game-theoretic emphasis on the problem of co-ordination. These studies often presuppose a common task, a pre-established co-operativeness, a collective intelligence and capability for problem-solving. It is of course true that one of the problems under study in DAI is precisely how collective or

decentralized control is achieved in a distributed problem-solving (DPS) system (Lesser & Corkill 1987, Durfee et al. 1987a,b). However, what is usually presupposed in DAI is a need for co-ordination. In other words, in a DPS system agents must objectify themselves to see where they fit in a co-ordinated process (Bond & Gasser 1988). The underlying idea is that co-ordination must be already *there* and agents must fit in it.

Owing to applicative reasons, AI is concerned with optimizing communication as well as with task and resource allocation among intelligent co-operative agents. Of course, task allocation may be addressed either *statically*, by a designer, or *dynamically* (see, again, Bond & Gasser 1988) by a set of agents which may use specific methods, such as **contracting** (Parunak 1987, Malone 1988). But even in this type of dynamic approach, tasks and roles are pre-established, and the matching between agents and available roles is a matter of negotiation (Malone 1987, Gasser 1988).

In short, agent co-operativeness is taken for granted, and there is little interest in a *radically bottom-up approach*. This type of approach basically consists of situating intelligent autonomous agents, endowed with cognitive capabilities and endogenous goals, in a common world, and letting them (inter)act. This is perhaps the only viable way for an observer to discover the agents' needs for sociality, be it co-operative or competitive, without presupposing them.

In a gradualistic approach of this kind, the weight of objective relations among agents, and between each agent and the external world, becomes more evident. Of course, even in some areas of DAI and MAS agents are involved in objective structural relationships (blackboards, global planner, contract-net). But these are special architectures provided by the designer. The resulting social structures are then compulsorily co-operative: co-operation does not emerge from agents' goals and interactional practice.

The hypercognitive fallacy

When agents are not forced into a pre-established co-operative architecture, they are conceived of in terms of what, in the introduction, we called a *hypercognitive view*. Therefore, while AI has inherited from game theory the emphasis on the problem of co-ordination, it has also inherited the hypercognitive fallacy from phenomenological, post-Wittgensteinian social theory. The following features seem to characterize such a view, although they do not necessarily co-occur in each model:

(a) *Lack of a dynamic perspective*: agents are so fully aware of the conditions under which they interact, that evolutionary steps of social actions are substantially ignored. It is to be noted that joint intentions are usually derived from individual intentions (Levesque et al. 1990), and the question is raised of why it is rational for agents to form joint commitments

(Cohen & Levesque 1991), whereas what is rational for the group is assumed to be rational for the agent (Rosenschein & Genesereth 1988). Even in such an attempt, however, **precognitive relations** – that is, objective relations neither wanted nor believed by the involved agents – are ignored: joint action is reduced to the mental states of the participants, namely to a "shared mental state", which is not derived, but simply postulated.

(b) *Social subjectivism*: social relationships are investigated only inasmuch as they are mentally represented, that is, only starting from what are considered as social goals and beliefs (agent believes and wants what others believe and want). This feature is linked to the preceding one.

(c) *Emphasis on communication*: as a consequence of previous features, social action is only conceived of in terms of communication aimed at modifying current beliefs and goals (Winograd & Flores 1986, Galliers 1988, Werner 1989, Cohen et al. 1990).

As opposed to both forced co-operation and the hypercognitive view of agents, we are likely to view social action as an emergent phenomenon. Indeed, if intelligent autonomous agents are placed in a common world, social relations are likely to emerge automatically and implicitly among them. Over time, these relations will have an impact on the agents' actions and mental attitudes. A multi-level – cognitive and extracognitive – pattern of social action and relation then emerges.

To work out a formal model of the objective relations is relevant not only to social theory but also, owing to the predictive power of such a model, to applicative aims. For example, a way of reducing the explosion of agents' communications in a DPS network implies making predictions on the grounds of their objective relations: given certain situations of dependence and concurrence among (some) agents, it is possible to foresee what kinds of interactions will take place, what messages will be send to whom, and for which goals.

In this chapter, a preliminary model of different types of *objective relationships* among cognitive agents is put forward. In the next chapter, an attempt is made to predict some fundamental types of cognitive social interactions.

Society is out there, and not only in the mind

Our main aim is to argue for the study of extracognitive social relations. More specifically, we believe that the following aspects ought to be investigated:

(a) *Objective bases* of social interaction. Any relation occurring either between two (or more) agents or between one single agent and the external physical world is defined as objective. To assess whether a relation is objective we must take the stance of a non-participant observer (namely, the scientist's point of view): objective relations are those relations that are described in the observer's mind, but not necessarily in the involved agents'.

(b) *Emergent finalities* (extracognitive as well) of actions intended and planned by cognitive agents.

Elsewhere (Ch. 9), we will deal with point (b) to some extent. Here, we concentrate on point (a). In particular, we will be dealing with precognitive objective relations, that is, those objective relations that hold independently of the agents' wants and beliefs (cf. Fig. 1.1).

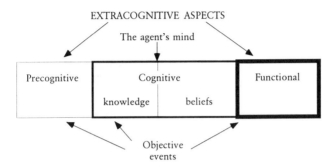

Figure 1.1 Cognitive and extracognitive aspects of social action.

A premise is needed concerning the meaning of what we call precognitive bases. A fundamental assumption concerning intelligent agents is that their actions are necessarily based on knowledge. What matters, some would say, are the agents' world models rather than the world as such. So why bother with precognitive bases of social action? All we need to account for are the agents' beliefs. Even if false, beliefs are still necessarily implied by actions.

This reasoning is correct but insufficient because the nexus between beliefs and actions is bi-directional. Action is regulated by, and is a testbed for, beliefs. In fact, *false beliefs* are likely to lead to *unsuccessful actions*; and *unsuccessful actions* are, in turn, likely to lead to *belief revision*; consequently *an unknown situation* which is *relevant* to the agent's achievements is likely to become *known*; and then *produce relevant actions*.

Matters of fact not only predict to some extent the agents' achievements and failures, but also their possible mental attitudes, and the acquisition of new beliefs and goals. As we will endeavour to show in Chapter 2, a factual **concurrence** among agents is likely to produce aggression, while factual **social dependence** is a predictor of manipulation, or at least of the dependent agent's **goal of influencing** its social **resources**.

Of course, the real predictive power of precognitive bases of sociality is conditioned by the existence of a formal model of the processes outlined above. What we need to develop is a formal account of phenomena ranging from unknown relevant situations and failures in planning up to belief revision. Indeed, existing systems of belief revision are able to maintain coherence among beliefs, but are separated from planning. Only recently (Galliers 1990) has the problem of pragmatic belief revision (belief revision oriented to interaction) been raised. On the other hand, those planning systems which are concerned with learning from failures, that is with adjusting failed plans (Hammond 1986, Alterman 1988), are separated from the management of beliefs. As usual, an integrated model is what is lacking.

Precognitive notions

As previously stated (Fig. 1.1), an objective relation is defined as precognitive when it is neither wanted nor believed by the agents involved.

Precognitive relations may be *non-social* (pre-social) or *social* depending on whether they imply a single agent or more than one. In the former case, precognitive relations hold between one agent and the external (non-social) world. In the second, they hold between at least two agents' behaviours or mental attitudes.

As we will endeavour to show, social relations are based upon, and derived from, some fundamental non-social objective relations. Of all sorts of possible objective relations, therefore, we will take into account those we believe are relevant to the goals and destinies of social agents and thus to the modelling of social action.

Precognitive notions relevant to the social domain

At least two types of relations between one agent and the external world are of some relevance from a social point of view: *dependence* and **interest** relations. Both produce social relations, and will prove useful for describing sophisticated types of social interactions. In a sense, they lie at the bottom of sociality: from the least to the most complex, social relationships represent a series of steps starting from, and based on, pre-social dependence and interest relations. The latter thus have a fundamental explanatory role in a theory of social action.

The relation of dependence

Dependence is undoubtedly the fundamental relation upon which the whole construction of sociality is based (see Castelfranchi et al. 1992b). As we tried to show elsewhere (Conte et al. 1991), full co-operation necessarily implies **mutual dependence**. But dependence seems to be responsible for other types of interactions as well: it lies at the bottom of **exchange** (mutual help; but, for a more technical notion see Ch. 2), influencing (attempting to make others pursue some goal they spontaneously would not be pursuing), and some forms of *exploitation* (taking advantage of others' actions).

However, dependence is not necessarily a social notion. A relation of dependence may be said to occur whenever:

- any object or event in the external world could increase, if used, the probability that a given state of the world be realized, and
- that world state is wanted by at least one agent.

In such a case, we say that the agent is dependent on the object or event. The latter will then be called a resource. Resources enter the structures of the actions (see also Parunak 1990). An **action** is a relation holding among agent(s), goal(s), and resource(s). Agents are said to be acting when using one or more resources to reach a given goal. We then say that anything that is involved in the action, except the agent, is a resource of that action.

Agents are usually dependent on the existence of resources. We will call this type of dependence **resource dependence**, to distinguish it from social dependence:

$$(R\text{-}DEP\ x\,r\,a\,p) \overset{def}{=} (A\text{-}GOAL\ x\,p) \wedge (RESOURCE\ r\,a) \wedge ((DONE\ a) \supset p)$$

in words: *x depends on resource r, when r is a resource for x to perform action a which achieves x's goal p.*

ADAM	WORLD
Goal ON R Y	
Action repertoire CLEAR c PUTON c_i c_j	

Figure 1.2 A one-agent world.

A set of resources is required for any act to take place (for a similar notion of resource, see Bond 1991). In our notion, cubes and table are resources in the blocks world. In Figure 1.2 we have an example. Adam is a one-armed robot. His goals are described on the left side of the figure, while the state of the world is described on the right side. In this world, only two types of action are conceivable: *PUTON* c_i, c_j, where c_i and c_j denote cube variables, and *CLEAR c* which means clearing a cube from the one sitting on top of it and putting the latter on the table. In the blocks world, one can put a cube on top of another cube only if both are clear. Therefore, in order to achieve his goal in the current state of the world, Adam must perform two different actions: *CLEAR* and *PUTON*. To act, Adam needs the following resources:

(a) the resources required by *PUTON* (clear cubes);

(b) the resources required for *CLEAR* (clear cubes and table).

In the social world, as we will see, others may be used as resources. This happens not only in exploitation but also in prosocial action: in help, in a quite abstract sense, the recipient is a resource of the action, give help.

The relation of interest

The notion of interest has a long tradition in the social sciences. In the last few decades, due to a typical hypercognitive misunderstanding, it has been considered heavily compromised with authoritarianism (both in politics and in philosophy; social philosophers wonder, indeed, who is given the responsibility for spelling out what is one's own interest). Consequently, its use is strongly discouraged in any sort of intellectual enterprise.

On the other hand, this rejection shows that interest is a typical objective notion, in the sense previously defined. Besides, interest is not necessarily a social concept either. A given world state is said to be an interest of an agent when it achieves some of its goals:

$$(INTEREST\ x\,q\,p) \stackrel{def}{=} (A\text{-}GOAL\,x\,p) \wedge (q \supset p)$$

in words: *a presocial relation of interest occurs between one agent with his mental states and some external state of affairs when a given state of the world q implies another world state p, and the latter is a goal or subgoal of the agent's* (when p is a subgoal, it often coincides with a pre-condition for a subplan). In other words, q (or, better, the event which produced it) is in x's interest. On the contrary, a world state which goes against an agent's interests is a counter-interest of that agent's:

$$(C\text{-}INTEREST\ x\,q\,p) \stackrel{def}{=} (GOAL\,x\,p) \wedge (q \supset \neg p)$$

It should be noted, the notion of interest points to what is useful for an agent. A world state by itself sufficient to bring about a state wanted by that agent is useful in the sense that it reduces the agent's costs: he finds (part of) his job done.

As an example, let us go back to Figure 1.2. Now, look at Adam's interests, that is, to the facts that are advantageous for Adam's goals: the fact that cube Y is *CLEARTOP* represents an interest of Adam's with regard to his goal of having R on top of Y. Conversely, the fact that G is on top of R is a counter-interest of

Adam's with regard to the same goal. However, cube G being *CLEARTOP* is in his interest with regard to the goal *CLEARTOP R*.

Dependence and interest

The two notions present evident similarities and one may drop into the other depending on the perspective taken by the observer. However, resource dependence is identified with regard to intended actions: one is dependent on those resources which are needed to act. Interests are identified with regard to (sub)goals, and they only refer to useful conditions. Events and the resulting states sometimes achieve the agents' (sub)goals, thus serving their interests. Conditions that need to be true for an agent to act create a dependence of that agent upon them. He cannot do without them.

Of course, the existence of required resources may be seen as an interest of the agent's. This is a truism: precisely because they are needed for the agent to act, existing resources reduce the agent's cost of acquiring them. An already realized action condition is an interest, while an action condition that ought to be realized is a resource.

Precognitive social relations

Let us turn our attention to the social side of the previous notions and to other social relationships that are based upon them.

Social dependence and the social structure

Our basic definition of social dependence says that an agent depends on another agent when, to achieve one of his goals, the former needs an action of the latter:

$$(S\text{-}DEP\ x\ y\ a\ p) \stackrel{def}{=} (A\text{-}GOAL\ x\ p) \wedge \neg(CANDO\ x\ a) \wedge (CANDO\ y\ a) \wedge$$

$$((DONE\ a) \supset p)$$

that is: *x depends on y with regard to an act useful for realizing a state p when p is a goal of x's and x is unable to realize p, while y is able to do so.* Look at Figure 1.3. Now, Adam is no longer able to clear cubes. However, the blocks world now includes a female robot, Eve, who is able to do so. In such a condition, we would say that Adam is dependent upon Eve with regard to his goal of having R on Y.

Social dependence is an objective dependence where resources are filled in by social agents. It sets up a social network among agents independent of, and often preceding, their awareness. Several dimensions are intertwined, such as the existence of alternatives, the degree of dependence, etc. (see Castelfranchi et al. 1992b).

In particular, **dependence** may be either **unilateral**, when only Adam depends on Eve, or **bilateral**, when they depend on each other. Note that, bilateral dependence is here said to be **mutual** when *agents depend on each other to achieve one and the same goal* (cf. Conte et al. 1991):

$$\left(M\text{-}DEP\,x\,y\,p\right) \overset{def}{=} \exists a_y\!\left(S\text{-}DEP\,x\,y\,a_y\,p\right) \wedge \exists a_x\!\left(S\text{-}DEP\,y\,x\,a_x\,p\right)$$

Bilateral dependence is said to be **reciprocal** *when agents depend on each other in order to realize different goals*:

$$\left(REC\text{-}DEP\,x\,y\,p\,q\right) \overset{def}{=} \exists a_y\!\left(S\text{-}DEP\,x\,y\,a_y\,p\right) \wedge \exists a_x\!\left(S\text{-}DEP\,y\,x\,a_x\,q\right)$$

In Figure 1.3, if Eve's goal were identical to Adam's ON R Y, the robots would be mutually dependent. Instead, if Eve's goal were ON Y R the robots would be reciprocally dependent (although their goals would be incompatible).

ADAM	WORLD	EVE
Goal ON R Y		Goal ?
Action repertoire PUTON c_i c_j		Action repertoire CLEAR c

Figure 1.3 Social dependence.

Social interference

We say that there is an objective social interference between two agents, x and y, when the achievement of one's goals has some effect on the other's pursuing, and then achieving, her[1] goals. Goals may interact in a positive or negative way.

Positive interference: **favour** relationships

In the positive case, we say that x favours y if he accidentally sets up a state of the world which is in y's interest[2]; y factually benefits from x's activity when at least one of the accidental consequences of x's coincides with a goal of y's,

$$(FAVOUR \; x \, y \, a \, p) \stackrel{def}{=} ((DONE \text{-} BY \; x \, a) \supset p) \wedge (A \text{-} GOAL \; y \, p)$$

that is x doing a is favouring y in her goal p, when a consequence of x doing a achieves y's goal p.

This relation differs from social dependence in that it is much weaker: in factual benefit, y could reach her goal p on her own, without x's intervention. However, things are such that y may have her job done thanks to x's accidental help. For example, if you raise your hand to greet someone passing by and in doing so you stop the bus I am waiting for, you are giving me unsolicited and unintentional help, but I cannot be said to be dependent on you.

ADAM	WORLD		EVE
Goal ON R Y		G	Goal CLEARTOP c
	Y	R	
Action repertoire CLEAR c PUTON c_i c_j			Action repertoire CLEAR c PUTON c_i c_j

Figure 1.4   Social interference: favour.

In Figure 1.4, Eve's achieving her goal to clear all cubes happens to favour Adam's goal. Although he does not need Eve's intervention, since he can accomplish his task by himself, Adam takes advantage of it.

Negative interference: conflict and concurrence

Social interference is negative when y reaching her goal prevents x from reaching one of his. This gives rise to some interesting precognitive social situations, such as conflict and concurrence, which, once known by the agents involved, often produce antisocial interactions of different sorts.

An objective conflict may lie between two goals when the agents have goals that are *per se* incompatible, that is contradictory. However, the more general case is represented by **interest conflicts**:

$$(I \text{-} CONFL \, x \, y \, q \, p^t \, z^t) \stackrel{def}{=} (INTEREST \, x \, q \, p^t) \wedge (C \text{-} INTEREST \, y \, q \, z^t)$$

or: *a conflict of interest between two agents with regard to a given state q occurs when q is an interest of x's goal that p be true at time t, while it is a counter-interest of y's goal that z be true at the same time*[3].

We do not have examples of this type of conflict in the blocks world (in such a world, it is implausible that agents do not realize their contrasting interests, thus transforming them into contrasting goals: in Figure 1.4 we have an example of incompatible goals in which Eve destroys Adam's move by clearing Y, while Adam in turn destroys her goal and so on in infinite regression). In the real world, on the contrary, an objective conflict is more often a conflict of pure interests: people are frequently unaware of their contrasting interests. The unemployed are interested in a lowering of work costs because in the short run they will be allowed to find a job at a lower wage than would be accepted by employed people. It is difficult to believe that the unemployed want wages to be lower: conflict holds between the interests of the two categories rather than between their goals.

ADAM	WORLD	EVE
Goal		Goal
ON TABLE c and	G	ON TABLE c and
ON R c	Y R	ON G c
Action repertoire		Action repertoire
CLEAR c		CLEAR c
PUTON c_i c_j		PUTON c_i c_j

Flgure 1.5 Social interference: conflict and concurrence.

Often, conflicts depend on resource scarcity. In Figure 1.5 an example is shown. Both Adam and Eve want to put a cube (each a different one) on another cube sitting on the table. Given the scarcity of this sort of cubes (there is only one), the two goals cannot be realized at once, even though they are not *per se* incompatible. From the above equation, we can derive:

$$\left(CONC\,x\,y\,r\,a_x^t\,a_y^t\right) \overset{def}{=} \left(R\text{-}DEP\,x\,r\,a_x^t\right) \wedge \left(R\text{-}DEP\,y\,r\,a_y^t\right) \wedge$$

$$\left(\left(DONE\text{-}BY\,x\,a_x^t\right) \vee \left(DONE\text{-}BY\,y\,a_y^t\right)\right)$$

in words: *x and y are in a relation of resource concurrence when they both depend on one and the same resource, and the resource cannot be used by both at once.*

It is easy to show that concurrence falls within the preceding case of interest conflict, since what is an interest to one agent is a counter-interest to the other: each robot wants to put its own cube on Y, and consequently doing it implies a counter-interest for the other.

It should be noted that concurrence could also be defined as shared dependence. In Figure 1.5 Adam and Eve both depend on a resource which cannot be used simultaneously for different goals. On the contrary, the sharing of interests or goals does not necessarily imply an antisocial relation. Indeed, the sharing of interests and goals tends to produce prosocial interaction at least in the case of mutual dependence. However, this is true when goals and interests are effectively shared, that is, when they overlap. It is not true when agents have parallel goals or interests (cf. Conte et al. 1991), that is, when their goals are identical in every respect but each mentions a different agent as achieving the goal in question. With parallel goals or interests, there is no real sharing. Rather, there is often concurrence: when any two agents want to eat one and the same cake, their goals overlap almost perfectly except that the eater is supposed not to be the same.

Recapitulation

In this chapter, current AI models of social action have been shown to suffer from either top-down (that is, pre-established) co-operativeness (see especially DAI, CSCW, etc.) or the hypercognitive fallacy (a view of social agents as mutually transparent and endowed with in-built social awareness), which is widely accepted in MAS.

In contrast to both tendencies, a model of social action based upon objective structural relations among the agents has been worked out. In this chapter, some relations which pave the way to such a model have been presented. In the next chapter, some deductions from the relations defined here will be shown and discussed. In Part 4 of this book, objective effects of social actions, that is, the role of emergent functionality among cognitive agents, will be described.

CHAPTER TWO
From precognitive conditions to social action: adaptive cognition

Social actions, social resources and social goals

On the grounds of objective relations, agents construct social actions. But what *is* a **social action**? In our view it is not simply any action that involves other agents. Indeed, this is unnecessary and insufficient for an action to be social:

(a) *insufficient*: actions may have other agents among their resources without being social: if x avoids y's inadvertent hit, x performs no social action since y is not treated as an agent but as an object;

(b) *unnecessary*: there are social actions that do not involve other agents among their resources: if x shuts the door in order not to be seen by y, he performs a social action even though the action "shutting the door" does not have y among its resources.

We define a social action as an action that achieves a social goal. In other words, at some level in the chain of a social action's goals one of these two alternatives is mentioned:

– an *action* performed by another agent y, or
– some *mental attitude* of y (goal, belief, or emotion).

y must be mentioned as an autonomous agent (endowed with mental attitudes and the capacity to pursue its own goals; for a discussion of this notion see Ch. 3) in one of x's goals. Note that actions sometimes are social only indirectly. In these situations, non-social actions are used to achieve a social effect. A given action's immediate goal may not mention any other agent (preparing a meal) but it might have a higher-level goal which does (offering the dinner to a friend who is coming over).

Types of social goals

We will now consider some fundamental types of social goals, which, when variously combined, represent the main origins, or bases, of sociality.

Goal adoption

The general form of a prosocial action is based on **goal adoption**, i.e. one pursuing another's goal. More precisely, we define goal adoption as the process by which a given agent comes to have another agent's goal as his own:

$$(G\text{-}ADOPT\ x\,y\,p) \overset{def}{=} \Big(R\text{-}GOAL\,x\,(OBTAIN\ y\,p)\big(BEL\,x\,(A\text{-}GOAL\ y\,p)\big)\Big)$$

in words: *x adopts a goal of y's when x wants y to obtain it as long as x believes that y wants to achieve that goal.* In other words, *x* has a new goal as a result of goal adoption. He has it, (a) *as long as* he believes that *y* has it, and (b) *in order for y* to obtain it. Thanks to condition (b), the present notion of adoption excludes all cases in which one is led to have a new goal by others pursuing the same goal (imitation). Instead, such cases are allowed by other definitions (e.g. Cohen & Levesque's (1990c) notion of helpful goals).

Adoption does not coincide with *benevolence*. A relation of benevolence, indeed, is an unconditioned adoption. Usually, benevolence is a built-in property of agents (in MAS research, agents are modelled as benevolent, that is, likely to adopt any request of the user's). However, several constraints might be conceived of which would render this notion closer to real-life benevolence. For example, benevolence by role occurs very frequently in real life: it holds when *x* is benevolent toward any agent belonging to a given category (e.g. friend, colleague, neighbour, etc.).

Goal adoption can be instrumental to the achievement of other goals. We will express a rule constraining adoption – allowing it to be chosen by autonomous agents – and will call it **adoption rule** (AR). This rule essentially says that an agent adopts a new goal if he can think of some benefit as a result of the adoption,

$$\forall p \exists q \Big(BEL\,x\,\big((G\text{-}ADOPT\ x\,y\,p) \supset (OBTAIN\ x\,q)\big)\Big) \supset (G\text{-}ADOPT\ x\,y\,p)$$

in words: *if x believes he can get something out of adopting any goal of y's, he will then adopt it.* We will get back to this rule and some types of prosocial action in Chapter 4. Here, let us say that the application of such a rule does not necessarily end up with the goal adopted being *achieved*. Among other factors contributing to such a conclusion, a *goal balance* (a comparison of different goals in terms of their utilities) occurs between the goal adopted and the agent's other goals.

Aggression

In aggression, *x* acts so as to prevent *y* from reaching one of her goals. More precisely, we will define an **aggressive goal** as follows:

$$(G - AGGRESS \, x \, y \, p) \overset{def}{=} \left(R \text{-} GOAL \, x \, \neg p \left(BEL \, x \left(GOAL \, y \, p \right) \right) \right)$$

in words: *x wants to attack y in her goal p, when, as long as x believes that y wants p, x wants y not to achieve that goal.*

Adoption and aggression are two fundamental types of social action, which often occur combined in several ways. Many actions are aggressive at a lower level of their goal chain, while their ultimate goal is prosocial, or vice versa. For example, in many complementary relationships (parent–child, teacher–student, and sometimes even professional–client), one party is said to act in the interests of the other even against the latter's will (compromising some of her goals). We will return to this issue in Chapter 4. A merciful lie is a further example of aggression for a good purpose (a lie is always considered detrimental, however slightly, since agents are by default expected to have an interest in learning the truth).

On the other hand, prosocial actions are sometimes deceitful and covertly aggressive. For example, if one party in an exchange succeeds in obtaining more than it has given, the exchange turns into a fraud.

Influencing

In research on MAS, heterogeneity among agents is seen as a source of conflict. In our view, however, conflict is not a necessary consequence of local differences among agents. As will be shown, a qualitative differentiation in the distribution of resources among agents may be a reason for prosocial action (exchange and co-operation). More generally, heterogeneous agents may try to take advantage of one another. This sometimes produces conflicts and aggressions, but often leads to the agents influencing one another, that is to say, inducing one another to set a new goal:

$$(INFL \text{-} GOAL \, x \, y \, p) \overset{def}{=} \left(A \text{-} GOAL \, x \left(A \text{-} GOAL \, y \, p \right) \right)$$

in words: *x has the goal of influencing y with regard to a given goal p, when x wants y to have the goal p.* In other words, if the influencing is effective, the addressee will end up with a new goal that she did not have before.

Since we are dealing with cognitive agents, the mechanism of influencing is usually a cognitive one. (Non-cognitive mechanisms might occur – think of drug inoculation; however, they are relatively infrequent and irrelevant in this context.) For a cognitive autonomous agent to have a new goal, she ought to acquire some new **belief** concerning the link between that particular goal and some other old goal (or interest) of hers. Therefore, cognitive influencing consists of providing the addressee with information that is pretended to be relevant for some of her goals, and this is done in order to ensure that the recipient has a new goal.

When is influencing effective? What sort of power is exercised by an agent when influencing someone? How is it acquired? Many aspects of this phenomenon deserve special attention and should be analyzed at some length (cf., however, Castelfranchi 1990). For our present purposes let us say that, despite what is commonly felt, influencing is not necessarily a form of manipulation: it is not always pursued indirectly (as when *x casually* tells *y*, who is about to go to work by car: "I really don't feel like walking all the way to the bus station today."). It may be extremely explicit ("Look, I've got your driving licence: you drive me to the bus station first, and then I'll give it back to you."). It might not even be self-interested (after arriving at the bus station: "Why don't you leave the car and get the bus too? You will save a lot of petrol.").

Cognitive social actions (adding beliefs and wanted effects)

Let us now address the questions of how and why precognitive relations of the type seen in Chapter 1 lead to various types of cognitive social actions.

The process from precognitive relations to relevant social action involves two steps:

– the agents *becoming aware* of the social relations they are involved in, and
– the subprocess *from relevant beliefs to social action*.

A satisfactory model of the first step ought to involve a formal theory of causal and default reasoning, perception and learning, which is far beyond the scope of the present work. However, we will express some preliminary ideas about pragmatic causal reasoning that are relevant for the agent modelling. More specifically, we will try to show which characteristics the agent ought to possess to acquire information relevant to its goals/interests. As for the second step, we will endeavour to show some of the social consequences of the agents acquiring relevant information.

In all the situations described below, we will assume the *postulate of introspection* (agents implicitly metabelieve everything they believe and want) and the **assumption of action competence** (if agents believe they have done a given action, that action has in fact been done). However, unlike our previous work on the same issue (Conte & Castelfranchi 1994) where agents' beliefs were incomplete but necessarily true, here agents are allowed to hold both incomplete and false beliefs. Finally, the process under study is triggered by default by some relevant event (that is, by some event that interferes positively or negatively with some goal of one of the agents). To simplify matters, we will also assume that this event will be perceived by at least one of the agents considered, and what is more that the event is believed by that agent to be consistently associated with a world state that will prove relevant to that agent's goals.

Adaptive cognition

Autonomous agents are adaptive systems, responsive to external conditions and capable of adjusting both their actions and their mental states to them.

In current usage (Agre & Chapman 1987, Brooks 1989, Steels 1990), adaptive and reactive systems are, by definition, non-cognitive systems. What is more, adaptation is traditionally considered as an alternative to cognitive learning. Mechanisms of adaptation are thought to operate through the external selection of a given behavioural response. In biological systems, for example, adaptive responses are evolutionarily selected and conveyed through the genes.

We reject the cognitive/adaptive opposition and would like to think of cognition as one mechanism of adaptation. Cognitive systems are also adaptive systems and, moreover, their cognitive equipment plays an important role in learning adaptive responses. In other words, these systems are endowed with an adaptive form of cognition.

Adaptive cognition is defined here as a set of mental states (beliefs, goals, intentions, etc.), and some basic principles and rules to manipulate them, that allow the system to behave adaptively. More explicitly, adaptive cognition is modified as a function of the effects resulting from actions. If negative outcomes are obtained by the performing system, that is, if the system fails to attain its objectives, it will start revising the cognitive ingredients of its actions.

Note that, here, the revision process does not exclusively focus on the system's beliefs, but also on its intentions, goals, and desires. Cohen & Levesque's (1990b) *postulate of realism*, which rules out belief-incompatible wishes, is a principle of adaptive cognition extended to wants. Likewise, we suggest that systems drop intentions and plans that have proved ineffective, and not helped the system achieve its objective, without necessarily abandoning the latter.

We will provide just a few elements for a model of adaptive cognition. In particular:
  – some *basic axioms and rules* as well as
  – some *specific beliefs, goals, and social actions*, derived, thanks to those axioms and rules, from objective relationships.

Learning from failures

An adaptive cognitive system is one that responds to external events actively modifying its behaviours in order to adjust to the environment. However, this is almost a truism, and does not get us very far. Several underlying questions should be clarified: to what type of event does a cognitive system respond adaptively? What does it mean to modify one's behaviour actively?

Following Alterman's (1988) notion of adaptive planning, we claim that the gist of adaptive cognition is a system's *capacity to learn from failure*. A cognitive system is truly adaptive when, once it has perceived that its action has failed, it will check the action done and possibly revise the whole internal process that led the system to performing it. In other words, a system of this sort does not give up at the first defeat and consider its goal impossible. Before abandoning it, an adaptive system will attempt what social psychologists call an internal attribution of the failure; it will search for errors in the process of achievement. As soon as it perceives a failure, an adaptive system will start revising the action that failed.

First, we need an assumption of competence with regard to one's failures. Reasonably, *we will assume that when an agent performs a given action for achieving a given goal and fails, it will then believe it has not obtained its goal.*

Assumption of failure competence

$$\left(\neg p \wedge \left(BEFORE\left(DONE\text{-}FOR\ x\ a\ p\right) \neg p\right)\right) \supset \left(BEL\ x\ \neg\left(OBTAIN\ x\ p\right)\right)$$

Furthermore, we need a rule that leads the agent to accomplish the aforesaid internal attribution of failure.

Pragmatic learning rule

$$\left(\neg p \wedge \left(BEFORE\left(DONE\text{-}FOR\ x\ a\ p\right) \neg p\right)\right) \supset \left(BEL\ x\ \neg\left(\left(DONE\ a\right) \supset p\right)\right)$$

or: *if x has just done action a in order to achieve goal p and p still is false, x will next believe that it is not true that if a is done, p will then be true.* In fact, by the assumption of failure competence, x will perceive its failure, and conclude that the causal belief responsible for the failed plan is false. This is so for the meaning of *DONE-FOR* as defined in the Appendix (p. 189). This amounts to saying that an action has been done by an agent, and that the agent believes that the action will bring about a wanted effect. Now, if that effect is believed not to have been produced, the action will be challenged by the system, which will conclude that the requested action does not in fact bring about the wanted effect. The latter conclusion may lead the system to a further extreme consequence, namely that action a did not bring about p simply because p is unrealizable. However, this is not necessary. Before dropping p, x will have ruled out the hypothesis that a does not bring about p, but another event e, different from a, does.

The agent cannot come up with the conclusion that the action required has not in fact occurred. In this model, the agent is competent with regard to its actions (cf. the assumption of **action competence** in the Appendix (p. 187)). In other words, since x is the agent of primitive action a, it is not possible that both x believes to have just done a and a has not occurred.

To sum up, as soon as it perceives it has run into failure, an adaptive cognitive system will:

– conclude that the action just done does not achieve the wanted effect;
– ascertain whether, in its beliefs, other actions do.

From interests to goals

One of the ways in which new goals are acquired via cognition implies that people learn that they have a previously unknown interest. Once having known this, for the **goal generation rule** (GGR) – which states that x will have as a goal any state which implies an achievement goal of his – x will have a goal corresponding to his interest. In other words, for the GGR, his believed interest is also a goal. This might appear too strong. Why, then, do people go on smoking or drinking or taking drugs when they know these habits are harmful? This question is notoriously a most difficult one. It has puzzled philosophers (for a philosophical reappraisal of the issue, see Pears 1984) and social scientists for many years, and we do not pretend we can make it more comprehensible. Let us get back to the notion of goal defined in the Appendix (pp. 185–6). In the present approach, a goal is not yet what the agent chooses to do. A goal may be rejected not only because it is found unachievable or already achieved, but also because it has been beaten by other goals, for example by hedonistic, even self-destructive but highly compelling, desires. By saying that a believed interest becomes a goal, then, we do not mean to say that agents always pursue what they believe to be their interests. The latter part of our deduction (from believed interests to goals) is ensured by the GGR.

The tricky question is how does such a knowledge emerge? How does an agent come to believe that something is in its interest (the former part of our deduction)? The right answer is: by trial and error. Indeed, if the agent does an action that does not achieve its goal, it will fail in obtaining its goal, and thanks to the assumption of failure-competence, it will also perceive such a failure:

$$\big((C\text{-}INTEREST\,x\,(DONE\,a)\,p) \wedge (DOES\text{-}FOR\,x\,a\,p)\big) \supset$$

$$\big(BEL\,x\,\neg(OBTAIN\,x\,p)\big)$$

that is: *if it is the case that doing action a is a counter-interest of x's with regard to its goal p but x, not knowing this, does a for p, it follows that x does not obtain p and perceive this failure.* This is so for the first premise (*a* being done is a counter-interest of x as for p) and for the assumption of failure-competence.

Now, *if x perceives its failure, for the learning rule expressed earlier it will conclude that a being done is not an interest of its own with regard to goal p,*

$$\big((C\text{-}INTEREST\ x\,(DONE\ a)\,p)\wedge(DOES\text{-}FOR\ x\,a\,p)\big)\supset$$

$$\big(BEL\ x\ \neg((DONE\ a)\supset p)\big)$$

This could be seen as an unsatisfactory conclusion, however. Adaptive agents are granted little intelligence concerning their interests. So far, all the knowledge that they have been allowed to draw from failure is about what is *not* in their interest. More useful information about their negative (counter-) and positive interests has not been allowed.

Indeed, there is at least one circumstance in which agents may extract positive conclusions about their interests from failures: while realizing some interests, agents may accidentally find out that their beliefs about other interests of theirs are wrong. Agents may learn from experience that what they believe to be a multi-purpose interest is in fact a conflictual circumstance, facilitating one goal and destroying another. For example, while finally reaching some important career objectives, you may find to your horror that these achievements have caused your marriage to break down. Or else, you may discover that although going on a diet does help you lose weight, at the same time it makes you sleepless and unhappy. In such situations, therefore, a given state q achieving a goal p (lose weight), is a counter-interest with regard to goal z (be happy).

Interestingly, counter-interests may be transformed into positive interests thanks to the following:

$$(C\text{-}INTEREST\ x\,q\,p)\supset(INTEREST\ x\ \neg q\ \Diamond p)$$

that is: *if q is a counter-interest of x with regard to p, "not q" is x's interest with regard to the goal that p will at least be possible.* Indeed, if "not p" follows from q, then either p or "not p" follows from "not q". In other words, if q implies "not p", "not q" does not imply the same consequence. Counter-interests should be avoided in order to make things possible, if not true. Giving up some work commitments will not secure you a long and happy marriage, but will at least save it from certain breakdown.

Therefore, knowledge about one's counter-interests will produce necessary, if not sufficient, measures for achieving your goals.

From benefit to exploitation

Let us consider what happens when y favours x with regard to some goal of the latter. Although this type of social relation might appear to be of extreme cognitive subtlety, it paves the way for interesting phenomena of social parasitism: to the extent that x believes y will act in x's interests (thanks to a process of the type described in the preceding section), he will probably wait for y

to act in his interests. Thus, in the situation described in Figure 1.4 (see the preceding chapter), Adam will wait for Eve to do part of his job.

Note that Adam is not allowed to conclude that Eve's action is intended to produce p, since he has no reason to believe that Eve has any corresponding goal. Therefore, Adam is not allowed to believe that Eve wants to help him. All he has got to believe is that he benefits from Eve's doing.

From unilateral dependence to influencing and adoption

In an objective relation of favour, to achieve his goal, it is sufficient for Adam to wait and see, since he believes that, sooner or later, Eve will act in his interests. In social dependence, on the contrary, this is not enough. If people believe that they depend on others (irrespective of any belief concerning factual benefit), they will try to influence others according to their needs. Formally:

$$\left(BEL\, x\left(S\text{-}DEP\, x\, y\, a\, p\right)\right) \supset \left(INFL\text{-}GOAL\, x\, y\left(DOES\, y\, a\right)\right)$$

that is: *if, to achieve his goal p, x believes he is dependent on y doing a, he will next want to influence y to do action a.* In Castelfranchi et al. (1992b), this was shown to follow from the definition of social dependence and the GGR: if x believes he cannot do a, which implies next p and p is a goal of x's, while y can do a, then x will have the goal to influence y to do a.

Look at Figure 1.3: beside the initial goal $ON\, R\, Y$, Adam has one more goal, namely that Eve has a new goal herself: to clear R.

If agents are reciprocally dependent (suppose Eve wants to have Y on G), Eve might decide to adopt Adam's goal that she clears R, in order for Adam to put Y on G in **reciprocation**. Of course, such a decision usually implies a belief that the other is committed to adopting one's goal in reciprocation (for more details on this, see Ch. 3). Another interesting process based on dependence is one from mutual dependence to co-operation. This was analyzed in some detail elsewhere (Conte et al. 1991; for details see again Ch. 3).

However, how do we derive Adam's belief that he is dependent on Eve? If Adam is in fact dependent on y but does not know it and tries to achieve his goal, he will certainly fail:

$$\left(S\text{-}DEP\, x\, y\, a_y\, p\right) \supset \forall a_x\left[\left(CANDO\, x\, a_x\right) \wedge \neg\left(\left(DONE\text{-}FOR\, x\, a_x\, p\right) \supset p\right)\right]$$

in words: *if x depends on y doing a_y to achieve his goal p, his attempt to achieve p on his own is not sufficient to achieve p.* This follows from the definition of social dependence, which implies that x cannot do the actions achieving p. Therefore, x's attempt to achieve his goal on his own will be unsuccessful.

Now, if p does not occur, x perceives his failure and concludes that he cannot perform the action required:

$$\left((DONE\text{-}FOR\,x\,a_x\,p)\wedge\neg p\right)\supset\left(BEL\,x\,\neg\left((DONE\,a_x)\supset p\right)\right)$$

that is: *if, after x's attempt to perform a for p, p does not occur, x perceives his failure and concludes that the actions he can do do not imply the desired state.* This is true for the learning rule expressed earlier: if x perceives that the action done failed to achieve the intended goal, he obviously concludes that none of the actions he can do achieve p.

So far we have shown that, from factual social dependence, a factual failure in the depending agent's attempt to achieve his goal follows, and consequently from his (probable) perception of failures the agent's awareness of being unable to reach that goal follows as well.

Suppose now that the same agent perceives another agent doing an action that achieves p. In such a case, the former agent will conclude he is socially dependent on the latter:

$$\left((A\text{-}GOAL\,x\,p)\wedge\left(BEL\,x\,\exists a_p\left[\left((DONE\text{-}BY\,y\,a_p)\supset p\right)\wedge\neg(CANDO\,x\,a_p)\right]\right)\right)\supset$$

$$\left(BEL\,x\,\exists a_p(S\text{-}DEP\,x\,y\,a_p p)\right)$$

in words: *if x believes there is an action done by y leading to p that he is not able to do, then he believes he is socially dependent on y.* This is true for the definition of social dependence provided in Chapter 1 and the **assumption of action ability** expressed in the Appendix (p. 190), which states that if an agent performs an action he can do it. In other words, x will believe that:

(a) y can do an action leading to p (action ability), and that
(b) he himself cannot do it (second premise), and that
(c) p is a goal of his own (first premise plus introspection),

all of which are the necessary and sufficient components of the notion of social dependence defined in Chapter 1. If y is believed by x to be able to perform the action a_p, which achieves x's goal and which x is not able to perform, x believes he is dependent on y to achieve his goal p.

From conflict to aggression and from concurrence to competition

Finally: *if Adam believes there is a situation of conflict between his and Eve's interests* (cf. Figure 1.4), *he will also have an aggressive goal towards Eve.* In formal terms:

$$\left(BEL\,x\left(I\text{-}CONFL\,x\,y\,q\,p^t\,z^t\right)\right)\supset\left(G\text{-}AGGRESS\,x\,y\,z^t\right)$$

in words: *if x believes there is a conflict of interest about world state q with regard to his goal p at time t and y's goal z at the same time, x will next want y not to obtain z at time t.* This is true for the definitions of conflict and aggression, as well as for the GGR. Indeed, if x believes there is a conflict of interests between himself and y, by definition he believes that q, which is an interest of his with regard to his goal p, is also a counter-interest of y with regard to her goal z. Therefore, for the GGR, x will want q to be true although he perfectly well knows that q implies "not z", which is a goal of y's. In other words, x will have an aggressive goal towards y. In Figure 1.4 Adam ends up with the goal that Eve does not achieve her goal *CLEARTOP Y*.

Adam's belief that his interests clash with Eve's is not easily derived from the objective conflict itself. Indeed, such derivation would require Adam to attempt to realize his interests in the presence, and in spite, of Eve. In return, Eve would probably destroy Adam's goal, and so on back and forth until either finds out what is going on. Therefore, two types of aggressive goals are pursued in order to avoid this stalemate:

(a) each agent tries to conceal his own achievement from the other,

(b) each agent tries to convince the other to abandon her goal[1].

Both goals are aggressive, since the latter is a deception and the former is an attempt to influence y to drop one of her goals without any real good reason – at least from y's point of view – for doing so.

As with conflict, believed *concurrence* is not a necessary but merely a highly predictable consequence of objective concurrence. When either agent gets hold of the contended-for resource, they keep on dismantling what the other has achieved until one discovers what is happening.

From believed concurrence a particular type of aggressive goal is derived:

$$\left(BEL\, x \left(CONC\, x\, y\, r\, a_x^t\, a_y^t \right) \right) \supset \left(GOAL\, x \,\neg \left(DOES\, y\, a_y^t \right) \right)$$

which is a special case of the previous equation. In words: *if x believes there is a concurrence between himself and y for resource r, x will next want y not to do the action that requires r at time t.* In Figure 1.5 Adam wants to put his cube on the only *CLEARTOP* cube existing and believes Eve wants to do the same. Hence, Adam will try to prevent Eve from performing that action (as usual, by threatening, deceiving, or even by simple request[2]).

Recapitulation

Here, cognitive social action is seen as an emergent phenomenon which results from objective relations holding between each single agent and the external (social or non-social) world. This view can shed light on the question of what the sources of sociality are, why intelligent agents need to interact, and what steps gradually lead from static matters of fact to social action. In a word, objective social relations are argued to have some predictive power, that is, to allow social beliefs and cognitive actions to be predicted. Furthermore, objective social relations pave the way to a reconsideration of social structures as not simply consisting of mutual knowledge, negotiations and commitments, but also resulting from common external conditions.

In other words, we believe that a model of multi-agent interaction confined within the limits of individual minds is insufficient. Mind is not enough. But shortcomings cannot be made good simply by constructing interactive subcognitive agents. The real methodological challenge of the present day, and the testbed of an emulative computational project consists, we believe, of working out an integrated simulative approach. In such an approach, simulations of models of minds should be flanked by that of dynamic systems, namely, of the composite selective effects of their actions. In concrete terms, the following simulations should be integrated:

- the *emergence of minds* from subcognitive units;
- models of *social minds* (such as models of the minds of co-operative vs. exchanging agents);
- *agents in interaction* (the emergence of sociality);
- *emergent finalities* among intelligent agents in interaction
- *emergent collective agents.*

In the following chapters, we will address the last three points, while leaving aside the first point, which is beyond the scope of the present approach. In *theoretical* terms, the second point is focused on throughout the book, the third has been examined here, while the fourth will be addressed to some extent in Chapters 8 and 9. However, in Chapter 11, *simulations* of both (c) and (d) will be presented and discussed at some length.

PART TWO

Others as inputs
to one agent's goals

CHAPTER THREE
Adoption of others' goals

Autonomous agents

In the last few years, the emphasis previously laid on intelligent systems within some AI subfields – such as DAI and MAS – has been shifted onto **autonomous agents**. Rather than a consequence of emulating real agents, this shift is due to applicative reasons.

Indeed, autonomous systems are required in all domains in which a central controller, arbiter, or co-ordinator would be unrealistic, computationally unfeasible or too costly, and generally less convenient than a distributed control. (Think of the costs and problems posed by the remote control of one or more robots, those of the centralized co-ordination of multi-agent co-operative structures, etc.) The relative convenience of autonomous distributed systems is increased by their greater flexibility and reactivity to the environment, and by their adaptiveness. Systems thoroughly programmed, which are granted little autonomous decision-making, unfailingly but blindly execute their plans and tasks: they are unable to react to unexpected and important events. Furthermore, the emphasis on autonomy is encouraged by the multi-agent context: the decentralized solution provided so far to the multi-agent co-ordination and co-operation problem is based essentially on negotiation.

The very notion of negotiation brings into play the question of autonomy, since local utilities and interests, and even preferences are matters of negotiation. **Self-interested agents** are, indeed, autonomous. However, it is hard to believe that the current artificial agents have preferences and tastes of their own. What is therefore a definition of autonomy useful for constructing a society of artificial systems (see Castelfranchi 1993a)?

Levels and types of autonomy

Needless to say, there are different *degrees* of autonomy. In a continuum from thoroughly programmed systems with no autonomy to unconstrained gods sitting in splendid isolation in their remote worlds, there is a wide spectrum of intermediate solutions. Real agents, for example, are somewhere in the middle, since many of their highest-level goals are built-in, but may and do in fact change over their life-time.

The quantitative difference can to some extent be explained as a difference in the possible *levels* of autonomy. Let us at least make the distinction between a higher-level autonomy and a lower-level one. The former has to do with the autonomy of goals and ends, whilst the latter is at the level of actions and plans. In other words, an agent endowed with its own goals is more autonomous than one that is only allowed to construct its own plans in order to achieve others' goals. We will come back to this issue in the next section.

Furthermore, there are several distinct *types* of autonomy.

Usually, entities are called autonomous when they stand on their own. In an open system, a software agent is autonomous when it exists independently from the others and the global task to accomplish (Hewitt & de Jong 1983).

In addition, agents are said (Hewitt & de Jong 1983) to be autonomous when co-operation is not pre-compiled, but based on rational choices (e.g. active requests for help) (cf. Bragato & Roberto 1993).

A special form of autonomy relies on belief revision processes: it is the tendency to select external information – instead of accepting it acritically – on the grounds of some rational criteria.

A further meaning, contrasting somewhat with the latter, is that of adaptiveness. Recently, autonomous systems have been equated with self-organizing systems (Bourgine & Varela 1991), that is, systems which modify themselves under the effect of environmental pressures in ways that correlate positively with their persistence over time. According to this notion, autonomous systems should be seen as reactive, undergoing external constraints and adaptively reacting to them.

Even without sharing this perhaps excessively weak view of autonomy, one cannot deny that autonomous systems are at the same time self-sufficient and reactive: they need to respond to environmental stimuli and events.

Agenthood and autonomy

An *agent* is a system the behaviour of which is directed towards implementing a specific state of the world; in a word, a goal-governed system. An agent shows special types of behaviours, called *actions*, that are neither accidental nor strictly speaking caused by external stimuli or events. An action is necessarily intentional: it is always performed in order to achieve a given intention (see the **assumption of action intentionality** expressed in the Appendix (p. 190)). Therefore, an action is always caused by an internal representation, and only indirectly – through this representation – by an external stimulus.

However, this is not yet sufficient in order to define an *autonomous* agent. Suppose that a robot is enabled only to execute orders and external requests, without taking any initiative. It is self-regulated in the sense that it carries out appropriate plans and actions. It may even be able to find solutions to some problems. Still, it cannot be said to be fully autonomous. Autonomy is something more complex: an autonomous agent has to have its own goals (Covrigaru & Lindsay 1991), in the pursuit of which it might refuse to do what it is asked to do. Two careful distinctions ought to be drawn here. First, a *goal-autonomous* agent should be distinguished from an intelligent but only **plan-autonomous** help-giver. The latter can only have goals as means to achieve goals of others (that can be either adopted by, or built into the agent). In sum, a plan-autonomous agent is enabled to plan autonomously how to achieve a goal that others want it to achieve.

This goes back to the higher- vs. lower-level autonomy discussed above. Consider Cohen & Levesque's famous example concerning commitment in help-giving systems (Cohen & Levesque 1987). Willie, a household robot, is asked to bring the speaker a beer. As it finds none in the house, Willie takes the initiative to ask the next-door neighbour for a beer. We would not say that Willie *is* an autonomous agent, although in some sense it *acted* in an autonomous, intelligent and creative way.

On the other hand, autonomous agents should be distinguished from selfish ones. Suppose that on its way to the kitchen, Willie is addressed by a further request: "Bring me a pill for my heart!" According to its specifications, the slavish robot keeps its earlier commitment as long as required – commitments must be dropped when fulfilled or impossible to achieve. Therefore, Willie trundles over with a beer in its gripper only to find the speaker on the verge of a heart attack. A slightly more autonomous robot would keep its commitment as long as needed: when some emergency occurs, it ought to be able to drop or interrupt ongoing and incompatible tasks to achieve more important goals. Now, this is an example of autonomous agenthood, even though it is not an example of selfish agenthood.

Therefore, an autonomous agent will be defined here as an agent that acts to achieve its own goals.

$$(G\text{-}AUTONOMOUS\ x) \overset{def}{=} \forall q [(GOAL\ x\ q) \wedge$$
$$\exists e(BEFORE\neg(GOAL\ x\ q)(HAPPENS\ e)) \supset$$
$$\exists p(R\text{-}GOAL\ x\ q(BEL\ x(INTEREST\ x\ q\ p)))]$$

in words: *an agent x is* **goal-autonomous** *if, and only if, whatever new goal q it comes to have, there is at least a goal p of x's in which q is believed by x to be instrumental.* In other words, x is an autonomous agent if it generates new goals as means for achieving existing goals of its own. Actually, it can be shown that this equation is allowed by the GGR. In other words, autonomous agents generate new goals thanks to GGR.

One corollary of this equation is,

$$\forall x(G\text{-}AUTONOMOUS\,x) \supset \exists e \forall q\big[(BEFORE\,\neg(GOAL\,x\,q)(HAPPENS\,e)) \supset$$

$$\exists p\big(BEL\,x\,(INTEREST\,x\,q\,p)\big)\big]$$

in words: *if an agent is autonomous, if it comes to have a new goal q, there is at least a further goal p of x which is believed by x to follow from q.* We saw an example of an application of this corollary in social reasoning, namely in planning the goal of influencing.

Social autonomy is a special case of goal autonomy. Socially autonomous agents choose whether to adopt or reject external requests in terms of goal autonomy. Unlike benevolent agents (cf. Cohen & Levesque's (1990c) notion), they do not limit themselves to rejecting those requests that clash with other goals of theirs. Furthermore, they reject those requests that they have no reason to accept. They will not accept a request that does not fit one of their higher-level goals, whether selfish or altruistic (cf. Harsanyi's (1990) notion of utilitarian goals) even if that request does not contrast with any of their existing goals.

Social responsiveness and limited autonomy

Both old-style reflex systems and current reactive systems ignore the fundamental role of mental representations in plugging the gap between external stimuli and the systems' responses. In reactive systems, perception is directly coupled to action: all the knowledge is extracted from sensors, and goals and desires are expressed by physical actions. In the multi-agent context, this is equivalent to saying that actions of one system are stimuli; inputs which activate another systems' behavioural responses. *This* notion of reactivity is not particularly profitable in a multi-agent context (but there are also doubts about its general applicability; see Castelfranchi 1993a) and should be replaced by the less abused notion of social responsiveness. Unlike reactive systems, which are usually and deceitfully opposed to deliberative ones, socially responsive systems could be defined as systems which react to actions and intentions of other systems – especially to their communications – thanks to a mechanism of *goal activation*. In cognitive systems, goal activation is necessarily initiated by a modification of the systems' beliefs: external stimuli (others' actions) might alter the systems' beliefs, hence activate more or less urgent goals of theirs, and finally, but only as an indirect consequence, induce their behavioural responses. What is generally needed is therefore a theory of belief-based goal activation, which applies to both the social and the non-social contexts. As a consequence, artificial systems would be allowed both cognitive autonomy and social responsiveness. But what is the main reason for responsiveness? Why should agents be responsive to actions and communications of other agents?

A fundamental answer to this question is found in the concept of *limited autonomy*. Indeed, as discussed at some length in the first chapter, the agents' sharing of a common world leads to all sorts of collisions and interferences, both positive and negative. Here, a more general notion of autonomy than that of self-sufficiency is proposed. Agents which are autonomous in the sense previously defined are not necessarily self-sufficient. Indeed, their autonomy in a multi-agent context is necessarily limited essentially for two reasons:

(a) *social dependence*: autonomous agents should not be viewed as necessarily capable of achieving all their goals on their own. In other words, agents might depend on others for the achievement of (a number of) their goals, which ultimately leads to their need to be adopted by these agents.

(b) *liability to being influenced*: agents can be influenced by others, that is, they can be induced by other agents to have some new goal. Obviously, this feature is mitigated by autonomy:

– Agents choose whether to have a new goal or not; they do so only to the extent that they believe such a goal to be a means to some higher-level goal of theirs.

– Furthermore, agents can only be influenced by means of their beliefs, that is, by receiving information incrementing or modifying existing beliefs. But, again, autonomous agents are not gullible: they do not acritically accept all information received. They are able to sift incoming information, retaining or rejecting it according to some internal criteria (consistency with previous beliefs, reliability of the source, etc.; cf. Galliers 1991).

To sum up, agents have limited autonomy in the sense that they are likely to adopt one another's goals. In the following, the issue primarily addressed is goal adoption and its relation to social dependence.

Goal adoption and autonomous agents

In autonomous agents, external inputs are *filtered* through the agents' choices. When receiving any new input, agents decide whether to simply ignore it or take it into account. As autonomous agents' goals are not generated anew, they must be related back to some higher-level, pre-existing goals of the agents'. As already stated, a goal-autonomous agent is one which generates new goals applying a GGR.

On the other hand, goals are not to be viewed only as the agents' desires that are compatible with the agents' beliefs. In fact, goals do not necessarily originate from more or less stable motivations, drives or urges of diverse nature. Some goals emerge from planning, means–end reasoning, pragmatic calculus, etc. Some might proceed from the external will. However, to avoid a view of multi-agent interaction based solely on either benevolent or slavish attitudes, autonomous agents must be allowed to choose whether to accept the external will or not, whether or not to transform this particular form of external input, a *request*, into an internal output, a *goal*. This special application of the filtering process is what we call the process of *goal adoption*. Goal adoption is a fundamental filtering mechanism allowing autonomous agents to interact with one another. It connects the autonomous agent with the social world.

Natural and unnatural means–end links: the rule of adoption

The adoption rule (AR) presented in Chapter 2 is but a special case of the general GGR provided in the Introduction. What is interesting about AR is that it points to a special form of means–end reasoning, namely reasoning about unnatural, that is, artificial or conventional, means–end links. Unfortunately, logical tools do not allow this peculiarity to be expressed explicitly. The AR implicitly extends to the unnatural means–end links, but does not explicitly model it. This is because the formalism used does not allow the means–end links to be explicitly modelled: the antecedent to the consequent relation is a sort of passe-partout which is commonly used to express a variety of relations: logical implication, causation, planning links, and more generally means-to-ends links. Although formally implicit, the notion of unnatural means–end links is extremely important and heuristic. It seems especially relevant to an understanding of the social world, at both the micro- and the macro-level. When an agent x applies the AR, the goal and action that x will have and perform are only extrinsically linked to the benefit x obtains in return: there is no natural link between the new goal (action) of x and the end that he expects to achieve through it. Suppose that x wants to free himself of his room-mate tonight, and to this end decides to lend her his car to go to the theatre. The action *LEND-CAR* is by no means naturally instrumental to the goal "free-oneself-of-room-mate". Thus x's plan is based upon someone else's will and plans. Indeed, social reasoning is, by definition, forged by external will and plans. Social reasoning is most typically characterized by unnatural means–end links. The application of means–end reasoning to social situations is paradigmatically based upon unnatural links, as happens in daily life micro-interactions.

This becomes even more evident at the macro-level: the reason why people adopt norms, play social roles, etc., is not intrinsically linked to the benefits that they obtain in return. Usually, these social behaviours are extrinsically enforced (through money, social approval, reputation, power, authority, etc.). This issue will be further analyzed in the following chapters.

Reasons for goal adoption

Durfee et al. (1987b) draw their model of *self-interested agents* from classic economic theory and utilitarian philosophy. In our terms, instead, the postulate of an agent who adopts other people's aims solely as a function of his own aims (which may also be defined as self-interested), does not necessarily coincide with a selfish view of the agent. The agent's own goals, for the purpose of which he decides to adopt certain aims of someone else's, may include benevolence (liking, friendship, affection, love, compassion, etc.) or impulsive (reactive) behaviours of an altruistic type (although only towards certain agents and only in certain circumstances). In our model, there are three families of goal adoption, depending on the motivation of adoption:

(a) *terminal* adoption, where adoption is an end in itself and x neither calculates nor expects any advantage or reward. Adoption is an end-goal in x's mind, or better, he has the end that y obtains some of her goals. x is truly benevolent towards y.

(b) *instrumental* adoption, in which x adopts a goal of y's in order to obtain some advantage in return (think of the AR), i.e. because adoption is useful for one of his goals. There are various types of instrumental adoption ranging from mere exploitation (x allows y to attain a goal because this achieves a goal of x's as well; e.g. x feeds a chicken in order to have its eggs; x replies to a question asked by y in order to impress z), to exchange (x does something that is useful to y if/in order for y to do something of use to x). We will examine exchange.

(c) *co-operative adoption*: co-operation in the narrow sense is merely one type of adoption; x adopts a goal of y's (and possibly vice versa) in view of a goal shared by x and y. In one sense, co-operative adoption can be seen as a type of instrumental adoption; x and y have a shared goal. They depend on one another in order to achieve it (i.e. x needs an action by y and vice versa). x adopts y's goal as a result of the shared goal (and vice versa) (Grosz & Sidner 1990).

Of these three families, only terminal adoption is currently realized in existing MAS. Therefore, we will examine the last two families of goal adoption in some detail.

Instrumental goal adoption: exchange

During the 1950s and throughout the 1960s, a social version of the utility theory became popular in most social sciences, thanks to the antimentalistic propositions rather formally and elegantly expressed by Homans (1959). In this theory, known as *exchange theory*, individuals participate in interaction to the extent to which the rewards obtained are higher than the costs encountered by each agent. Such a simplifying principle was considered the most fundamental category of social interaction.

In research on distributed systems, which also draws on utility theory, the most general category is that of co-operation. However, sometimes it is not clear whether the notion of reference is exchange or co-operation.

Here, the two notions will be distinguished in terms of the mental ingredients that are needed for agents to be engaged in each of them. In other words, how are the minds of exchanging agents shaped? Do they differ in any significant way from the minds of co-operating agents?

Castelfranchi and Parisi (1984) proposed an incremental notion of exchange starting from a minimal factual notion and step-by-step derivation of a cognitive model of exchange.

(a) *bilateral adoption*: x adopts y in q and y adopts x in p. Father (x) adopts his daughter's (y) goal to have a new car to avoid being obliged to drive her to school, and y will adopt x's goal to go out and buy cigarettes and magazines in order to show off her new car. Here, there is no true exchange in the agents' minds nor any **reciprocation**, only a two-way goal adoption. Actually, there is something more: x's adoption favours y's adoption. This general notion of exchange may be of interest for a variety of reasons. For example, it allows unintentional and even functional exchanges (like exchanges in animal societies, or the functional role of such habits as the Trobriandese *potlatch*, a well-known example of collective exchange of gifts, found among the inhabitants of the Trobriand islands, and usually resulting in a global resource redistribution, etc.) to be explained.

(b) *adoption and reciprocation*: x adopts y and y adopts x in reciprocation. Here, reciprocation is defined as a special case of the goal to obtain adoption:

$$\left(RECIPROCATE\ x\,y\,p\right) \overset{def}{=} \left(G\text{-}ADOPT\ x\,y\,p\right) \wedge$$
$$\exists q\left[BEFORE \neg\left(G\text{-}ADOPT\ x\,y\,p\right)\left(BEL\,x\left(G\text{-}ADOPT\ y\,x\,q\right)\right)\right]$$

or: *x reciprocates y when, before x adopting whatever goal of y's, he believes that y has adopted one of his goals.* Reciprocation is induced by adoption. This is a frequent situation in social life. It is usually called *social exchange* although it is not characterized as such from the cognitive point of view. For example, *x* invites *y* to come over for dinner to enjoy her company. Feeling grateful, and to discharge her obligation, *y* brings *x* a present. Next, she will return the invitation. Here, there is reciprocation but no goal to be reciprocated, nor to obtain adoption. Consequently, these situations are not true exchanges, although they may be considered as forerunners of exchange (cf. Blau 1964).

(c) *adoption for reciprocation*: *x* adopts *y* to obtain her reciprocation, and *y* reciprocates. Although very similar to exchange, this is not yet a true exchange. Take the example of flattery: an employee (*x*) ingratiates his director (*y*) to obtain a promotion. Flattered by *x*'s praise, *y* wants to return *x*'s adoption and decides to promote him. In this situation, *x* wants to obtain reciprocation and decides to adopt *y*. From this example, therefore, we learn that autonomous agents share a norm of reciprocation (Gouldner 1960). In his deontic moral system, Jasay (1990) elaborates a set of precepts of the *honesty* system. In particular, this system is endowed with the promise-keeping precept, defined as a precondition of any social life. As observed by Radnitzky (1993: 19): "It is to social life what truth-telling is to communication." We will return to this issue in Chapter 6, after having introduced our normative notions.

(d) *adoption conditioned to reciprocation*: *x* adopts *y* on condition, and in order, that *y* reciprocates, and vice versa. This is exchange in the strictest sense. What was only an expectation in the preceding case, namely *x*'s expectation to obtain adoption as an effect of giving adoption, becomes a necessary condition here. This is precisely what Blau (1964) meant when he conceived of economic exchange as a simultaneous give-and-take adoption. Probably, the most fundamental aspect of real exchange is not simultaneity but rather mutually conditioned adoption: I will do an action for you as long as I believe you will do something for me in return:

$$(EXCHANGE\,x\,y\,p) \stackrel{def}{=}$$

$$\left(R\text{-}GOAL\,x\,(OBTAIN\,y\,q)\left(BEL\,x\left[(A\text{-}GOAL\,y\,q) \wedge (RECIPROCATE\,y\,x\,p)\right]\right)\right) \wedge$$

$$\left(R\text{-}GOAL\,y\,(OBTAIN\,x\,p)\left(BEL\,y\left[(A\text{-}GOAL\,x\,p) \wedge (RECIPROCATE\,x\,y\,q)\right]\right)\right)$$

that is: *x and y engage in exchange when x adopting y is relativized to x's belief that y reciprocates, and vice versa y adopting x is relativized to y's belief that x reciprocates.* In other words, each adopts only as long as the other reciprocates. This is the *paradox of exchange*: if there is no adoption, there cannot be any reciprocation. On the other hand, if there is no guarantee of reciprocation, there is no adoption. By accepting exchange with another agent, each agent *commits itself* to reciprocate (cf. Castelfranchi 1993b). In the absence of a model of *commitment*, we cannot fully account for the phenomenon of exchange. We will get back to this in Chapter 6.

The agents' goal to exchange follows from their belief that they are reciprocally dependent:

$$(BMB\, x\, y\, (REC\text{-}DEP\, x\, y\, p\, q)) \supset (EXCHANGE\, x\, y\, p\, q)$$

in words: *if x and y mutually believe they are dependent on each other each to achieve his/her goal, they will enter into a relation of exchange.* By AR, in fact, each will decide to adopt the other's goal on condition that the latter reciprocates. Interestingly, if y does not share x's belief that they are reciprocally dependent, x will try to convince her: x will come up with an influencing goal toward y.

Cheating in exchange

In the definition of exchange proposed, the partners' beliefs play a fundamental role: if the agents adopt each other, they believe that a reciprocation will necessarily follow. In other words, the achievement of y's goal is not sufficient for x to obtain reciprocation. In exchange, the reward must be perceived: if y is reciprocated but she believes she has not yet been reciprocated, nor will be later, y will not adopt x's goal. Certainly, the achievement of y's goal is not even necessary to obtain reciprocation from her: suffice to say that y believes she has achieved her goal. This artful practice of exchange has been transformed into a theoretical model[1] that has contributed to the spreading of a standard subjective bias in AI and cognitive science. In our analysis, conversely, what y asks is the satisfaction of her goal. She did not ask x to make her believe that her goal was achieved. The major forms of cheating are therefore ruled out. Partners in exchange are expected to honour the agreement in all its parts, and to give each other what has been agreed upon. They are bound to fulfil their partners' goals, and not simply make them believe they have.

However, this clause does not rule out some subtler forms of cheating. In exchange, agents are not expected to query the real utility of the contract for all parties involved. In other words, they are not expected to question the rationality of each other's decision. If, in a boutique, a short and heavy lady asks for a long fur, the assistant is not required to tell her that the fur does not suit her. He is obliged to sell her a fur at its right price. He may be held to give the lady some information that might discourage her from purchasing the fur (e.g. a fur needs frequent cleaning, it should not be exposed to too much humidity, etc.), but he is by no means held to take into account the real needs of the customer. In exchange, agents may profit from their partners' irrational decisions and cannot be reproached for this[2]. The agents are rather indifferent to each other's real needs, nor do they appear to be required to take them into account.

Mutual dependence and co-operation

Co-operation occurs when two or more agents intentionally achieve a common goal, that is, a goal with regard to which the agents depend on one another. In other words, co-operation is a multi-agent plan, i.e. a plan that necessarily requires more than one agent for it to be accomplished successfully (cf. Castelfranchi et al. 1989). In a multi-agent plan, the subplans required of each agent are tasks or roles, and the co-operating agents are task performers or role players. In its fullest sense, a co-operative plan occurs when agents mutually believe that they depend on one another to achieve one and the same goal:

$$(M\text{-}COOP\,x\,y\,p) \stackrel{def}{=} \big(BMB\,x\,y\,(M\text{-}DEP\,x\,y\,p)\big) \wedge$$

$$\exists a_x \exists a_y \Big[\big(GOAL\,x\big((DOES\,x\,a_x) \wedge (DOES\,y\,a_y)\big)\big) \wedge$$

$$\big(GOAL\,y\big((DOES\,x\,a_x) \wedge (DOES\,y\,a_y)\big)\big)\Big]$$

in words: *two agents x and y mutually co-operate when they mutually believe that x depends on y doing a_y and that y depends on x doing a_x and when they have the identical goals that both actions be performed.*

Indeed, mutual co-operation can be derived from mutual belief of mutual dependence:

$$\big(BMB\,x\,y\,(M\text{-}DEP\,x\,y\,p)\big) \supset (M\text{-}COOP\,x\,y\,p)$$

or: *if two or more agents mutually believe that they are mutually dependent for the purpose of achieving their goal p, they will ultimately mutually co-operate.* Owing to GGR, each agent has the goal that both actions be done, and then the goal to do what they can do themselves; owing to mutual knowledge of dependence, each agent wants to have the other in turn doing what s/he can to obtain the common goal. Therefore they will co-operate.

Co-operation leads to some form of instrumental adoption. Indeed, x believes he is dependent not only on y doing something, but more generally on y achieving a certain goal. For example in the blocks world, x depends on y achieving the goal that $cube_i$ is CLEARTOP, so that x can put $cube_j$ on top of it and the common goal that $cube_j$ is on top of $cube_i$ will be achieved. By AR, x will adopt y's goal. Suppose $cube_i$ is red, and x has control over red cubes. Let us assume that in our blocks world, a pre-condition for acting on cubes is that the agent has access to cubes. Let us also assume that one has access to cubes either when cubes are not controlled by anyone (i.e. they are *free*), or one has asked and received access to the cube by the agent controlling that cube. Since x adopts y's goal, he will give her access to $cube_i$. The same happens with y: since she depends on x to achieve the same goal, and has control over $cube_j$, she adopts x's goal and gives him access to $cube_j$. Both agents adopt each other's goals. Moreover, they do so in order to get the other to do the same and in the belief that s/he will. In a sense, co-operative adoption may be seen as a form of conditioned adoption. What is the difference, if any, between exchange and co-operation?

Exchange and co-operation

Both in AI and in other formal approaches (e.g. game theory), co-operation is the only type of social action considered. The game-theoretic view of co-operation (Kreps et al. 1982, Axelrod 1984, Axelrod & Dion 1988, and many others), which AI social studies inherited, presents several problems:
  (a) *co-operation is viewed as a fundamentally emergent*, as opposed to deliberate, phenomenon;
  (b) *co-operation* is essentially *equated to* either *co-ordination* (avoiding negative interferences; cf. Ch. 4), or conflict resolution; since the game-theoretic structure does not allow positive mutual dependence, a higher-level, more robust notion of co-operation is not conceivable within the game-theoretic view;
  (c) *local co-operative action is meant as a generic prosocial action*; the difference between adoption, exchange, co-operation and other forms of positive social actions are not allowed.
  In our view, exchange and co-operation may be instrumental to each other. In other words, two agents can either:
  (a) *co-operate to allow exchange*: for example if, in order to enjoy your company, I adopt your goal that we have dinner together, we will co-operate to prepare the meal; or
  (b) *exchange to allow co-operation*: in the previous example from the blocks world, x and y exchange control over given resources in order to achieve a common goal.
  However, between these two fundamental categories of social interaction, there is a difference of vital importance. As said earlier, in exchange, adoption is exclusively oriented toward obtaining reciprocation. In co-operation, adoption is also driven by the final goal, which is common by definition. In

other words, while co-operation is a multi-agent plan, exchange is not. Indeed, exchange cannot even be modelled as a unique plan. It results from two individual plans that overlap to some extent. In our blocks world example, x wants y to achieve her goal because this is a means for a final goal that is also his own. Therefore, x gives y access to the resource she needs. He does so because he really adopts her goal. We could say that x is co-interested in y having access to x's resource. In the next chapter, we will discuss this in greater detail together with other phenomena related to the notion of interest. Furthermore, in Chapter 11, we will show some important effects of the difference that we are making here in some AI applicative domains.

Recapitulation

A really autonomous agent has been defined here as goal-autonomous, that is, as a self-interested agent capable of rejecting other agents' requests when these requests are incompatible with its own goals, whether selfish or altruistic.

How is social action possible among goal-autonomous agents? In a common world, autonomous agents encounter a fundamental limit to their autonomy. This is not only due to head-on collisions, but also to the fundamental phenomenon of social dependence. Others may represent resources for a given agent. Agents need one another's help to achieve their goals. They need to have their goals adopted by others. The mechanism of goal adoption is the core of social life. It represents a filter of others' requests: agents adopt one another's goals either as an end in itself, or when they see some advantage in doing so, when they can profit from the others' achievements, or obtain their reciprocation, or, finally, when they are co-interested with others. Some suggestions have been provided for each of these alternatives, and the role of goal adoption in different forms of social interaction – exploitation, exchange, and co-operation – has been analyzed.

CHAPTER FOUR
Adoption of others' interests

Adoption beyond the others' wishes

What are the limits within which goal adoption occurs? In real life, adoption does not necessarily presuppose an explicit will. Sometimes, recipients need to *read* beyond the speakers' requests in order to provide them with a useful answer. Sometimes, goal adoption is spontaneous: it is not even dependent on either explicit or implicit requests. These phenomena point to the crucial issue; the contours and limits of goal adoption. Furthermore, they seem to address the puzzling question of whether adoption is possible when the would-be recipient has no goal to receive adoption. In other words, is adoption beyond the others' wishes possible?

Degrees and levels of adoption

As widely known in Human Computer Interaction (HCI), one of the first questions that an intelligent help system ought to face is: to what level in the user's recognizable plan should the system's answer apply? Up to what goal does the system need to reconstruct the user's plan in order to give a proper and useful answer?

In the field of HCI, this is also known as the phenomenon of *over-answering* which is only an applicative example of a theoretical problem that has received a great deal of attention within pragmatic theories of communication. We can neither address such theories nor analyze the question of over-answering, but we can at least clarify some crucial issues. These issues are not only relevant in a descriptive–theoretical sense – that is, to provide a model of adoption that approximates, as closely as possible, help among real agents – but also for reasons of efficiency. As we will endeavour to show, in order to be really useful, the helper often needs to go beyond the recipient's request. In other words, in help giving, agents take advantage of one another's intelligence and autonomy. Indeed, they receive and interpret one another's requests. Help givers evaluate the requests for help from the recipients' viewpoint, against their goals and interests. Let us examine when and why they do so:

(a) *Indirect requests.* The first and most frequent problem encountered by conversants and theorized by students of communication and pragmaticians is that of indirectness of communication. For a variety of reasons which we will not discuss here, including economy and courtesy rules, requests may be, and often are, *disguised* or conveyed in an indirect form. In these phenomena the speaker's real will is sufficiently comprehensible to the hearer. No specific interpretation is needed, since the meaning of the request is unambiguously established by convention.

(b) *Beyond communication.* A much less obvious use of communication is when the speaker's will is left deliberately implicit. In other words, the communication made is meant to achieve some quasi-hidden goal of the speaker. Consider an agent asking someone who is about to go out: "Are you going anywhere?" in order to be invited to join her. Here, the hearer is not assisted by conventions. She needs to accomplish some more complex and speaker-oriented inferential work. The reason why the speaker leaves his ultimate goal implicit is usually self-defensive: in this example, since the speaker's intention to get an invitation is implicit, any answer, including rejection, could be left implicit as well, for example: "I am rushing to work." Furthermore, an implicit request allows the hearer to take any initiative she likes: the hearer could answer: "Nowhere in particular. Do you want to come for a walk with me?" In such a case the speaker's intention is catered for with no need to refer to it explicitly. Now, implicit communications point to one of the most interesting aspects of interaction: when is the hearer entitled to reconstruct the speaker's plan? And when is it sufficient to answer only the explicit part of a request?

(c) *Beyond the actions wanted by the recipient.* Sometimes, help is not forthcoming in the form in which it is asked. The helper does not always perform the actions desired by the recipient, and yet his answer may still be helpful. Indeed, if he carried out the actions desired by the recipient, the latter would have gained less of an advantage, if any. In the definition suggested by Cohen & Levesque (1990c), the helper is a mere mindless executive, since his help consists of executing all actions the recipient wants him to do. Now, a mindless executive is not a helper. Consider, for example, y's asking x, "Have you got a light?". x understands the indirect speech act, "Give me a light", and understands that y's aim is to light a cigarette; x has a cigarette lighter and is in a position to help y solve her problem in a slightly different way. But according to the previous definition, if x were to stick to y's request, he should answer, "No, I don't have a light" and that would be it.

(d) *Beyond the recipient's plans.* Let us take another case: y has a bad stomach ache and asks x for an aspirin to relieve the pain (y does not know that aspirin is bad for the stomach). Suppose x has got some aspirin but is aware of its side-effects. According to the previous definition, nonetheless, x will be helpful if he does what is asked of him. Intuitively, instead, x is truly helpful if he adopts not only whatever is asked of him, but also the goals and higher-level goals of the request. From this point of view Grosz & Sidner's (1990) claim that in plan recognition, agents will be interested only in those [plans] that are intended to be recognized to be insufficient. Helpers are not only interested in the recipients' plans. Real helpers should provide the recipients with information that is necessary for them to attain even some extra-plan goals. It is in fact possible that the plan produced by y is useless or detrimental to her goals and x might discourage her. In her plan theory, in distinguishing between the agent's and the observer's beliefs, Pollack (1990) stressed the fact that some of the listener's beliefs concerning means–end links might differ from those of the speaker's. The former might therefore change the latter's plan, suggesting different approaches. However, this implies new levels of goal adoption and a less executive concept of helpfulness. In order to be truly helpful x must be an autonomous planner and adopt the recipient's higher-level goals.

(e) *Beyond the recipient's goals.* The second restrictive aspect of current definitions of adoption, co-operativeness or helpfulness refers to the fact that we must view the benevolent agent as being capable of spontaneous adoption, that is, of adopting y's goals even independently of y's requests and expectations. Sometimes, goal adoption is not even implicitly requested. The helper does not infer any implicit request: he simply attributes to the recipient some goal that he has decided to adopt. This is done either in a top-down process – the recipient is a member of a class which, in the helper's agents' models, has that goal – or on a circumstantial basis – as when a passenger picks up and hands you the glove you have inadvertently dropped. Indeed, the recognition of the sentence plans has a lot in common also with the recognition of the plans of non-communicative actions: also the goals that y does not intend to communicate are perceived. In some cases, a truly helpful system may tend towards adopting other important goals of the recipient's, which may be temporarily inactive, or even her interests (that is, advantageous situations that may be neither known to, nor wanted by, the agent; see Ch. 1).

Intrusive and legitimate adoption

Autonomy may render help intrusive. High-level helpfulness, especially that which goes beyond the recipient's goals, may be dangerous both in human relations and in an artificial friendly system. Imagine an expert system that, to the request to book a table in a given restaurant, replies: "Are you sure you can afford it? It is very expensive." or "I shall not book it for you because the food is very hot and you are elderly." Clearly a limit must be set to the helpfulness of agents, so that they do not become intrusive. Let us consider another example (Castelfranchi 1990): y asks x to pass her a hammer and x replies: "Here's the riveter, it's easier." Here, x has not only understood the goals that y communicated to him so that he can adopt them, but also her higher-level goals, i.e. her overall plan. Indeed, x does not adopt the subgoal suggested to him but proposes another plan to her (other actions and resources). In this case, x is highly co-operative: he adopts y's interests (to achieve her goal more easily, more quickly). This is possible because x sees no conflicts between y's goals and her interests. A limit could conventionally be set to x's adoptiveness: that he should adopt only those interests and inactive goals of the recipient's that are compatible with her present goal, the one for which she wants help; on the contrary, the helper should not adopt those interests of the recipient's that clash with the goals she is autonomously pursuing. In natural interaction this limit does not apply but there are rules about who is entitled to interfere and from whom we accept interference. These rules are however based on roles and relations (e.g. close friends, parents, spouses) that have not yet received adequate treatment in the field.

Interests of other agents represent one of the inputs to any given agent's goals. Some questions arise here:

- *Why do agents need other agents to pursue their interests?*
- *Why* should one agent decide *to adopt other agents' interests?*
- More generally, *is there any significant difference between adoption of interests and goal adoption?*

The gap between interests and goals

A fundamental answer to the first question is found in the hiatus between agents' interests and their goals. In fact, by definition, agents' interests are advantageous states which are neither necessarily wanted nor believed by the interested agents. As was shown in Chapter 2, it is possible to show both that adaptable agents finally become aware of their interests, and, thanks to GGR, that they will also produce new goals from their beliefs about their interests.

Interests and beliefs

As was shown in Chapter 1, beliefs about interests are true when they overlap with objective interests, that is, with interests as perceived by an external observer. In this case, we say that interests are *known*. Otherwise, if there is no correspondence between believed and objective interests, interests are only *pretended*. Finally, objective interests are *ignored* when they are not represented at all within the agent's beliefs. This happens rather frequently, but the ratio between known and unknown interests varies over the agent's life-time. For example, it may be expected to decrease with experience. This can be observed empirically. Believed interests have a fundamental pragmatic role: they help the agent to reason about actions and in planning. Obviously, ignoring one's interests may lead to their impairment. Therefore, since pragmatic cognition is adaptive and tends to be amended through experience, false beliefs about interests are likely to be discovered and rectified. Consequently, previously ignored interests tend to become known. This does not imply that interests are realized only if they are known to the agents. Nor is it implied that ignored interests are realized only accidentally. Sometimes, actions realizing one agent's interests may be objectively induced by the circumstances in which that agent finds itself. Without knowing what its interest is, that agent will produce a state of the world that achieves one of its goals (see the working-class example discussed in Ch. 2).

Conflict of interests (prevailing interest)

Ignoring one's interests leads to their impairment. One's capacity to forecast events and analyze situations in the light of one's own goals may be so severely limited that some interests are never detected. This effect is even more dramatic when an immediate, comprehensible interest contrasts with a long-term one. The gap between interests and goals is not simply due to the agents' lack of information. This is only one of the limits to agents' rationality. Conflicts of interests within the same agent are here considered to be an additional source of irrational behaviour. Quite on the contrary, utility scientists (e.g. Luce & Raiffa 1990) hold a harmonious view of agents' interests:

> The distinction between an individual and a group is not a biological–social one but simply a functional one. Any decision-maker . . . which can be thought of as having a *unitary interest* motivating its decision can be treated as an *individual* in the theory. Any collection of such individuals having *conflicting interests* which must be resolved, . . . will be considered to be a *group*." (20, our italics)

In this view, within one and the same agent unitary interests are taken for granted, and the phenomenon of conflicting interests is seen as a fundamentally inter-agent phenomenon; the question of how individual agents eventually achieve their unitary interests is not raised. The possibility of intra-agent conflicts is not denied but not addressed explicitly either. Two objections should be made:

(a) *conflicts also occur within one and the same individual*. Conflicting interests within the same agent motivate this agent to decide how to solve the conflict, and sometimes, intra-agent conflicts of interest are solved via inter-agent decision-making, that is, thanks to suggestions, requests, or prescriptions from others. Therefore, unitary interests are not only inputs to individual agents' decisions; they are also *outputs* of both intra- and inter-individual agents' decisions. The relationship between agents, interests and groups is more complex than is found in utility theory. It is not true that unitary interests are to the individual agents what conflicting interests are to groups. In both, the same question arises: how does an agent, individual or collective, solve conflicts among its several interests?

(b) *Social processes may be found at the origin of individual agents' decisions.* Sometimes, a conflict resolution cannot be achieved by a single agent for reasons that will soon be clarified. Therefore, other agents may enter the conflict resolution process, turning it into a social process; into social decision-making.

In sum, the existence of other agents in a common world is not a necessary evil. The individual agent's autonomy is not only limited by others interfering, but also by its own private constraints. It is not true that, were other agents not out there, each agent could realize its interests totally. Agents represent both a limit to and a resource for one another's achievements. Not considering both aspects will produce a partial and somewhat misleading account of the individual to group relation. For example, a most crucial question would not be easily answered: since autonomous agents do not only endure their fellows, but they also *decide* to join groups, why should they do so?

A single agent's interests may be conflicting for several reasons:

(a) *End-conflict*: since interests are defined with regard to goals, agents may also have conflicting interests that depend on their conflicting goals.

(b) *Means-conflict*: furthermore, goals that do not appear to be in conflict may be achieved by conflicting states. This is a classical problem of means–end reasoning which concerns interests as well.

(c) *Potential goals*: interests may be related even to inactive and potential goals. An agent's goal is inactive when it is not currently examined (for example, if it is already fulfilled or is unachievable) but its status may change depending on circumstances. A goal is potential when an agent is expected to have that goal some time in the future. This change is not expected to depend on circumstances but on an implicit theory about normal personality and its development. Therefore, conflicting interests may be identified even when no actual goal conflict occurs. This is often the case when agents cling to apparently irrational behaviours. Children, for example, do not have the goal to be healthy. This is at most a potential goal, that is, one that children are expected to have sometime in the future, as adults. Nonetheless, their parents try to get them to avoid harmful behaviour and habits here and now.

These considerations, especially the latter, could help us understand why agents may not realize what their interests are. The gap between interests and goals is not only determined by a lack of or inadequate information. It may also be due to circumstantial change and the development of the individual agents over their life-time. Goals may change, but interests are identified here and now, even when they refer to future goals.

This points to the fundamental notion of **prevailing interest**[1]. Here, an agent x's prevailing interest will be defined as that which will favour x most with the highest probability and at the lowest cost: x's prevailing interest is a state that, by keeping constant the probability of being realized, achieves either the highest number of x's goals or the most important ones (including inactive and potential goals) and jeopardizes the least. For example, as a consumer I may welcome a slackening of the inflation rate, whereas as a wholesaler I would like to see it speed up. Other things being equal, the latter is my current prevailing interest. Under conditions of inflation, I gain more by selling goods than I lose by buying them.

Tutorial roles as a way to fill in the gap

To identify one's *prevailing interest*, an external observer is required. The observer is usually a scientist. Any of the people we encounter daily may also be observers: parents, friends, experts, etc. Each of the above characters may form a representation of the agent's goals and their development. Each may confront this representation with the model of the current and predictable world each already has, and suggest which states would be most convenient to the observed agent given her goals. Unlike the scientist, however, the real life observer, x, usually plays a participant role: instead of being neutral, x will try to influence the observed agent, y, to act in her own interests, whatever x believes them to be. Between x and y, there will be a tutorial relation: x will act as a tutor towards y.

Tutorial relationships can easily be found between teacher and pupil, adult and child, director and directed. A relationship between x and y can be called tutorial if three conditions are verified:

(a) *x adopts y's goal p*, or a subset of y's goals (out of affection, philanthropy or because his social role prescribes him to do so etc.);

(b) *y does not act in her interest q with regard to her goal p*;

(c) *x wants y to have the goal q*.

The tutorial relationships are characterized by one party's having tutorial goals *vis-à-vis* the other. To be clearer, x has a **tutorial goal** vis-à-vis y, when x has an influencing goal towards y that, once achieved, is believed by x to realize a given interest of y's:

$$(T\text{-}GOAL\,x\,y\,q) \stackrel{def}{=}$$

$$\exists p\Big(R\text{-}GOAL\,x\big(A\text{-}GOAL\,y\,q\big)\big(BEL\,x\big(INTEREST\,y\,q\,p\big)\big)\Big)$$

in words: *x has a tutorial goal towards y, when x has an influencing goal q that y wants relativized to x's belief that q is an interest of y's with regard to her goal p.*

How can tutorial goals be derived?

It could be asked where tutorial goals come from. Indeed, from *x*'s adoption of *y*'s goal *p*, by GGR, we can easily derive *x*'s goal *q*. But what about *x*'s goal of influencing *y* to want *q*?

Tutorial goals also represent a special case of adoption. They occur at the intersection between adoption and influencing. As we know, influencing goals are not necessarily benevolent: they are often pursued independently, and even in spite, of the other's interests. However, there are also situations in which influencing goals originate from adoption, and even interest adoption. These are called here tutorial goals. In other words, a tutorial goal is an influencing goal that implies *x*'s adoption of (some of) *y*'s interests. However, adoption is not yet sufficient to derive an influencing goal. An additional belief is needed, namely *x*'s belief about a further interest of *y*'s:

$$\forall q \forall p\Big[\Big(\big(BEL\,x\big(\big(INTEREST\,y\,(GOAL\,y\,q)\,p\big)\wedge\neg(GOAL\,y\,q)\big)\big)\wedge$$

$$(G\text{-}ADOPT\,x\,y\,p)\big)\supset(T\text{-}GOAL\,x\,y\,q)\Big]$$

in words: *if x believes that y is interested in having q as a goal with regard to her goal p and believes y does not have goal q, and if x adopts y in p, then x will have a tutorial goal towards y.*

This is true for GGR: if *x* adopts *y* in *p* (second premise), by definition of adoption *x* wants *y* to obtain *p*. Now, if *x* believes that *y* wanting *q* is an interest of *y*'s with regard to *p* (first premise), by definition of interest, *x* will also believe that *y* wanting *q* leads to *y* obtaining *p*. For the GGR, therefore, *x* wants *y* to have the goal *q*, and this implies *x*'s belief that this is an interest of *y*'s. By definition, this conclusion means that *x* has a tutorial goal *vis-à-vis y*.

Tutorial roles: aggressive or adoptive?

There are many examples of tutorial goals and relationships in real life. The parent–child relationship offers a bountiful observatory. A paradigmatic example is a parent wanting a child to do her homework. Of course, the parent could do it in place of the child. In that case, adoption would not be tutorial. Instead, the parent usually chooses to try to influence the child to act in her own interests.

Two observations can be drawn from this example. First, tutorial behaviours are often considered aggressive. Our analysis of the subject matter accounts for this evidence in at least two ways. As already stated, x's tutorial goal implies his belief that y does not have q as a goal. This in turn implies x's belief that:

(a) *y does not know her interest* with regard to her goal p (otherwise, for GGR, she would have q as a goal); or

(b) *the goal p favoured by q is not a current goal of y's*;. or, finally,

(c) *she does not correctly estimate her current prevailing interest*. For example, she wants to do well at school, but also wants to go out with friends. She knows that doing her homework would impair the latter goal. Since to have fun is more compelling for y than doing well at school, she finally gives up the latter goal. The parent, instead, thinks that her prevailing interest should induce y to stay home.

In other words, x believes that either:

(a) y has *incomplete* or *wrong beliefs* (about her interests); or

(b) y has illegal or *immature goals*, and consequently x thinks that they could, or actually should, be ignored in the interest of y.

Essentially, x's beliefs diminish y's competence, and his goal is aggressive.

In sum, if the parent does the child's homework, he will adopt her preferences, maybe even her short-term interests, e.g. getting high marks for the homework, but not her prevailing interest. The parent replaces his child completely – for brevity, let us call this type of adoption surrogate adoption – but, so to speak, he respects her will. On the other hand, if the parent does not do the homework but asks his child to do it, he will not replace her but ignores and opposes her wishes. What is more, he may exercise his authority to the point of overruling his child's wishes: ("If you don't do your homework, you won't go out!") Therefore, there seems to be a sort of trade-off between surrogate adoption and tutoring. Tutoring does not imply acting in the pupil's place. In this sense, it is less intrusive but more aggressive than surrogate adoption.

However, in surrogate adoption, x is less co-interested in y achieving her goals. Consequently, adoption is usually less effective than tutoring. In other words, if x really knows[2] what y's interests are, x's tutorial goal achieves y's interest better than surrogate adoption would. In the latter case x would limit himself to realizing y's interest q, without worrying about y doing it. He does not equip y with tools to deal with future occurrences of the same problem.

Why do agents adopt the interests of other agents?

One's adopting another's interests seems to imply one wanting the other to *obtain* some achievement. Let us provide a definition of interest adoption:

$$(I\text{-}ADOPT\,x\,y\,q\,p) \stackrel{def}{=} \big(R\text{-}GOAL\,x\,q\,(BEL\,x\,(INTEREST\,q\,y\,p))\big)$$

that is: *x adopts y's interest q as long as x believes that q is an interest of y's (with regard to y's goal p).*

This is tricky, though, because interests have been shown to refer even to what are not (yet) goals of the recipient. Now, how can an agent *obtain* something that she does not want? This is possible in a rather peculiar sense: *x* adopts *y*'s interests when these favour those goals of *y*'s that *x* assumes *y should* have. Therefore, one could argue that adopting someone's interest should imply a tutorial goal, concerning the goal with regard to which interest is adopted. However, this argument would be worth a more detailed analysis than can be done here.

Thanks to the mechanism of adoption, both the goals and interests of others may be inputs to one agent's goals. By the rule of adoption, an autonomous agent needs reasons for adopting the goals of other agents. As we know, he is sufficiently motivated to do this whenever he thinks he may get something in return. For example, we argued that the agents usually plan to adopt others' goals to obtain reciprocation from them.

As far as interests are concerned, however, things are not so simple. Why should an autonomous agent adopt someone else's interests? This type of adoption is less rewarding than ordinary adoption for two reasons:

- given the objective nature of interests, *recipients may not realize that they have been adopted.* Or, if they do, they may feel mistreated and abused for the reasons examined above, and consequently unlikely to give adoption in return.
- furthermore, *the adoption of interests is an unnecessary and rather expensive way to obtain reciprocation.* To fulfil someone's goals is both sufficient and cheaper, since people's goals are somewhat more accessible than their interests.

Why on earth, therefore, should autonomous agents pursue one another's interests? By analogy with goal adoption, we will distinguish three fundamental types of interest adoption:

- *terminal*: an agent *x* adopts another agent *y*'s interest *q* as an end in itself. The paradigmatic example is precisely the parent–child relationship, where the former agent pursues the latter agent's interests – and not only her goals – out of affection.
- *co-interested*: an agent *x* adopts someone's interest *q* in order to achieve a common interest or goal *p*. In social life, there are many examples of common interests, that may be more or less relevant to predict social

phenomena.

– *instrumental*: interest adoption is instrumental when x adopts y's interest to gain something in return. Instrumental adoption of interests is but a special case of the AR.

While the first two are very similar to the corresponding forms of goal adoption, the third is substantially different since reciprocation is relatively less likely in interest-adoption than in goal adoption. What kind of benefit is therefore expected from adopting the interests of others?

Social prescriptions and interest adoption

When it is terminal, interest adoption is a spontaneous phenomenon. Indeed, the recipients of such a form of adoption are not always aware of it; often, they are not particularly grateful for it either. Think of the parent–child example, or of philanthropists: the adopting agents do not mind the recipients' ungratefulness since they do not choose to adopt their interests in order to be reciprocated by them, to obtain something in return. They choose to behave this way because they are interested in the recipients (parents), or because they are internally and spontaneously motivated to help others (philanthropists).

Besides the internal motivations of the adopting agents, interest adoption may also fulfil some social expectations. In other words, there are many situations in which given agents are expected, required, and even prescribed to realize either some specific or prevailing interests of other agents. Actually, on more careful scrutiny, in some cases the adoption of interests is both spontaneous and socially prescribed. The adopting agents do not (necessarily) choose to adopt the recipients' interest in order to comply with this prescription, but the prescription is there. Its most important consequence is a strong social pressure and disapproval of agents who violate the prescription, disappointing expectations. For example, parents are prescribed to adopt their children's interests, and this is also what parents in fact do. The parents' real motivations are probably related to their biological bases, attachment, affection, etc. Still, a rather heavy social stigma attaches to those parents who do not pursue their children's interests, or do so insufficiently and inconsistently.

Typically, interest adoption is socially prescribed when it is instrumental. In social life, there are many situations in which people are required to adopt the interests of others. In sporadic interactions, agents may be held to consider one another's interests. Consider the following exchange:

y: "Excuse me, sir, do you know where the nearest post office is?"

x: "Certainly, madam, but it will be closed by the time you get there!"

Here, a passerby is asked for logistic information. Instead of fulfilling the request, he adopts the asker's current prevailing interest, namely not to waste resources pursuing a goal with little or no chance of success.

Let us examine this example more carefully. One could wonder why x bothers with y's prevailing interest. Unlike parents with their children, x feels no internal motivation to realize y's interests, but does so only because he believes he is bound to do so.

There is probably more than one answer to this question[3]. One possible answer is that x complies with some social norm prescribing him (as a member of the community) to adopt some interests of other members, at least on given conditions. In other words, x is not *directly* adopting y's interests, but rather someone else's (let us say, society's) request, and hence, but only indirectly, y's interests. With its norms and prescriptions, society is concerned with y's interests. In the example provided, x's behaviour is not much different from, say, that of a driver stopping at a red light.

In addition to its other drawbacks, this answer is insufficient: it does not account for the reason why x complies with social prescriptions. We will return to this question in the next two chapters. Here, we want to argue that interest adoption follows from some pre-existing goal adoption: it is an indirect form of adoption that presupposes the existence of a *third party* and its goals.

Interest adoption and multi-agent links

Often, agents choose to play roles that involve the achievement of others' interests, and even the performance of tutorial tasks. To put it differently, social roles (for an initial formal treatment of this notion see Werner 1988) are construed as complex patterns of goals, action and plan repertoires, knowledge, skills, obligations, etc. In some cases, role goals and tasks include the pursuit of interests of a given set of agents. These interests may be more or less specific and more or less vital. For example, bodyguards are required to watch over the supreme good, i.e. the life of those they protect to the point of sacrificing their own lives. To a lesser extent, Members of Parliament, as well as leaders and spokesmen of trade unions and workers' organizations, are selected to defend some well-defined interests of the categories that they are supposed to represent.

Finally, some roles are tutorial. This is frequent in complementary role relations, especially in the professional–client relation. The interaction between doctors and patients, lawyers and defendants is interspersed with attempts by the professionals to persuade their clients to undertake certain behaviours (to go on a diet, to come to terms with their adversary in a court case, etc.). These moves are suggested in the interests of the clients, even if they clash with the clients' wishes and claims.

All these examples attract our attention to the following apparent inconsistency. On one hand, some agents play a given role to get something in return, usually to be paid. They are not motivated to adopt the interests of the beneficiaries *per se,* for the latter's own sake, but only to the extent that the realization of these interests earns them something (say, a salary or fee). On the other hand, the agents who play the roles in question are indeed called upon to concern themselves with the interests of the beneficiaries. Their role tasks and obligations compel them to do so, even when these interests are not acknowledged by the beneficiaries, even, as in the bodyguard example, when fulfilling the role task could cost the agent its own life. How can this apparent paradox be resolved? How can interest adoption be directed towards obtaining a reward, especially a monetary one?

Social action has been defined as the domain of unnatural means–end reasoning. Planning in social life is actually even more complex than this. The social world is not a set of dyadic interactions with each interaction occurring in a vacuum. On the contrary, at least two sets of constraints pre-exist (cf. Castelfranchi et al. 1992a), social norms and multi-agent links. No interaction is really dyadic, but almost all have consequences on, and are allowed by, a network of agents. As unnatural links play a fundamental role in social planning, so multi-agent links have a strong impact on the adoption of interests and tutorial relationships. In other words, when interests are brought into play, inter-agent negotiation and adoption is not exclusively a two-party process, but involves some third party, a mediatory entity. The three parties are:

– x, the agent acting in the interests of another agent; let us call him the *beneficent agent*;
– y, the agent whose interests are adopted, or *beneficiary*;
– z, *the entity who adopts y's interests terminally*, for y's own sake.

A complex interrelationship holds between them: z wants x to realize y's interests, and x adopts z's goal, thus indirectly adopting the interests of y. Take baby-sitting as a simplifying example. A baby-sitter (x) takes care of a child (y) on behalf of, say, the child's mother (z). x is asked by z to take care of y when she is absent. To do this, x is promised a salary. x accepts the request because he needs to earn a living and adopts z's goal. Consequently, x has the goal to take care of y when y's mother is absent. However, since z's goal is to realize y's interests, x has to adopt y's interests as well. This is not really expected, though, in ordinary situations of exchange. In the example considered, however, the baby-sitter is expected to mind the child's interests even in the absence of any explicit request by the child's mother. At nights, if the child wakes after its mother has gone out, the baby-sitter is expected to get the child to sleep as soon as possible, instead of allowing it to watch the TV while he is on the phone. Even though z is not aware of any such possibility and has not given x any explicit instructions, x ought to ask himself what is the prevailing interest of the child he has been entrusted with. In short, x should behave as if the child were his own child.

This points to a fundamental aspect of tutorial roles, and more generally of those roles that imply the role player adopting the interests of some complementary category of agents: although based on exchange, these roles demand a *commitment* of the role players which goes far beyond the commitment demanded by ordinary exchange. When roles imply interest adoption, role players are required to act towards the beneficiaries as if their adoption were terminal. To play such roles implies some costs which are not compensated by the reward that the role players obtain[4] (their salaries or fees). These costs are similar to those implied by norm-abiding behaviour (see the next two chapters): norm-abiding behaviour is more costly than spontaneous, endogenous behaviour. Otherwise, it would not make sense to call it norm-abiding. Analogously, roles include some role prescriptions, and role playing leads to compliance with those prescriptions, involving commitment to certain role-abiding behaviours.

In the next few chapters, in which the notion of obligation will be introduced, the question of the costs incurred by the agents who achieve normative goals will be addressed.

Recapitulation

In the previous chapter, it was found that agents can deal with others' requests and wants. Here, they are found dealing with others' objective necessities and welfare.

This phenomenon points to two equally important conclusions.
   – *interest is a fundamental objective notion that helps explain both the individual and the social action*; not only one's own interests but also the interests of others provide inputs to one's actions;
   – there is a fundamental paradox of real societies: *self-interested agents*, that is, agents motivated to action by their own goals and needs, *display actions which are intended to achieve goals and needs of others*.

How can this paradox be solved? To provide an answer to such a question means providing the most fundamental solution to the question of the micro–macro link. Although self-interested and therefore autonomous, a social agent may be used as a *device* to facilitate multi-agent co-ordination and co-operation.

Indeed, the right answer to this question depends on a heuristic formulation. The problem is not really how social forces and constraints can act in spite of autonomous agents, but rather whether and how they profit from, and take advantage of, the mental potentialities and resources of autonomous intelligent agents. As the mechanism of adoption seems to show, the agents may render one another a valuable service. In particular, the phenomenon of interest adoption suggests that help may be extended far beyond the boundaries of the recipients' will. The possibility that one obtains reciprocation from a third party – e.g. society at large – if not from the recipient, makes it possible that one provides help even at the level of the recipients' interests. Indeed, it becomes rational, that is, rewarding for one agent to concern itself with others' welfare, even when no terminal benevolence is involved. It is through indirect mechanisms of this sort that social laws and obligations obtain the hardest and most challenging of results, namely rational co-operation and help giving among autonomous agents.

Now, we will turn our attention to a further external input: normative prescriptions. Here, more than before, the question is of course why and how an autonomous agent comes to accept external requests that may not be useful for its own achievements.

PART THREE

Macro-social inputs to micro-level action: the case of norms

CHAPTER FIVE
The normative coin

... either where one of the parties *has* performed already; or where there is *a power to make him perform*; there is the question whether *it be against reason ... to perform*, or not.
(Hobbes, *Leviathan*, p. 95, our italics)[1]

The role of norms in MAS

The study of norms is a recent but growing concern in the AI field (cf. Moses & Tennenholtz 1992, Shoham & Tennenholtz 1992a), while theories of norms began to appear long before in the social sciences, notably in game theory (cf. Schelling 1960, Lewis 1969, Ullman-Margalit 1977).

The normative dimension is essential to social life. An explicit model of this dimension is crucial for any theory of social action. Notions such as social commitment (cf. Cohen & Levesque 1990b, Gasser 1991b, etc.), joint intentions, teamwork (Cohen & Levesque 1991), negotiation (Davies & Smith 1983), social roles (Werner 1989), etc. would be purely metaphorical if their normative character was not accounted for.

Indeed, one's committing oneself to someone else causes the latter to be entitled to expect, control, and exact the action the former agent has committed himself to (Castelfranchi 1993b). Hobbes had seen this quite clearly when he proposed that the only possible way to avoid belligerent attitudes among humans consists of a *network of contracts*, that is, mutual commitments leading to the *investiture of a sovereign*, who is responsible for the peacekeeping (see Gauthier 1969). Social commitment is a customary, if not the most frequent, source of entitlement in everyday interaction: a promise creates an entitled expectation in the addressee, namely a belief that the promised course of action will be realized. As a consequence, the addressee feels entitled to exact the action expected, that is, to control its occurrence and react if it is not performed. In particular, the addressee is entitled to express a public protest and receive the consent and support of the community of witnesses before whom the action of commitment occurred.

Furthermore, there is no true negotiation without control of cheaters and a norm of reciprocation (cf. Gouldner 1960). When social agents negotiate the exchange of resources, they actually set up the value of the exchanged resources, that is, what each is *entitled* to expect from others given the resources invested. Without a norm of reciprocation, such expectations would not be fulfilled if the exchange, as is often the case, does not occur simultaneously (as Hobbes realized). The utilitarian agent would spontaneously respect the agreement only if the partner is regarded as stronger. Otherwise, he would try to get off scot-free. In a word, he would try to cheat.

Analogously, joint intentions and teamwork arise from true negotiation and create *rights* based on commitments. Finally, roles are but sets of obligations and rights.

Although norms are now considered essential for both understanding social behaviour and implementing good MAS, the existing treatment of norms is still unsatisfactory precisely in view of implementing norms in an *autonomous* agent architecture. Let us see why.

The game-theoretic view of norms

Within game theory, social norms are essentially seen as *conventions*, that is, behavioural conformities that do not presuppose explicit agreements among agents, and emerge from their individual interests (cf. Schelling 1960, Lewis 1969). The function of these norms is essentially that of permitting or improving co-ordination among participants. A well-known example (Lewis 1969, p. 5) is that of two people unexpectedly cut off in a telephone conversation. They both want to continue the conversation and each of them has to choose whether to call back or wait. A convention gradually emerges from interactional practice, establishing who should do what. *Norms of co-ordination*, therefore, do not stem from a conflict of utility. Indeed, the solution of a problem of co-ordination is such that, if one agent succeeds, so does the other. The single's utility implies the joint one, and vice versa.

The emergence of norms

Ullman-Margalit (1977) actually provides an account of norms that goes far beyond mere conventions and norms of co-ordination. She endeavours to provide a formal (in the sense of abstract and structural) treatment of different types of norms, including (a) *norms of co-ordination*, (b) *Prisoners' Dilemma (PD) norms*, originating from a conflict of utility among interactants, and even (c) *norms of inequality*, aimed at maintaining a state of affairs in which one party is favoured or privileged at the expense of another. The fundamental concern of the author is for the origins of norms and, more specifically, the reasons for given types of norms.

Even in Ullman-Margalit's opinion, it is not the game-theoretic paradigm in its most general form that provides a reason for norms. Only a special case of it, the generalized PD structure, can be found at the onset of norms. Essentially, the argument is as follows: in reiterated games (as opposed to the one-shot type, where participants interact once, and simultaneously), the higher the number of players – and consequently the lower the probabilities of the same agents interacting repeatedly – the more destructive, either jointly and separately, the players' options. Consider the classical pay-off matrix of the PD game (see Table 1, p. 7), where the most rational choice for each player is to play Defeat when their opponent has played Co-operation. The consequent obvious question is how a co-operative answer can be made possible. Game theorists have generally searched for a strategic solution to this question in reiterated versions of the game and/or in the absence of mutual knowledge among the players. In other words, a co-operative choice can be expected when either player wants to prevent their opponents' defections by showing a co-operative attitude, or they are uncertain as to the rules applied by their opponents – for example, player 1 can be expected to resort to a co-operative choice when he does not expect player 2 to follow a rational rule, which should lead her to play Defeat in response to Co-operation. Conversely, a co-operative answer is less likely to occur, game theorists say, in cases of:

– *low chances of punishment*: the expected chances that one's defection be *punished* by the other players are low, and
– *free-riding*: comparatively, the expected chances to participate in a joint positive outcome are relatively independent of one's choice, as happens in large groups. Think of public goods: even if you do not pay council taxes for street lighting, you still expect it to be available.

Moreover, it can easily be shown that the non-co-operative answer tends to become all the more stable: the more often the agents play Defeat, the more rational it is for them to cling to such an option.

This is, Ullman-Margalit would say, where the PD structure "calls for" norms. In a game-theoretic account, norms are called for whenever the agents' choices tend to produce a state of affairs that is both individually and socially undesirable.

That one of the functions of norms is to solve conflicts among members of a social group cannot be denied. The theory developed by Ullman-Margalit has the merit of having brought into play this type of norm and, at the same time, of having shown the potential and inadequacies of a game-theoretic account.

However, we think that there are additional important inadequacies within this account, besides those pointed out by Ullman-Margalit. In a sense, these inadequacies pertain to the author's conception itself. As for this conception, indeed, the following considerations seem to apply.

Emergence of norms or limited rationality?

What Ullman-Margalit seems to have formulated is a theory of the limits and insufficiencies of the game theoretic, and for that matter of the utilitarian, approach at large. Indeed, that norms can do what utility cannot is an essentially correct statement. In our view, however, this seems to suggest a limitation of the utilitarian approach, rather than its contribution to explain the emergence of norms.

How do norms work?

From moral philosophy Ullman-Margalit borrows (Hart 1961) an interesting notion of norms, defined as "a *prescribed* guide for conduct or action which is generally complied with by the members of a society" (Ullman-Margalit 1977: 12; our italics). In particular, Hart characterizes what he calls *rules of obligation* according to the following features:
  (a) their *prescriptive force*
  (b) their expected *necessity for social life*
  (c) expected *clashes between norms*, on one hand, *and interests and desires* of the agents who owe the duty, on the other.
  Although a vague concept – what is meant by social life (b)? What kinds of conflicts do norms produce at the local, individual level (c)? – this notion is quite interesting, especially thanks to its explicit reference to the prescriptive role of norms. However, as used by Ullman-Margalit, this notion loses part of its appeal, since the game-theoretic framework does not allow for an explicit treatment of the prescriptive role of norms (see "Prescriptions and game theory", p. 80). Moreover, what is lacking is a theory of *how norms are implemented in social systems*. How do prescriptions work? How can they "guide" the conduct of agents? Certainly, these questions are not objectives of Ullman-Margalit's analysis, but without answering them, the emphasis on the prescriptive character of norms has a flavour of mere speculation.

Social effects of norms: distributive vs. collective

Although somewhat sceptical about the validity of the game-theoretic paradigm applied to norms, Ullman-Margalit seems less doubtful about the validity of the *methodological individualistic* assumptions. According to her (1977: 14), methodological individualism is the view according to which statements about social collectives can be reduced to statements about individual human beings, their actions, and the relations among them.
  If a methodological individualistic assumption is applied to the author's

analysis, a fundamental question seems to arise: should norms necessarily benefit all members of the social group? Indeed, the answer implied by a methodological individualistic assumption seems to be: yes: given such an assumption, the *social effects* of the single agent's options are necessarily intended as *distributive*, rather than collective. In other words, the social effects of the agents' defections are negative for *all participants*, rather than for the social group, and those of co-operation are good for all. Therefore, if the social group is not to be taken as a *whole*, as a collective, but as an aggregate, only the norms that produce positive distributive social effects would be rational for all agents. In such a framework, all norms protecting some categories of agents (handicapped people or property owners) over the remaining ones would become inexplicable. How, indeed, could we differentiate the norms of inequality from mere abuse from the point of view of the non-privileged party, if any such difference should be maintained?

Social interference vs. social complementarity:
game theoretic vs. Hobbesian rationality

This is interwoven with the preceding consideration. We should like to discuss Ullman-Margalit's view according to which the Hobbesian solution to the problem of order is but a game-theoretic solution. We do not mean to raise a philosophical contention, but rather to grasp the opportunity to unveil an incompleteness of the game-theoretic approach, which Ullman-Margalit does not seem to have perceived. In our view, due to this incompleteness, the game-theoretic view is superseded by the Hobbesian view of sociality.

In the passage quoted by Ullman-Margalit, while explaining why it is not unreasonable (that is to one's detriment) for one to honour a social contract, Hobbes formulates a theory of collective entities based upon social dependence:

> . . . in condition of war, wherein every man to every man, for want of *a common power to keep them all in awe*, is an enemy, there is *no man* who *can* hope *by his own strength*, or wit, *to defend himself from destruction, without the help of confederates*; . . . He therefore that breaketh his covenant, . . . cannot be received in any society, that *unite themselves for peace and defence,* . . . ; and therefore *if he be left, or cast out of society, he perisheth*; (quoted by Ullman-Margalit 1977: 68–69; our italics).

Ullman-Margalit reads this passage in the light of game theory. The Hobbesian scenario is seen as a "Hobbesian game", namely as a generalized PD game, in which agents are interfering with one another, and therefore need to resort to an agreement preventing destruction and self-destruction. This interpretation follows from the game-theoretic view of society as the realm of what in

Chapter 1 we called *social interference*, positive or negative, and game theorists call *strategic interdependence*. According to such a view, any agent's choice bears consequences for all the others, but each agent is perfectly at ease on its own. Society puts together a bunch of self-sufficient beings, which thereafter ought to take one another's doings into account.

We claim that this view of society is reductive, and so is the above interpretation of the Hobbesian passage. Indeed, there is a supplementary type of interdependence, not incompatible with the preceding one, which plays a fundamental role in social action. This is what we have so far called social dependence, referring to an objective pre-condition of social action. In it, agents are not completely self-sufficient, but are *complementary*. Some of their goals and interests cannot be achieved in isolation, but call for the skills of other agents.

In the Hobbesian passage, both forms of sociality are shaded: on one hand, society keeps peace among interfering members ("every man to every man . . . is an enemy"); on the other, confederations protect their *complementary* members, which would perish if "cast out of society". In contrast, the game-theoretic scheme seems to admit only of the former.

The difference between these two forms of sociality carries a fundamental consequence. While the former, interference, calls for a network of mutual contracts among agents, the latter, complementarity, is more likely to produce multi-agent co-operations, in the sense defined in Chapter 4. The former leads to *distributive aggregates*, the latter is more likely to lead to *collective entities*. Norms emerging from interference are advantageous for all participants (*distributive rationality*); norms emerging from complementarity are advantageous at the global level, and for the group as a whole (*collective rationality*). (For a more extensive account, see Ch. 10.)

To sum up, we believe that a theory of social dependence in the sense of complementarity is needed to account for collective rationality, and that game theory, not being able to grasp complementarity, cannot account for collective rationality. As a consequence, it cannot give a full explanation of norms (as well as of other institutions) which do not always produce distributive advantages, but often only collective ones.

Norms as conditioned preferences

Within the game-theoretic literature, the work by Bicchieri (1989, 1990, Bicchieri & Dalla Chiara 1992) deserves special attention.

Following Ullman-Margalit (1977), the work specifically focuses on the emergence of norms; however, it is intended to go a step forward. It is not meant simply to describe the game-theoretic conditions that call for norms, but also to apply a truly evolutionary model to the question of the emergence of norms. The work stems from the fundamental question of how knowledge allowing co-operation among rational agents emerges; as Ullman-Margalit says, game theorists usually tend to consider this knowledge to be already there, without investigating its origin. The work proceeds by combining a game-theoretic model with an evolutionary approach (Maynard Smith 1982).

Furthermore, it endeavours to account for the "exogenous" character of norms. It tries to do justice to the important insight that a behaviour oriented towards and controlled by social norms ought to be clearly distinguished from merely rational behaviour, that is, behaviour "endogenously" derived from the premise that the agents are rational (cf. also Elster 1987). This intuition implicitly shades the prescriptive characterization of norms, but in a rather generic way.

Unfortunately, Bicchieri's attempt to combine such philosophical insight with a game-theoretic framework is unsatisfactory. Bicchieri defines a social norm as an equilibrium, a combination of strategies such that "each maximises his expected utility by conforming, on the condition that nearly everybody else conforms to the norm." (cf. Bicchieri 1990: 842). Notably, in order to distinguish it from (a) a *moral imperative*, and (b) a *mere habit*, a social norm is defined as a conditioned preference.

However, such a model raises the following problems:

- *social norms vs. moral imperatives*: while Bicchieri tends to emphasize the difference between *norms* and *moral imperatives*, it would be nice to show also their possible *similarities*; for example, these two notions are much closer to each other than each of them is to mere habit;
- *conditioned preference vs. exogenous motivation*: preferences are often intrinsically conditioned: consider the preference "not to live in a multi-ethnic district" (cited by Bicchieri). Although this preference is fulfilled on condition that all other people in the same district have the same preference, this preference *per se* is by no means exogenous. Nor normative. It is an endogenous preference that, in order to be fulfilled, requires conformity.

Prescriptions and game theory

Notwithstanding the contribution of moral and rational philosophers, the game-theoretic approach does not seem to have produced a general theory of norms as *prescriptions*, that includes norms of co-ordination, i.e. conventions, as well as other types of norms. Let us now turn our attention to some general aspects of the game-theoretic framework, that are not suitable, in our view, for a theory of norms as prescriptions.

Spreading of individual mutations vs. spreading of norms

In the game-theoretic literature (cf. Kreps et al. 1982. Axelrod 1984), the focus is not so much on the emergence of norms, but rather on the emergence of *prosocial regularities* (co-ordination and co-operation). A multi-agent context is seen as a reiterated PD game with *n* players. Usually, the object of inquiry consists of concurrent interactional rules built into the players (say, *tit for tat*, which leads agents to play as their opponents have done in the preceding tournament; or *unconditioned defection*, which leads to Defeat always being played), and how equilibrium among them is achieved. Other questions that are usually raised concern the conditions under which a given rule – for example, Co-operation – is preferred to all others. Examples of such conditions are, as has been said, the extent to which agents know one another, the structure of the game, the ecological conditions, the group size (on these last two aspects, see, for example the work carried on by Huberman and collaborators (Glance & Huberman 1993)), and so on. Which will be the frequency of each strategy after *n* tournaments? How do strategies spread, and what mechanisms of learning are implied (cf. Fudenberg & Kreps 1988)? These are rather interesting questions, which have an evolutionary and functionalist appeal (cf. Maynard Smith 1982).

However, when applied to social norms, this approach proves inadequate. A co-operative strategy can be seen as a built-in *mutation*, but in this case it is *not* a *normative* option. Intuitively, there is a large difference between one feeling like co-operating and one feeling socially requested, or expected, to co-operate. In sum, the problem faced by game theorists is a *two*-dimensional problem, including *behaviours* and *mental mutations* (the rules followed by the players). The normative problem, instead, is a *three*-dimensional problem, consisting of behaviours, personal motivations and *social prescriptions*. Where do the latter come from? How do they modify the behaviours? How do they interact with the agents' (endogenous) motivations?

Normative expectations and the costs of transgressions

As a consequence of the preceding consideration, normative expectations and their role in discouraging transgressions cannot easily be observed in a PD game situation. Indeed, in order to observe the impact of normative expectations, which seems rather strong in real life, the players ought to be allowed to get some benefits/costs out of fulfilling/violating the normative expectations *per se*.

In a game-theoretic approach, instead, the costs of transgressions are essentially superfluous in explaining the players' decisions. Of course, a given option can be encouraged/discouraged by the expected reaction of the opponent (for example, a defection is expected to be returned by the opponent). However, the opponent's defection is not necessarily viewed as a punishment or retaliation. The use of such terminology, frequent in the literature, is both metaphorical and deceitful since the reason why a player who co-operated and was deserted in a reiterated PD game plays a Defeat on the successive tournament of the same game is *not*, as is usually interpreted, to *punish* his opponent, but to *reduce his own losses*. Since he obtained the worst result in the preceding tournament (i.e. CD; note that the preference order in a classical PD game is DC>CC>DD>CD), he will now resort to a cautious strategy, which is expected to reduce his costs. There is no theoretical need for any normative or didactic motivation – that would imply teaching the opponent how to behave in social settings.

Expected benefits vs. encountered costs

The game-theoretic literature on the emergence of co-operation (cf. Kreps et al. 1982, Axelrod 1984) investigates the increasing frequency and the reproduction rate of a given rule in terms of its pay-off value (the higher the pay-off value of a given strategy for the agents using it compared to the values of other existing strategies, the higher the probability that it will be used in the future). The agent is expected to *choose* among several options in terms of their relative advantages. What game theorists seem to ignore, however, is that already encountered costs play a no less relevant role than expected benefits, at least as far as normative behaviours are concerned. In other words, the question is not only how agents choose a given strategy, but also what happens when agents have chosen a given, i.e. normative, strategy. This question may shed light on the issue of the spreading of norms. As we will try to show in Chapter 7, the costs of a normative choice play a fundamental role in its spread: once a normative option has been chosen, the compliant agents want other people to do the same in order to balance the respective costs!

In sum, game theory successfully accounts for the spreading of certain behaviours over a population of strategic agents. In a word, it can explain *conventions* and social *conformity*, but does not fully justify the crucial aspect of the normative mechanism that plays a role in the spreading of normative behaviours, namely the normative request. Hart's (1961) notion of *rules of obligation*, notably his intuition that norms are *imposed* obligations, did not receive an adequate formal handling within the game-theoretic approach. No account was provided of the agent wanting others to conform to norms. Usually, *people,* including transgressors[2], *want norms to be observed.* Such a desire can be conveyed in many different ways: from simple *expectations* (note that the term expectation is often used to refer to a hybrid mental object, namely a *goal/belief*: if you expect the weather tomorrow to be sunny and warm you both believe it will and wish it to be so), to explicit commands and requests; from implicit disapproval of transgressors, to explicit reproaches, etc. The game-theoretic view of norms as emergent, *epiphenomenal* effects of complex social systems does not account for this aspect.

Norms in MAS research

Although based on a different assumption, the view of norms proposed in MAS research is similar to the game-theoretic one. For example, Shoham & Tennenholtz (1992a) claim that norms are *not* simple epiphenomenal effects of social systems, but rather should be built into the action representation of the system. The question is what type of representation should be given of these peculiar objects. The attempt made by Shoham & Tennenholtz (1992a, b) to offer such a representation is still unsatisfactory because it is essentially conventional and useful only with poorly autonomous agents. Indeed:

– it still relies on a *behavioural notion*: norms are seen as constraints on the agents' action repertoires
– therefore, again, it does not allow agents to accept or reject norms deliberately; in short, *it does not allow for* any truly *normative choice*
– it is *aimed* essentially *at improving co-ordination* within the social systems themselves (cf. Moses & Tennenholtz 1992). However, that of co-ordination is only *one* of the functions of norms. Other functions may be explored.
– although it does not share an epiphenomenal assumption, *it explains the spreading of norms essentially in terms of optimization of MAS behaviour* (Shoham & Tennenholtz 1992b), while putting aside the question of normative learning and decision-making. In other words, it does not answer the questions (i) how the single agent comes to have a given constraint and (ii) why it decides to observe some norms. For obvious reasons, both questions become more crucial when dealing with autonomous agents.

Objectives of the present approach

Norms are ultimately merely an external source of action control. This statement is not a *reification*[3], however, as long as it is associated with a model of *how* such control is achieved.

The present approach, thanks to some proposed notions, i.e. the process of goal adoption and the external goals, will endeavour precisely to show how it is possible for norms to guide and control behaviour. Indeed, they are seen as a fundamental connection between micro and macro. When they refer to autonomous agents, norms bring into play a classical problem of the social sciences, namely, how can autonomous agents be controlled from the outside? How can autonomous agenthood and external (including, but not coinciding with, normative) control be reconciled?[4] In order to answer such a question, norms ought to be seen not only as an essentially social but also as a mentalistic notion. In other words, an integrated approach to social theory is sought, in which both the extracognitive aspects of social action – that is, the social nature and utility of norms including, but not reduced to, improving co-ordination among agents – and its cognitive aspects – that is, the mental constructs that allow autonomous agents to display a normative behaviour – is accounted for.

Furthermore, as we will endeavour to show next, compliance with norms is one of the cases in which behaviour is controlled through unnatural, artificial means–end links (which were introduced in Ch. 3). The normative control of autonomous agents' behaviours takes advantage of the capacity for artificial means–end reasoning and planning which autonomous agents have. Norms, in other words, are but a special case of a general social law: in order for autonomous agents to accept others' requests (including normative ones), they ought to find some convenience for doing so. That such a convenience coincides or not with the request's reasons and objectives is irrelevant. Analogously, the reasons why agents adopt norms often have nothing to do with the norms' functionalities. In this sense, the mechanism of **norm adoption**, as well as that of goal adoption seen in the previous chapters, is based upon artificial means–end reasoning and planning. Elster's (1987) intuition that normative behaviour is motivated by exogenous reasons is correct, but this motivation does not characterize norms in a specific way: all social interaction is characterized by this feature. Therefore, we need a theory of norms that brings to light these similarities, the fundamental mechanisms that norms share with other social inputs.

In the following two chapters, we will propose, (a) *an integrated approach to* the study of social norms, in which *norms* are seen as *both macro- and micro-objects*, useful *social objects* and *mental constructs*, circulating within a MAS; and (b) *a model of norm adoption* – i.e. of the agents' decisions to accept normative requests – as a special case of goal adoption, which is the most fundamental aspect of social reasoning and is *based upon artificial means–end links*.

In particular, we will endeavour to track the norms in the following steps:
1. the *circulation of norms in the social system*: from the Sovereign to the Addressees of a norm;
2. the *route followed by norms in the agent's mind*:
(i) from beliefs about normative requests to normative goals;
(ii) from normative goals to normative actions;
3. the *spreading of norms in the social system*: from a normative action to the goal of defending the norm.

The multi-agent nature of norms

Norms are typically social phenomena. This is so not only because they stem from, and presuppose, some sort of community, but also, and more interest-

ingly, because they are a multi-agent object:
  - *they involve more than one agent* (norms usually concern a class of individuals);
  - intuitively, *they express someone's desires* and assign tasks to someone else (a class which may, or may not, include the normative source itself);
  - consequently, *norms may be regarded from different points of view*: the social circulation of norms involves different *social characters*; in each of them, norms play a different cognitive role, be it a simple belief, a goal, a value, or something else.

In principle, at least four characters (but the list could be extended) may be distinguished within a model of the circulation of norms, all contributing to some extent to the understanding of different aspects of this process (empirically, however, some of these characters may be found to be lacking or to overlap):

  (a) S *(Sovereign)*: she is entitled to issue a (set of) norm(s);
  (b) A *(Addressee)*: he is implicitly or explicitly mentioned in a given norm either as active executor(s) of a task (paying bills), or as passive target(s) ("Don't smoke"). Norms usually mention a class of As. An A may be unaware of one or even all the norms concerning him. This does not prevent him, at least in the case of legal norms, from being punished when he transgresses these norms. Thus, a norm may be in force even when it is not acknowledged by its As. However, the less a norm is acknowledged by its As, the lower its force. Usually, As are normative reasoners, that is, their decision-making includes a cognitive manipulation of those norms that concern them. This does not entail, however, their sharing these norms, nor even their compliance with them.
  (c) D *(Defender)*: she watches over the norms. She checks that norms are enforced (judge or policeman). In Chapter 6, this character will be examined not in its strictly juridical sense, but as one possible facet or dimension of **normative reasoning**. It is possible to argue, indeed, that an A tends to ensure norms are respected by other existing As. Therefore, an A is also (or becomes) a D.
  (d) O *(external Observer)*: he acknowledges and describes norms that do not concern him. This character has a crucial methodological role in this work, since it allows a descriptive use of normative beliefs to be distinguished from other uses, such as that involved in normative decision-making. An ethnographer describing the customs and rules existing in the society he is observing is supposed to recognize the norms concerning some or all of its members. Sometimes, he may even exhibit a behaviour corresponding to the norms observed (in order not to hurt the feelings of his sample) without considering himself an A of the same norms.

In the following, we will try to show the cognitive correlates of at least the last three characters.

Valid, operating, and effective norms

For a norm to be *valid* (in force), it is sufficient that it mentions a given (class of) agent(s) as executors of a constrained action. A norm necessarily implies some addressees: no addressee, no norm.

However, it is conceivable that no A of a given norm believes that that norm concerns him (all As are totally ignorant of that norm). In that case, the norm will not enter the A's decision-making and we would be facing the quite extreme case of a non-operating norm. For a norm to be *operating*, in fact, it is necessary and sufficient that it enters the decision-making of its As. Thus, an A must be aware that a given norm concerns him, but this is not yet sufficient: a norm is operating in A's mind, if A is deciding whether to comply with that norm or not.

The outcome of A's decision-making is two-fold: it might produce either a behaviour compliant with, or transgressive of, the norm. We will say that a norm is *effective* if:
  (a) it is *reflected in the behaviour* of its As;
  (b) the existence of that *norm is the main causal factor* of the spreading of that behaviour. In other words, the increasing frequency of the behaviour in question is *not* due to other factors, i.e.
    – *objective conditions* (for example, ecological events forcing rational decision-makers into a unique, hence uniform course of action);
    – *functional mechanisms* (which reproduce a given behaviour or trait by selecting positively the entity displaying that behaviour or trait; for a re-discussion of social functions see Ch. 7);
    – *the make-up of agents* (imitation): for example, let us take an artificial society where agents are so constructed as to apply the routines most frequently encountered in interacting with others (see Shoham & Tennenholtz (1992b) for a comparison of this strategy with others, e.g. apply the routine one has most frequently used in the past).

Indeed, the spreading of a norm does not necessarily entail any normative reasoning; thus, whether norms are effective or not does not necessarily imply that they are operating in the As' minds. However, it does imply some level of normative reasoning if what is spreading are not only the normative behaviours, but also the normative goals. Finally, norms are effective to differing degrees: the greater the correspondence between what a norm states and what the As do, the more effective the norm.

The normative coin

In the following, we will assume the following postulates:
  (a) the more organized a MAS, the more likely it will be to pursue its own

goal (see the notion of *purposeful systems* as used in organization theory; e.g. cf. Donaldson 1985); consequently, the more organized a MAS, the more autonomous[5] it is;

(b) the *goals of an autonomous MAS are pursued through the actions of its members* and, if these too are autonomous, through their goals.

Therefore, members may be assigned tasks by the system they belong to. Social norms are but tasks that an autonomous MAS assigns to its members in order to achieve its own goals. A social norm is therefore a two-sided object. Its external, or social, side is precisely the task prescribed by the MAS (for an initial analysis, cf. Castelfranchi & Conte 1991). Its internal, or mental, side is the set of mental states that allow the autonomous members of the system to accomplish the tasks they have been assigned.

The external side

To circulate inside the social system, a norm must be a recognizable, observable entity. As observable entities, norms can be either communicated, or embedded in non-communicative behaviours.

(a) When *communicated*, norms are mainly conveyed in a linguistic form: uttered sentences (by the Sovereign or Defender of a norm), or written texts (codes, sentences and rules). A huge amount of taxonomic work (to cite only the best-known examples, cf. von Wright 1963, Ross 1968) has shown that the most common forms under which norms are generally communicated are:

(i) *explicit commands* (e.g. "Honour thy father and thy mother")

(ii) *deontic declarations* ("One must do this" or "You must do that"), which are not mere descriptions, like an observer's recordings of the norms in force in the culture under study, but indirect requests

(iii) *explicit evaluations* ("Cheating is evil", "Deceit ruins society" etc.)

(iv) *indirect evaluations* ("Good children don't lie")

None of these convey norms: they may be taken as mere information; what is perhaps a bit less obvious, however, is that these become prescriptive if:

(v) they aim to influence the listener, and if, to this end,

(vi) they use an evaluation or a command as a means.

In the following exposition, this will become clearer:

(b) Norms may be conveyed in a *non-communicative* way:

(i) Through exemplary conduct: others' conduct can have an educational role. People often model their own behaviour upon that of others not in order to be like them (imitation) but in order to learn how things should be done, what is proper and correct, etc.

(ii) Through behavioural reactions: agents may infer norms and normative evaluations from others' behavioural reactions (as when the last to arrive would like to jump the queue but refrains from doing so because of the whispers and glances of disdain).

Recapitulation

In this chapter, the classical view of social norms as conventions, or behavioural regularities, has been questioned. In line with Hart's (1961) definition, norms are seen as prescriptions, which control the behaviour of autonomous agents by modifying their beliefs and influencing their goals. It has been argued, indeed, that an integrated approach is essential to account for norms as two-sided (social and mental) objects, that is, as a fundamental connection between macro (social) and micro (mental).

Furthermore, normative reasoning has been claimed to represent a special case of social reasoning, which, in the preceding chapters, was shown to be typically based upon artificial means–end links. This view of norms should allow us to understand what philosophers call the exogenous character of norms (Elster 1987). In our terms, it will also endorse the inclusion of normative prescriptions in a general theory of social requests. The external, social side of norms has briefly been examined, while a model of the internal, mental side will be proposed in the next chapter.

Some normative characters (Sovereign, Addressee, Defender, and Observer) have been defined.

In the next two chapters we will endeavour to model each normative character in an explicit way, following at the same time the transitions from one character to another, that is, the impact of the Sovereign on the Addressees' minds, the conditions under which an Addressee becomes a Defender of norms, and those under which an Observer becomes an Addressee. The whole set of these transitions is what we will call the circulation of norms in a MAS.

CHAPTER SIX
The route of norms in the mind

The internal side of the normative coin

Here, a cognitive approach to the study of norms[1] is presented. A cognitive study of norms is defined as a model of an explicit, symbolic representation of norms and of the mental operations that can be performed on that representation. The leading question will then be: what is a norm as a mental object, if any such object exists? How are norms represented in an agent's mind? The focus is on both the various cognitive aspects of norms (normative beliefs, goals, rules, etc.) and the mental processes involved in norm-governed action (rules of *normative reasoning* and *decision-making*, etc.).

What is of interest here is the cognitive processing of norms or normative reasoning in a general sense. Normative reasoning, as implied by normative judgement, has received considerable attention from both philosophers and students of moral development. Less attention, on the contrary, has been paid to the role of norms in general reasoning and planning.

Objectives

In the preceding chapter, it was claimed that norms are not yet sufficiently characterized as mental objects. Here, some crucial problems concerning the mental nature of norms will be raised and some initial solutions proposed. The problems are as follows:
  – *how are norms represented in the agents' minds*? Should they be seen as a *specific* mental object, and if so, what?
  – *what relation do they bear to beliefs and goals*? How can they regulate the agents' behaviours?
  – *how is their prescriptive* (and not simply conventional) *character* (that is, a more or less explicit request and the corresponding duty) *expressed*?
  – *why does an autonomous agent comply with norms*, thus fulfilling others' expectations?
In this chapter, in particular, two fundamental issues will be addressed:

(a) *from Sovereign to Addressee*: what is a *normative belief*? How is a normative belief formed? What is the difference between a simple request (and the relative belief) and a normative request (and the relative belief)?

(b) *the route of norms in the mind*: how can normative beliefs control the action of autonomous agents? Norms will be defined as *hybrid mental constructs*, including beliefs, goals and rules for the normative reasoning and decision-making. The process leading from normative beliefs to normative goals will therefore be examined.

Normative behaviour and normative reasoning

A fundamental objective of a cognitive study of norms is to disentangle the behaviour corresponding to norms from the cognitive processing of norms, and show the variety of situations beneath a norm-abiding behaviour. Normative reasoning is neither necessary nor sufficient for a norm-abiding behaviour to occur.

(a) *It is by no means necessary* since it might occur either accidentally or out of simple imitation;

(b) *it is not sufficient* since normative reasoning and decision-making may produce a transgression of norms; this happens, for example, when the normative goal is defeated in the confrontation with other goals of the agent's. It may also be the case, as we will see, that a normative goal is not generated and, nonetheless, a norm is somehow represented in the agent's mind at some level, whatever the format.

Therefore, to model the normative reasoning does not imply modelling a norm-abiding system. However, a large share of the normative behaviours displayed by autonomous agents is the output of a cognitive processing of norms.

Alternative ways of implementing norms in MAS

As stated, norm-abiding behaviour does not necessarily imply the cognitive processing of norms, nor does a normative mind necessarily produce a behaviour corresponding to norms.

A fully normative, or **norm-governed behaviour** is defined herein as a norm-abiding behaviour that implies some internal representation of the norm and some normative decision-making, that is, a decision to comply with a norm. Of course, quite a number of different reasons (avoidance of punishment, a desire to please, a need for praise, moral values of different sorts, etc.) might explain norm-governed behaviour. What cuts across these reasons is the very fact that norms come into the decision-making of the agent. This in turn implies that norms are in some way a mental object, participating in the agent's mental life. A fully normative behaviour is the output of a process in which a norm is weighed against some internal criteria. In this process, that norm must be integrated in the agent's knowledge base, and should give rise to some sort of normative goal, which is confronted with any other goals. Eventually, the normative goal can be abandoned. Therefore, to model normative reasoning does not imply modelling a norm-abiding system. Consequently, one might wonder what is the use of modelling a **norm-governed system**.

Of course, it is easy to prove that a substantial share of human agents' practical reasoning deals with norms, if only to reject them. Norm-governed systems are a subset of autonomous agents. Therefore, the advantages of norm-governed systems are essentially a special case of those of autonomous systems – e.g. avoiding useless, stupid and self-destructive behaviour as favoured by the rigid execution of routines, as well as the spreading of errors and deviations produced by pure imitation, etc. Provided that it would be helpful to have both (a) autonomous artificial agents, and (b) norm-abiding systems, then we ought to be able to construct autonomous agents with a capacity for applying norms.

Obviously, the proof of the pudding is in the eating: the only way to assess to what extent a norm-governed system is more useful than a norm-abiding system is to observe the respective performances. However, let us put forward some specific hypotheses.

Let us say that there are at least three distinct ways of implementing norm-abiding systems, each endowed with a different representation of norms (see Table 6.1),

(a) *built-in constraints*: from a theoretical point of view, we have discussed this option with reference to Shoham and Tennenholtz' (1992a) work; we can sum up the effects of a MAS with constraints of this sort as follows:
   – high reliability: the constraints will always be executed;
   – no learning: new constraints would be implemented when the system is off-line;
   – no novelty: constraints reduce available actions; only proscriptions, that is, prohibitions ("Don't . . . "), can be represented in such systems, but not prescriptions ("Do . . . ");
   – no repair: agents are not endowed with the capacity for modifying unsuccessful constraints.

(b) *built-in ends*: in this case, cognitive agents would be allowed to choose among their (competing) goals (instead of simply applying procedures and routines) but they would treat norms like any other of their goals. Let us consider the following consequences:
   – low reliability: goals may be abandoned when they clash with competing, more urgent needs;
   – average learning: built-in ends should be added when the system is off-line; in principle, rational autonomous agents should have the capacity

to seek out useful actions, but social norms are not necessarily always useful at the local level (see later in this chapter);

- novelty: built-in ends may correspond to prescriptions and not only to prohibitions; but since learning is not granted, there ought to be a one-to-one correspondence between social norms and internal goals with a consequent high computational complexity;
- repair: in principle goal-oriented systems ought to be able to try out several solutions and choose those that achieve their goals to the highest degree, before giving up their goals; however, the issue of differing degrees of achievement of one's goals has only recently been addressed (cf. Zlotkin & Rosenschein 1991);
- no social control: agents may have preferences corresponding to norms or not; they may cling to these or abandon them as a function of circumstances; as a consequence, in the MAS, there will not be any social control over each agent's actions.

(c) As explicit and specific mental objects, namely *built-in obligations*, distinct from ordinary goals and beliefs; note that a built-in obligation differs from a constraint, on one hand, since it does not automatically reduce the set of actions available to the agent; and from a goal, on the other hand, since it is not immediately transformed into a goal:

- average reliability, lower than in (a) and higher than in (b): agents may give up **normative goals**, but this will cost them more than abandoning ordinary goals – this will become clearer later on in the chapter;
- learning: normative goals are autonomously produced on the grounds of normative beliefs, and in principle beliefs may be acquired when a system is on-line;
- novelty: normative beliefs may be formulated as prescriptions, and not as mere prohibitions;
- repair: as with any other kind of goal, plans for normative goals are subject to change and repair with the limitations set out in (b);
- social control: since normative goals are a special type of goals, and normative actions have specific costs, agents can be shown to be interested in some monitoring of norms.

Table 6.1 Alternative representations of norms inside the agents' architectures.

	Reliability	Learning	Novelty	Repair	Social control
Constraints	+	–	–	–	no need
Ends	–	±	+	+	–
Obligations	±	+	+	+	+

Now, all these hypotheses should be tested computationally. Unfortunately, we are far from being able to execute such a test, which, *inter alia*, would require a fine-grained make-up of the agents. However, some future simulations of aspects of the mental model of norms that we are proposing will be discussed in Chapter 11.

From normative requests to normative goals

Norms are generally considered as prescriptions, directives, commands (Ross 1968). Even when expressed in some other type of speech act they are meant to *direct* the future behaviours of the agents subject to them, their Addressees.

To this end, they ought to give rise to some new goal in an Addressee's mind: for autonomous agents to undertake (or abstain from) a course of action, it is not sufficient for them to know that this course of action is wanted by someone else. It is necessary for these agents to have the goal of doing so. Norms may act as a mechanism of goal generation. Indeed, they represent a powerful mechanism for inducing new goals in people's minds in a cognitive way. How is this possible?

First of all, some beliefs about norms ought to be represented in an Addressee's mind. Let us start from beliefs about requests. A simple request, before succeeding and being accepted, produces a belief in the recipient's mind, namely a belief about a desire of the sender's. More specifically, the recipient believes that what the sender requires of him is to do an action planned for a given goal.

Two questions arise here:
- What is the *difference*, if any, *between* this type of belief, that is, a belief about an *ordinary request*, and a belief about a normative or *prescriptive request*?
- How do we go *from* a belief about a normative request, that is, *a normative belief* to the goal to comply with it, that is, *a normative goal*?

The normative belief

Let us begin with the first question. What do we actually mean by normative belief?

A first answer to this question is a *decentralized* one. According to such an answer, a normative belief is a belief about a *general*, or collective request or desire. In other words, an agent x has a normative belief n relative to a MAS if, and only if, x believes n is a goal shared by all its members.

This answer is interesting and fits the DAI field rather well, as great attention is generally paid to shared mental states, collective actions, teamwork, etc. Such an answer might be seen as a computationally feasible and useful way to handle the question of social norms in multi-agent co-ordination. Consider, as an example, Bond's (1991) notion of commitment. An agent is defined as a locus of control that sets up commitments, and, much as in Shoham's & Tennenholz's (1992a) notion of social law, a commitment is a constraint uniting a bunch of agents, it is essentially social and implies expectations on the part of one agent concerning the others' actions. However, this view presents three drawbacks:

(a) the current notion of joint intentions or goals is *fundamentally distributive*. A collection of agents is said to have a joint intention when this intention is shared among them and this sharing is mutually believed. We will give a critique of this notion in Chapter 10. For the time being we shall merely say that the notion of general or collective wanting is something different and not reducible to a distributive notion. A different, more relevant notion of collective wanting does not necessarily imply that the desire is shared by all the agents in a group, but rather that the goal is to achieve a prevailing, global interest of the group itself.

(b) As a consequence, the decentralized answer does not solve our problem. *It brings into play a collective wanting*, which is a further notion to be explained.

(c) The decentralized answer is not sufficient either, since *it does not provide a truly normative basis*; a normative belief seems to be grounded on something more than a collective wanting. In real life, not all the requests and desires of a group may be considered as normative. Your whole team badly wants you to win the race tonight, and you know it; still, this is not yet a normative request. What else is needed?

A second possible answer to our initial question suggests that a normative belief is based upon a notion of obligation. In other words, agents have normative beliefs, when they think there is an obligation on a given set of agents to do some action. The general form of a normative belief may be expressed as follows:

$$\left(N\text{-}BEL\, x\, y_i\, a\right) \overset{def}{=} \left(\Lambda_{i=1,n}\left(BEL\, x\left(OUGHT\left(DOES\, y_i\, a\right)\right)\right)\right) \qquad (5)$$

in words: *x has a normative belief about action a relative to a set of agents* y_i *if and only if, x believes that it is obligatory for* y_i *to do action a.* The predicate *OUGHT* here stands for an *obligation for a set of agents* y_i *to do action a.* A few words are needed to explain the semantics of our predicate *OUGHT*. As said in the Introduction, this stands for an operator of **obligation** about any given state of the world. However, it should be taken in a somewhat weaker sense than what is usually meant by obligation in traditional deontic logic. In fact, while in traditional deontic systems, p necessarily follows from obligation (that is to say, it is not possible that at the same time p is false and obligatory), in other systems (Jones & Pörn 1986), two concepts need to be distinguished, one referring to deontic necessity and the other to another type of obligation. The latter is defined as the circumstance in which a given proposition is both obligatory and possibly false in some subideal world.

Such a notion of obligation has several advantages over traditional deontic operators:

– it accounts for our intuition that *obligations are different from necessities*
– it *allows for exceptions*, that is to say, violations.

Indeed, intuitively, the notion of obligation seems to imply a further ingredient that is not contained in Jones and Porn's definition: while necessity may be imposed on any sort of proposition, an obligation seems to imply that it refers exclusively to actions or world states resulting from actions. In other words, obligations imply actions, and therefore goals. This has an interesting consequence precisely with regard to the issue treated in this book. Obligations provide inputs to goals. Goals are not necessarily chosen desires; they may be derived from obligations as well.

However, both the conceptual analysis and the formalization of the notion of obligation need further refinement. We will therefore draw on the notion of obligation developed by Jones and Porn which presents evident advantages over the preceding deontic operators.

Getting back to the normative belief, the question is: What relation does the last equation bear to a belief about an ordinary request? This relation is allowed by means of a *normative source, a Sovereign,* and the related belief. Now, several beliefs are implied, corresponding to as many requirements of a normative source.

Additional normative beliefs: about normative influencing

First, let us define a **normative influencing goal** as the goal to generate an obligation for a set of agents to do a given action:

$$(N\text{-}INFL\text{-}GOAL\,x\,y_i\,a) \overset{def}{=} \big(GOAL\,x\,(OUGHT(DOES\,y_i\,a))\big)$$

that is: *x has a normative influencing goal* vis-à-vis y_i *if and only if, x wants* y_i *to have an obligation to do a given action a.* Therefore, a *normative belief implies a belief about a normative influencing goal,*

$$(N\text{-}BEL\,x\,y_i\,a) \supset \exists z\big(BEL\,x\,(N\text{-}INFL\text{-}GOAL\,z\,y_i\,a)\big)$$

where z *belongs to a set of agents* y_j *not smaller than* y_i. In words, *an agent x has a normative belief about action a if x believes that someone belonging to a superset* y_j *including* y_i *wants it to be obligatory for* y_i *to do a.*

This is a minimal condition, since z, which is the source of the norm, the Sovereign, may in turn be a set of agents. It might even coincide with the whole superset y_j. In the latter case, the Sovereign overlaps with the MAS. But this is not necessary. Suffice it to say that a normative belief relative to a MAS implies that a subcomponent (one- or multi-agent[2]) of the system is believed to issue a given norm. In x's belief, what makes a request normative is the very fact that a given z is believed to want the members of a subset of agents, y_i, to have an obligation to do a.

Let a normative prescription be compared with coercion. In coercion, the aggressor does not want the victim to believe she has any abstract obligation to do something. All the aggressor needs to do is to persuade her that she is forced (i.e. threatened) to do what the aggressor wants. On the contrary, a normative request is believed to create a mental state of abstract obligation, independent of any personal desire or need. In other words, z is not (believed to be) happy with any member of y_i doing a in virtue of z's personal request (be it coercive or not). By default a normative request is one that wants you to form an obligation, and not simply the goal, to do something.

Disinterested Sovereign

Therefore, and more explicitly, a Sovereign is believed to issue a norm independently of and beyond her own interest. At least, she is believed to have the corresponding obligation:

$$(N\text{-}BEL\,x\,y_i\,a) \supset$$

$$\left(BEL\,x\left(OUGHT\,\neg\left(R\text{-}GOAL\,z\left(DOES\,y_i\,a\right)\left(BEL\,z\,\exists q\left[\left(DONE\,a\right)\supset\left(OBTAIN\,z\,q\right)\right]\right)\right)\right)\right)$$

that is: *an agent x has a normative belief if he believes that there is an obligation on the agent who issued the norm, z, not to have the goal of issuing the norm relativized to the belief that if the action required by the norm is done, z will obtain something as a consequence.*

This is necessary in order to distinguish Sovereigns from cheats. Even if this requirement may in fact be unfulfilled, as is often the case, in principle a Sovereign *ought* to set up norms independent of her personal interests.

Norm-based Sovereign

Besides, a Sovereign is believed to be grounded on norms. This accounts for the fact that a Sovereign is entitled to issue a norm. She does not act on her own personal initiative; she is granted the necessary authorship. Indeed, her authorship is based upon a norm.

Now, there are two ways to account for this fundamental intuition,

(a) a Sovereign may be characterized as being *held to* issue some norms. In other words, a Sovereign may be said to have an obligation to do so:

$$(N\text{-}BEL\,x\,y_i\,a) \supset \exists z\left[BEL\,x\left(OUGHT\left(N\text{-}INFL\text{-}GOAL\,z\,y_i\,a\right)\right)\right]$$

in words: *a normative belief implies a belief that it is obligatory for z to want members of y_i to form an obligation to do action a.* However, this may appear as too strong a requirement.

(b) A weaker ground for authorship lies in the notion of an entitled, or *legitimate* request. This, indeed, could be considered as a sufficient source of obligation. A **legitimate goal** can be defined as follows:

$$(L\text{-}GOAL\,x\,p) \overset{def}{=} \forall y \exists q \big[(G\text{-}CONFL\,x\,y\,p\,q) \supset (OUGHT\,\neg(GOAL\,y\,q))\big]$$

in words: *p is a legitimate goal of x's if and only if for all agents y that happen to have a given goal q conflicting with p, it will be obligatory for y to give up q.* In other words, a legitimate goal is watched over, protected by a norm against any conflicting interest. In a sense, rights and legitimacy could be said to help, i.e. go to the rescue of, those who cannot defend themselves against aggression and cheating.

Global vs. local utility

Finally, a normative request, and its Sovereign, are required to be means for some goal of the group at large, that is, of the superset of agents y_j, which includes y_i. A Sovereign is required to adopt some goal of the group in which the norm is in force:

$$(N\text{-}BEL\,x\,y_i\,a) \supset$$
$$\big(BEL\,x\,(OUGHT\,T(R\text{-}GOAL\,z\,(DOES\,y_i\,a)$$
$$\big(BEL\,z\,\exists p\,[INTEREST\,y_j\,(DONE\,a)p]\big)\big)\big)$$

or: *x has a normative belief if he believes that it is obligatory for z to have the goal that y_i does action a relativized to z's belief that if a is done, a given goal p of the superset y_j will be achieved.*

It is to be noted that a norm is expected to be convenient not necessarily to its Addressees (distributive rationality), but to the whole MAS in which it is in force (collective rationality). Or, which is the same thing, a norm is not necessarily expected to be convenient at the *local* level, while it is at the *global* level. This is an additional and perhaps more important reason why the decentralized solution to the question raised above is unsatisfactory: norms may increase the so-called global utility of the system, and, at the same time, clash with the goals, and perhaps even with the current or future[3] interests of some subcomponents of the MAS. We will come back to this point later on in the chapter.

To sum up, an agent has a normative belief if, and only if, that agent believes that there is an obligation for a given set of agents to do a given action. On more careful examination, however, the normative belief appears to imply that:

(a) a given action is *prescribed*, that is, requested *by*

(b) *a norm-based authorship,* a Sovereign, who has the following requirements:
- to create an obligation (and not simply a goal) for the Addressees to do a given action,
- to be disinterested, and
- entitled to issue the norm, thus realizing
- some global interest of the group in which the norm will be in force.

Of course, a normative belief does not imply that a given norm has in fact been deliberately issued by some Sovereign. Social norms are often set up by virtue of functional *unwanted* effects. However, once emerged, a given social norm is believed to be based upon some normative authorship, if only an *anonymous* one ("You are wanted, expected (not) to do this . . . "; "It is generally expected that . . . "; "This is how things are done . . . ", etc.).

The present model of normative beliefs is *recursive*. A request is believed to be normative if it can ultimately be related back to some norm. This is not to say that norms are irreducible objects. Of course, the origins of norms call for an explanation which unavoidably brings into play the community of agents, their interests and their interactional practice. However, in the agents' representations there is no need to keep a record of such a history. In the agents' beliefs a norm is always represented as an entitled, legitimate, even norm-driven, prescription. The present model attempts to give an account of this intuition.

In sum, we would like to propose a view of the relation between cognition and external conditions that overcomes the isomorphism implicit in rational theory: cognition does not necessarily reproduce the cause–effects links that occur in the reality out there, and nonetheless it may work rather adaptively. The very fact that a given effect of some action is a necessary explanation of the recurrence of that action does not imply that the effect is also represented in the minds of the agents who brought it about. This is so, not only because the agents' rationality is limited and biased by personal interests, but also because given cognitive structures, independent and separated from real processes, may sometimes turn out to be especially efficacious in ensuring given effects. With norms, something of this sort occurs: often, the cognitive reasons for applying norms have nothing to do with the real functions of the norms. Still, the cognitive normative apparatus works rather well and, paradoxically, renders rationality superfluous: it obtains better and more consistent results (behaviours) than rational calculus probably would.

The route of norms in the mind

Turning to the question raised above – how do we go from a belief about a normative will to the goal to comply with it, that is, to a normative goal? – a normative belief is only one of the ingredients of normative reasoning. As mental objects, norms are actually hybrid configurations of beliefs and goals. As defined so far, a normative belief is actually only descriptive: it does not constrain or regulate the believer and his decisions. Indeed, an observer's description of a society's rules does not influence his decisions to any significant extent. What is needed for an agent to regard himself as subject to, addressed by, a given norm?

The pertinence belief

First another belief is needed, namely a pertinence belief: for x to believe that he is addressed by a given norm, he needs to believe that he is a member of the class of agents addressed by that norm:

$$(P \text{-} N \text{-} BEL \, x \, a) \overset{def}{=} \left(\wedge_{i=1,n}(N \text{-} BEL \, x \, y_i \, a) \right) \wedge \left(V_{k=1,n}\left(BEL \, x \, (X = y_k) \right) \right)$$

where *P–N–BEL* stands for **normative belief of pertinence**; in words: *x has a normative belief of pertinence when he has a normative belief relative to a set y_i and an action a, and believes that he is included in y_i.*

Now, x's beliefs tell him not only that there is an obligation to do action a, but also that the obligation concerns precisely himself.

The normative goal

Still, the above equation is not much less descriptive than the one before. We have not seen any normative goal yet. A normative goal is defined here as a goal always associated with and generated by a normative belief. Let us express a normative goal as follows:

$$(N \text{-} GOAL \, x \, a) \overset{def}{=} \left(R \text{-} GOAL \, x(DOES \, x \, a)(P \text{-} N \text{-} BEL \, x \, a) \right)$$

or: *x has a normative goal concerning action a when he has the goal to do a, relativized to his pertinent normative belief concerning a.* A normative goal of a given agent x about action a is therefore a goal that x happens to have as long as he has a pertinent normative belief about a. Ultimately, x has a normative goal in so far as he believes his is subject to a norm.

Therefore, a normative goal differs, on one hand, from a simple constraint, which reduces the set of actions available to the system, and, on the other, from ordinary goals (cf. Table 6.1).

(a) *With regard to behavioural constraints*, a normative goal is less compelling: an agent endowed with normative goals is allowed to compare them with other goals of his and, to some extent, to choose which one will be executed. Only if an agent is endowed with normative goals, can he be said to comply with, or violate, a norm. Only in such a case, indeed, is he making a truly normative choice.

(b) *With regard to ordinary goals*, a normative goal is obviously more compelling: when an agent decides to give it up, he knows he is both thwarting one of his goals and violating a norm.

Now, the question is: How and why does a normative belief come to interfere with x's decisions? What is it that makes an agent responsive to the norms concerning him? What is it that turns a normative belief into a normative goal?

Goal and norm adoption

There seem to be several ways of accounting for the process leading to normative goals as well as several alternative ways of constructing a normative agent. There also seems to be a correspondence between the process from a belief about an ordinary request to the decision of accepting such a request, which we have called (cf. Ch. 3) goal adoption, and the process from a normative belief to a normative goal, which by analogy will be called here **norm adoption**.

In situation 1, (*conditional action*), we find some sort of production rule: in goal adoption, any time a request is received by a system endowed with such a rule, a goal that a be done is triggered. Analogously, in norm adoption, any time a norm belief is formed a norm goal is triggered. Now, this is a rather cheap solution: agents are granted neither reasoning nor autonomy. It is simple machinery that could help cut short some practical reasoning, or avoid collisions and improve co-ordination, but is insufficient as far as the modelling of normative reasoning is concerned. However, such a rule seems to account for a number of real-life situations. Think, as far as *slavish* goal adoption is concerned, of the habit of giving instructions when asked by passengers, and in the case of *automatic* norm adoption, of the routine of stopping at the red light (of course, in situation 1, it is hard to differentiate goal adoption from norm adoption).

In situation 2 (*instrumental adoption*), agents are granted greater autonomy: adoption is subject to restrictions. In goal adoption, on the basis of this rule, x will self-interestedly adopt only those of y's goals that he believes to be a sufficient condition for y to achieve some of his. Typically, but not exclusively, this rule depicts situations of *exchange*. A utilitarian norm adoption rule says that for all norms, x will have the corresponding normative goals if he believes he can get something in return (avoid punishment, obtain approval, praise, etc.).

Table 6.2 The route of norms in the mind.

	Goal adoption	Norm adoption
1. Conditional action	Slavish	Automatic
	$IF\big(GOAL\,y\big(DOES\,x\,a\big)\big)THEN\,a$	$IF(P\text{-}N\text{-}BEL\,x\,a)THEN\,a$
2. Instrumental adoption via (GGR)	Self-interested $\forall y\forall q\exists p\big[(G\text{-}ADOPT\,x\,y\,q)\supset$ $\big(BEL\,x\big((OBTAIN\,y\,q)\supset$ $(OBTAIN\,x\,p)\big)\big)\big]$	Utilitarian $\forall a\exists p\big[(N\text{-}ADOPT\,x\,a)\supset$ $\big((P\text{-}N\text{-}BEL\,x\,a)\wedge$ $\big(BEL\,x\big((DONE\,x\,a)\supset(OBTAIN\,x\,p)\big)\big)\big)\big]$
3. Co-operative adoption via (GGR)	Co-interested $\forall p\exists q\big[(G\text{-}ADOPT\,xyq)\supset$ $\big(BEL\,x\big((INTEREST\,xqp)\wedge$ $(INTEREST\,yqp)\big)\big)\big]$	Value-driven $\forall a\exists p\big[(N\text{-}ADOPT\,x\,a)\supset$ $\big((P\text{-}N\text{-}BEL\,x\,a)\wedge$ $\big(BEL\,x\big((INTEREST\,y_{j}(DONE\,a)p)\big)\big)\big)\big]$
4. Terminal adoption	Benevolent $\big(\wedge_{y=1,n}(G\text{-}ADOPT\,x\,y\,p_{y})\big)$ with p_y being the set of y's goals	Kantian $\big(\wedge_{x=1,n}(N\text{-}ADOPT\,x\,a_{x})\big)$ with a_x being the set of norm-actions required of x

In situation 3 *(co-operative* or *co-interested)* goal adoption occurs whenever an agent adopts another's goal to achieve a common goal. Norm adoption is co-operative when it is *value-driven*, that is, when the agent autonomously shares both the end of the norm and the belief that the latter achieves that end. This type of norm adoption can be seen as some sort of moral co-operation since the effect of the norm is shared (in the Addressee's beliefs) by the Addressee and the normative source.

The last situation, situation 4, is *terminal adoption*. This is not a rule, but a *meta-goal* which is defined, in the case of goal adoption, as *benevolent* (*x* is benevolent with regard to *y* when she wants the whole set of *y*'s goals to be achieved), and, in the case of norm adoption, *Kantian* (*x* wants to observe the whole set of norms addressing him as ends in themselves).

In situation 1, the rule is a typical production rule. Its output is an *action*. In situations 2 and 3, the rules output some specific *goals*. In situation 4, a meta-goal is described. In all situations, as far as norm adoption is concerned, the agent is endowed with a new type of goal, namely normative.

As said, the internal side of norms can be represented as a hybrid configuration of goals, beliefs and rules (cf. Fig. 6.1).

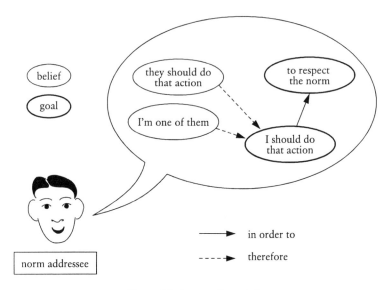

Figure 6.1 A normative mind.

A normative goal, in fact, is not sufficient for an agent to comply with a norm. Several factors occurring within the process leading from normative goals to normative actions may cause the agent to abandon the goal and violate the norm. Among others (more urgent conflicting goals, low expected chances of being caught red-handed, etc.), what is likely to occur is a confrontation with other Addressees. As is known, a high rate of observed transgression discourages one's compliance. Vice versa, and for the same reason, it is possible to show that if one has complied with a given norm, one will be likely to influence other agents to do the same (normative equity). Indeed, it can be argued that normative influencing plays a rather relevant role in the spreading of normative behaviour over a population of autonomous agents.

This we will do in the next chapter.

Norm adoption and commitment

It could be observed that norm adoption is but a form of commitment. Commitment is one of the notions in vogue within social AI. It is usually (Cohen & Levesque 1990b) meant in the very broad sense of personal commitment to an action (implied in the notion of intention) useful for increasing the degree of robustness of the system's performance.

Internal commitment, as found in Bouron (1992), corresponds to the notion of commitment defined by Cohen & Levesque (1990b) (on the basis of Bratman's analysis). It refers to a relation between an agent and an action. An agent has decided to do something; it is determined to execute a certain action (at the scheduled time); its goal (intention) is a persistent one. We prefer the term internal to that of individual because even a group or team may be attributed internal commitments.

On the other hand, there exists a notion of **social commitment** (Bond 1991, Gasser 1991b), which overlaps with collective commitment. What is lacking is a notion of social commitment as distinct from either personal and collective commitment, as well as a model of the links holding between each level of commitment and the successive. Here, we will claim that these levels share a normative foundation, which has been ignored by the existing models of commitment. Norms provide the connection between individual, social and collective commitment. In other words, commitment is a specific normative notion, it points to a special normative phenomenon which plays a fundamental role in social action, especially whenever a pact has been established among several agents. We will endeavour to show that commitment is but a social goal which implies norm adoption. When a given agent decides to pursue that goal it will also decide to adopt the norm associated with that goal.

Let us start with a notion of social commitment. In the sequel, we will not provide formal definitions, since our model of this notion is in progress (for more details see Castelfranchi 1993b). Our main concern here is to show how norms enter such interactions as exchange and co-operation rather than define a notion of commitment.

Social commitment

We need a notion of commitment as a medium between the individual and the collective one. A social commitment, in our view, is *not* an individual commitment shared by many agents. Rather, it refers to a process through which a number of agents commit themselves to one another (see also Bond 1991).

One might say that social commitment is just an internal commitment of x to do a and that this is known by y. In fact, this condition (though necessary) is insufficient. Let us suppose that y is aware of some intention of x to do an action a. This does not authorize us to say that x is committed to y to do a. Nor is it sufficient to suppose that x is aware that y knows his intention, etc. (mutual knowledge). Suppose we all know that John intends to play a nasty trick on Paul, and John becomes aware of the fact that we have understood his intention; nevertheless, John persists in his plan, relying on our silence. We may keep silent and become party to his trick. Even in this case, it cannot be said that John is committed to us to play a trick on Paul. If John drops out of his commitment, we may be surprised, but we are not entitled to protest.

We believe there are *at least* two additional conditions:

(a) *goal adoption*: x is committed to y to do a, if y wants a to be performed, or has an interest in it. Therefore, x and y share a goal that a be done as a result of x's adoption of y's goal or interest. Note that:
- x and y have an identical goal, but by virtue of x's adoption of y's goal
- this goal is an intention of x's (since it is his own action).

(b) *Emergence of a right*, namely y's legitimate (see the definition that we have provided above) goal to:
- ascertain that x does what he has promised;
- exact or require that he does it;
- complain or protest to x if he doesn't do a;
- (in some cases) make good her losses (pledges, compensations, retaliation, and so forth).

In actual fact, things are not so simple. What are the grounds on which y's right is based? x's intention to adopt y's goal *per se* creates no right, only expectations. Suppose y believes that her husband, x, intends to buy her a fancy bracelet that he knows she wants for her birthday. However, on his way to the jewellers, x sees a new shop and buys y a silk dress. y, who does not like the dress, will be disappointed. Still, no commitment on x's part was ever made; x did not promise anything. Therefore, y's right does not emerge from her belief that x intends to adopt her goal, but from her belief that x has committed himself to doing so. In commitment, the agent who commits himself gives notice to the recipient that he accepts being *bound* by his own promise to do the promised action.

(c) On the strength of the speech act theory (Searle 1969), we can say that, by committing himself to an action, an agent x *deliberately creates* an agent *y's right* to expect and exact that he does that action. The very act of committing oneself to someone else creates a right in the recipient. Before the promise, y has no rights over x, y is not entitled to exact his action. She can do so only after x's promise.

(d) While promising, x *makes one or more norms* ("Be trustful"; "Respect others' rights", etc.) *concern him*. What has been said implies that if x is committed, he has a duty; he ought to do what he is committed to and he does know it (pertinence normative belief).

(e) *Agreement*. It is insufficient that x intends to favour one of y's goals (even if there is common awareness). An agreement is also needed on y's side, together with x's recognition that such an agreement occurred. In other words, y ought to accept x's action.

Interestingly, commitment does not need to be explicit. Think of the girl who believes she is engaged to get married to a young man, and discovers that he, whom she considered her fiancé, never formed such a project in his mind. He contends that they never spoke of marriage, and that he did not commit himself to such a resolution. On the other hand, the girl says that he gave her a ring, and that she was introduced to his family. Who is right? Probably both. The girl may have coveted a dream in her mind. On the other hand, the young man may have let her believe that they were engaged. Looking at the whole deal from the girl's point of view, the two were implicitly committed to each other through symbolic acts rather than words. Conversely, from the young man's viewpoint, a terrible misunderstanding took place, caused by the girl's wishful thinking.

Commitment in social exchange

In Chapter 5 exchange was defined as being based upon reciprocal dependence. Essentially, we said that two agents enter into an exchange when each adopts a goal of the other in order to be reciprocated by the latter.

However, we believe that when exchange is realized on contractual grounds, it implies a reciprocal commitment; in other words, when two agents agree to enter into a relation of exchange, each is committing himself to reciprocate the adoption received. This is why cheating is not necessarily a rational solution for the agent who has already received adoption from her partner, even when the latter is not perceived as stronger. Cheating implies the cost of normative transgression, which ought to be taken into account and weighed up against the cost of obedience. At the same time, reciprocal commitment implies a right, namely that of receiving the expected compensation. Therefore, x and y are in a relation of exchange with regard to x's goal p and y's goal q if both have a legitimate goal that the other will reciprocate the adoption received, and each has a normative goal to do a given action, which leads the partner to achieve her goal.

Commitment in co-operation

In our words, co-operation is based upon mutual dependence. More precisely, true co-operation has been defined in terms of mutual knowledge of mutual dependence relative to an identical goal of x and y.

In Chapter 3 we defined co-operation as follows: x and y co-operate when they mutually believe they are in a relation of mutual dependence and each have two identical goals that each does its share of a common plan.

Now, we believe that co-operation implies social commitment as well. At least for full co-operation to occur, mutual commitment ought to take place, and that is the agents' reciprocal commitments each to do a share of a plan for a common goal. This explains why each agent is entitled to expect and exact that the other does her job. Therefore, full co-operation implies each co-operative agent having both a right and a duty: if x and y co-operate to achieve p, each has a legitimate goal that the other does the action she is competent to do, and at the same time each has a normative goal to do the action he is competent in.

Recapitulation

The focus of this chapter is the internal side of the normative coin. After a short discussion of the relative advantages of different normative architectures (built-in constraints, goals, and obligations), a fundamental distinction has been introduced between norm-abiding behaviour, which appears to correspond to some norms, and norm-governed behaviour, which instead results from some cognitive processing of norms and implies a mental representation of norms.

A normative belief has been defined as a belief about an obligation for a set of agents to do a given action. This was shown to imply some further beliefs about a normative source, the Sovereign. This is expected to fulfil a number of requirements: (a) to create an obligation for a subset of agents to do some action; (b) not to act in its own personal interests; (c) to be entitled to issue that norm; and (d) to act in the interest of the group. Now, these further aspects play a substantial role, especially within the process leading from normative goals to normative actions.

However, a normative belief is not yet sufficient to yield a norm-governed behaviour. A complex mental representation of norms is needed, which includes several types of beliefs (normative belief, pertinence normative belief), goals (normative goal), meta-goals, and rules of normative reasoning (rules of norm adoption). Several mechanisms leading to norm adoption have been examined. Finally, a notion of commitment implying both norm adoption and legitimate goals has been shortly discussed.

In the next chapter, a further type of normative goal, namely the Defender's goal will be identified.

CHAPTER SEVEN

The normative influencing

Cognitive factors of the spreading of normative behaviours

Aspects of normative decision-making, namely those aspects that lead from normative goals to either compliance with or transgression of a norm, will be examined. Furthermore, some steps in the circulation of norms from one character to another – i.e. from Addressee to Defender – will be reconstructed. This will be called normative influencing and will be argued to be crucial in the spreading of the normative behaviour.

Within a game-theoretic framework, the spreading of norms is not distinguished from a pure spreading of behavioural regularities. Here, instead, it will be argued that the spreading of regularities over a population of autonomous agents is also owing to a truly normative mechanism. In addition, while the game-theoretic approach emphasizes the impact of expected outcomes in the spreading of a given interaction rule, here the role of encountered costs in the spreading of normative requests will be investigated.

The chapter is organized as follows:

1. in the next section, *a model* is proposed *of the cognitive process leading from normative goals to normative actions*;
2. in the following section, the phenomenon of *normative influencing* will be explored;
3. finally, *the functionality of norms at the global level* (collective rationality) will be confronted with the local level one (distributive rationality), and some ideas about the cognitive ingredients of the normative mechanism, essential for the implementation of collective–rational norms, will be discussed.

Effective norms: from normative goals to normative actions

So far, we have been dealing with *operating* norms. What else is needed for a norm to become *effective*? What is the process leading from normative goals to normative actions?

In this chapter, we cannot dwell on a general model of decision-making.

We will limit ourselves to examining only some aspects of normative decision-making. Furthermore, we will ignore the process of confrontation between a normative goal and one or more other goals possibly stacked up in a module containing active goals. Suppose a normative goal is right on top of the stack. The question is whether it will be implemented or not.

One way of answering this question is the classical function of expected utility: a given normative goal will be executed if, say, the costs of transgression exceed those of obedience[1]. But what are the concrete costs of transgression/obedience? The following are fairly preliminary intuitions. As will be shown, here the role of D (the Defender) comes into play: another share of the circulation of norms in the MAS will be followed, namely *the transition from A to D*.

Some costs of transgression

It is generally believed that the *certainty of punishment* acts as a fundamental deterrence mechanism. The costs of transgression are then determined by the intensity of punishment and the probabilities of being caught red-handed. The latter, in turn, seem to be largely determined by the effectiveness of surveillance (see Table 7.1). To predict how likely punishment is often requires at least the following tests:

(a) *Existence of surveillance.* "Shall I park here? Certainly there is a no parking sign. However, this neighbourhood is out of the way: surely, there's no policeman around.". Here, pre-existing knowledge about the world makes the agent infer that there is no surveillance. Sometimes, it is the high rate of transgressors that makes the agent infer that surveillance is non existent: "Look at that wall! There is a no bill-sticking sign and yet everybody has stuck up their own sign. Evidently policemen don't bother about these bills.".

(b) *Hindrance to surveillance.* Beliefs about the rate of transgression may produce an expectation of impunity in a more subtle way: the higher the

Table 7.1   Costs of transgression.

Expected costs of transgression for a given crime i	$e_i p_i$ where e and p stand for the degree of pain and the probability of being discovered
Expected probability of being discovered	$p_i = \dfrac{s_i(\%)}{t_i(\%)}$ where s_i and t_i stand, respectively, for surveillance and transgression rates for crime i

The higher the rate of transgression, the lower the expected costs of transgression rate, the lower the probability that I will be discovered. If, say, nobody buys a train ticket, why should I, among thousands, be caught red-handed? To be discovered in this situation is highly unlikely and, as a consequence, *unfair*.

Some costs of obedience

On the other hand, a high rate of transgression seems to increase the costs of obedience: if expected costs of obedience are inversely proportional to the others' investments, as perceived by a given agent (see Table 7.2), it follows that the higher the perceived rate of transgression then the higher the expected costs of obedience for any single agent. If a given norm is known to be usually violated, the costs for a single agent to comply with it are proportionately higher. Note the difference between this claim and the free-riding paradox, where to choose a given option (e.g. to pay the municipal fee) is irrational for agents expecting to obtain a given benefit (e.g. a share of the public goods) irrespective of whether they have sustained the costs of the option or not. The main difference between the free-riding problem and our view of the normative decision-making resides in the fact that, as we have endeavoured to show in the preceding chapter, normative transgression *is* costly. Therefore, the decision to comply with a norm is not necessarily irrational. However, some normative decision-making is needed for ascertaining under what conditions transgression is more rational than obedience and vice versa.

Table 7.2   Costs of obedience.

By normative equity, expected costs of obedience for a given crime i	$r_i t_i$ where t_i stands for the transgression rate for crime i and r for the sources invested

The higher the rate of transgression, the higher the cost of obedience

Now, it is reasonable to assume that a high rate of transgression increases the costs of obedience. First, this is so for the reason mentioned above ("It is unfair that I should be found out. I am *entitled* to get away with it: why, then, should I take the trouble to observe the norm?"). Secondly, owing to the norm of reciprocation (Gouldner 1960), obedience is more costly when transgressions are frequent: "I comply with a norm if other Addressees of the same norm comply with it. If they don't, why should I? Am I different from others? Am I more gullible and naïve?"

Indeed, it seems that this reasoning is based on a rule of exchange applied to normative decision-making: "I will respect norms if you (other Addressees) respect them as well; I will not respect norms if you do not". In norm obedience a special case of the general principle of distributive justice applies. Since norm obedience is costly[2], why should we bear a cost that others do not bear?

From Addressee to Defender: normative influencing

From what we have said above, it can be inferred that an agent complying with norms is likely to become a Defender (D) of the norms. Interestingly, in Kelsen (1934) it is found that what defines a political asset as democratic is precisely the process by means of which the Addressees of norms participate in the issuing of norms. In our terms, this theory should be re-formulated as a theory of the transition from Addressee (A) to Sovereign (S). Without going so far, we think that an Addressee becomes at least a Defender, not in a particular type of political institution, but as a result of a normative decision-making which has led to compliance with a norm. The opposite is even more apparent: it is commonly held that one is entitled to evaluate the behaviour of others and their observance of the norms, only as long as one has committed oneself to the norms. Let us see why there is such a strong link between A and D.

The norm-defending goal

We will assume that a goal to defend any given norm exists, and define it as the goal that a given norm be respected:

$$(D \text{-} N \text{-} GOAL \, x \, y_i \, a) \stackrel{def}{=} \left(\Lambda_{i=1,n} \big(R \text{-} GOAL \, x \, (HAPPENS \, a)(N \text{-} BEL \, x \, y_i a) \big) \right)$$

in words: *x has a norm-defending goal* vis-à-vis *the set of agents* y_i, *if and only if, as long as he believes that there is an obligation on* y_i *to do action a, he has the goal that what is required by the norm will happen.* Essentially, a norm-defending goal is a generalized normative goal. Indeed, this equation should be intended as implying not simply that *the action* required by the norm *be performed*, but more generally that the *norm be fulfilled*. This means that a norm-defending goal is achieved when either the action prescribed is done, or the transgressors are punished (either in the specific forms laid down by the norm, or by any other customary penalty; see Fig. 7.1). Therefore, we will take *HAPPENS a* as meaning that the norm is to be respected.

Where does the norm-defending goal come from?

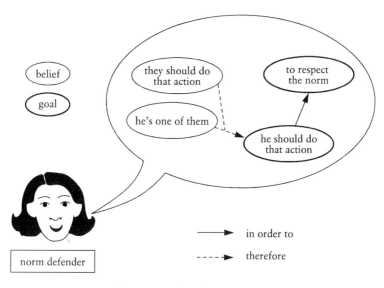

Figure 7.1 The defender's mind.

Normative equity

Once a norm has been observed by a given Addressee, we believe that the latter will come up with a new normative goal, the goal that that norm be respected also by the other Addressees. In our view, this is a necessary consequence of the *equity* principle, namely of a special application of it, that we will call the **normative equity principle**. In other words, if (a) we accept that agents want their costs to be no higher than those encountered by other agents, the benefits being equal[3], and (b) assume that doing the action prescribed by a norm implies a cost, we will conclude that agents want their normative costs to be no higher than those of other agents subject to the same norms, the benefits being equal.

Of course, it is reasonable to believe that before complying with norms the normative agent has to face two alternatives: (a) complying with and *defending norms*; (b) *giving up* the normative goal (when obedience is more costly than transgression).

But what happens once a norm has been fulfilled? In other words, if x has complied with a norm that he is subject to, he will have a norm-defending goal *vis-à-vis* y_j (a subset of y_i including all the agents addressed by that norm minus himself). This is a consequence of normative equity: in order for his costs to be no higher than those of others, x wants the other addressees either to comply with the norm that x himself has already observed, or to be punished. More generally, x wants the normative costs to be equally distributed among agents in his own world. This is interesting because it shows a consequence of norm-abiding behaviour that is usually ignored even though it plays a fundamental social role: the spreading of the normative requests. As anticipated in Chapter 5, we believe that, in the current formal approach to norms two phenomena are under-estimated:

(a) *post hoc social comparison*, in game theory, the behaviour of others is investigated only in order to decide which option to choose and before doing so. Although important, this is only one function of social comparison. There is at least one *post hoc* comparison, which occurs after the execution of the action decided upon, and this is to monitor the others' pay-offs. One could ask why this is so. In order to reduce undesirable discrepancies is the right answer. But how can discrepancies be reduced? This points to the second phenomenon neglected by game theorists;

(b) *normative influencing*, in game theory, an agent investigates the others' behaviours in order to comply with or adjust to them. In our view, the agent also attempts to modify the others' behaviours according to its own needs and goals.

Types of norm-defending goal

There are at least three types of norm-defending goals:

Directly preventing transgressions

Sometimes, the goal of preventing transgressions is achieved in a non-cognitive way, as happens with those drivers who accelerate in order to prevent the driver behind them, who's flashing his lights for them to get out of the way, from overtaking them in an unlawful fashion. In this example, the norm-defending goal is achieved by creating an obstacle, a physical condition hindering potential transgressions.

Punishment

A norm-defending goal may take the form of a goal that transgressors of norms (which instead x has observed) be punished. Now, this goal is often derived from normative equity plus the belief that in given circumstances a norm has been violated, and is strengthened or triggered by the fact that one actually usually complies with that norm, or has just done so – maybe to one's own cost: ("Look how they park their cars. When I think that it took me half an hour to find a parking place! I hope they get a fine!"). To set up a new balance, therefore, others ought to bear the cost of the transgression.

Normative reputation bulletin

An interesting form of normative behaviour consists of the agents *reporting on* one another's normative conducts. Indeed, a fundamental aspect of social life is **reputation,** which social psychologists have been studying in the last two decades (think of Goffman's (1959) notion of *face*).

Roughly speaking, this notion is usually meant as referring to the whole set of evaluations[4] that social agents make about one another. Within this large set, many different clusters may be found: evaluations concerning physical looks and attractiveness, internal resources and qualities, power and status, etc.

A subset of these evaluations can be expected to concern the agents' respectability, trustworthiness, etc., in a word their *moral reputation*. However, it can be assumed that the agents are evaluated also with regard to their normative behaviour, that is, how likely or unlikely it is for them to comply with norms. Compliance with norms, as well as transgressions, are recorded by the observers, be they *actors* on the normative stage – to use a Goffmanian metaphor – or mere *audience*, and contribute to form a platform upon which the reputation of the protagonists of the normative scenario is gradually constructed.

The utility of making a realistic appraisal of the normative, as well as moral and social, habits of one's acquaintances is evident. The more realistic such an assumption, the lower the probability of being cheated, attacked, and generally damaged by one's social surroundings.

A much less obvious question is rather why agents *report to others* on what they believe to be the moral and normative reputation of the actors observed. There seem to be at least two reasons:

(a) *adoption of the others' interests*: agents aim to prevent others, whom they are protecting for some reason, from trusting the wrong persons;

(b) *punishing transgressors and defending norms*: when the bulletin is intended to tarnish reputation, which is often the case, its effects are generalized blame on the ill-reputed agents, who thereafter tend to be deserted by the group and rejected as partners for exchange.

The normative reputation may be hypothesized to play a fundamental role in the spreading of normative behaviour. Indeed, the effects of one's behaviour upon one's moral reputation may have a far stronger deterrent impact than any other pain. In Chapter 11, the implementation of normative reputation in a MAS, and the observance of its effects in experimental computer simulations of the spreading of normative behaviour in artificial societies, will be discussed.

Influencing

In many circumstances, the goal of punishment is a special case of the goal of influencing, which is often involved in the expression of disdain or blame:

$$\left(\Lambda_{j=1,(n=1)}\left(N - INFL - GOAL\, x\, y_j a\right)\right)$$

in words: *agents x wants y_i (a subset of y_i including all the agents addressed by that norm minus x) to comply with it.* Examples of influencing distinct from punishment occur when one warns someone else against transgressing a norm ("Do you have a lighter?"; "Yes, but there is a "No smoking" sign over there"), or reminds the agent that he is doing something wrong (as happens when a driver proceeding in the opposite direction flashes his lights to warn you that yours are not on).

To sum up, the Defender's goal might be viewed as heavily responsible for the spreading of norms through a population of autonomous agents. *The more agents comply with norms, the more they will try to get other agents to do the same.* Once a norm has become effective, its rate of spreading should speed up dramatically as an effect of the norm-defending goal. Analogously, but on the other hand, as soon as some norm starts to be violated, the costs of obedience become higher and agents will be proportionately discouraged from observing that norm. The observance of norms is a cost *per se*, since it is represented by the agents as wanted by an external, although entitled authorship. However, such a cost cannot exceed a given threshold. In particular, it cannot be higher than that incurred by the other agents. Therefore, on one hand x is driven to defend the norm he has complied with, but, on the other, he is likely to abandon his normative goal and violate a norm which has been already violated by other agents subject to it. The problem of course is: what is the critical point, when does the rate of transgression start to discourage the single agent from complying with a norm? In other words, when does a single agent decide to comply with a norm and then persuade others to do the same, and when, instead, does he give up the normative goal himself?

About the functionalities of social norms

In this section, we will come back to the question of the functions of norms, not to provide a new taxonomy of norm functionalities but rather to emphasize and summarize some considerations scattered in the last three chapters, and which revolve around the question of collective vs. distributive rationality. As game theorists would do, we define as distributively rational with regard to a set of agents y_i, a state of the world that leads, in the long run, to the best possible outcome, or the least possible harm, for all agents included in y_{is}. A world state is instead rational in a collective sense, when it leads, even in the long run, to the best possible outcome for a collective entity c even though it does not imply the best possible outcomes for all its subcomponents – but those following from the maintenance of the collective entity itself[6].

The norm functionality most generally assumed and warranted in formal and computational studies is that of co-ordination, in the general sense of avoiding negative social interferences.

However, norms seem to produce other social effects, which apparently bring into play collective, rather than distributive, rationality. Consider, among others, the function of identification. Good manners, for example, improve identification rather than co-ordination: on the grounds of good manners, in-groups can be identified.

Moreover, one should consider that there are at least two types of norms of co-ordination:

(a) those which are aimed at *improving the agents' performance*, reducing head-on collisions[7], as well as destructive and self-destructive choices, e.g. what Ullman-Margalit calls PD norms, and, in some respects, Jasay's (1990) rules of *first occupation*, such as first come/first served, finders-keepers, etc.;

(b) those which are intended to *reduce physical attack*, such as again, the finders-keepers precept.

Now, if (a) norms can be expected to lead to the best possible outcome both at the individual and social level, it is not altogether clear what type of rationality should be assigned to (b) norms. Indeed, it is not so obvious why aggression should be irrational, even in the long run, for the *stronger* agents. In such a case, indeed, norms seem to play an *equalizing* role, which favours the weaker party at the expense of the stronger. As claimed by Jasay (1990), non-unanimous rationality is frequent in the domain of collective choice, and non-unanimous collective choice implies a fundamental evil: "by definition, it imposes Pareto-inferior solutions on some members of the community" (quoted in Radnitzky 1993: 19).

Goals, interests and norms

There are several distinct relations holding between norms, on one hand, and the goals and interests of the members of the MAS in which norms are in force, on the other:

(a) *distributive tutoriality*: actions prescribed are in the interests of all members of the system. Think of the norms prescribing the fastening of seat-belts, the wearing of helmets when riding motor cycles etc., which protect the individual's interests against his own will;

(b) *partial tutoriality*: actions prescribed are in the interests of a subset of the MAS at the expense of the rest; these are either the norms aimed to restore equity, protecting the interests of underprivileged categories, or, conversely, norms which favour inequality, protecting the interests of the privileged party (e.g. norms defending private property);

(c) *collective tutoriality*: actions prescribed in the interest of the MAS as a collective, but independent of and outside the interests of its members, like the norm prescribing the defence of one's home country from enemies, even at the cost of losing one's life.

Artificial cognitive utility vs. natural collective rationality

If norms clash not only with what the agents wish to do, but also with their interests, how do we account for the evidence that autonomous agents, indeed, observe a perceptible, although smaller than desirable, number of norms?

The rules and types of norm adoption discussed in the preceding chapter provide a formal answer to this question. Indeed, normative decision-making is a special case within the *gender* of goal adoption, leading to acceptance/rejection of the others' requests. The *specific* difference has also been shown: a normative belief is a belief about an obligation imposed by a normative authorship belonging to a given set of agents on a subset of agents. A normative authorship may be stretched until it overlaps with the whole larger set. What is necessary for a belief to be normative is that the request be believed to instigate norm rather than simply goal adoption, and is also believed to be entitled, disinterested, and oriented to do the interest of the larger set of agents as a community. In the present view, therefore, norms are represented, in the agents' minds, as a special type of request that the agents examine and decide upon, rather than accept acritically.

What is interesting about norms is that they are useful social objects that give birth to a new utility in their Addressees' minds, namely the utility to comply with that particular norm. As happens with requests, the means–end links are *artificially* created. It had probably never occurred to you to think about fixing an aperitif as a means to having the dishes washed after dinner, but this is exactly what your husband, coming back home after a long day at work, has proposed to you: you fix the aperitif now, and afterwards he will take care of the dish-washing.

Actually, norms do something more. Especially when they are useful only at the collective level, they create an *artificial utility* as well. In other words, the normative mechanism acts so as to create local reasons, e.g. personal goals, for compliance. As is widely known, artificial utility includes avoidance of punishment as well as social and self-approval, normative reputation, etc.

The artificial utility of norms does not coincide with their collective, social functionality, although the former is a means to achieve the latter. To use Ullman-Margalit's terminology, we can say that the artificial utility of norms is called for by the necessity to implement norms in societies of autonomous agents. It is not meant to deny that the true, *natural* functionality of norms may sometimes be represented in the minds of these agents, but this is absolutely not necessary. The normative mechanism evolved so as to act universally, independently of the idiosyncratic cognitive capacities and moral attitudes of the subjects. Hayek (1948, 1976, 1978) has theorized the evolution of a particular moral system, the *moral horde* or solidarity system, as based upon dominance and caring. It has been said that such a system is "deeply ingrained" [in the] "*emotional* make-up of the agents" (cf. Radnitzky 1993: 14; our italics). Our idea is that humans[8] have evolved not only the emotional ingredients of solidarity, but more generally the cognitive ingredients of norm adoption, implied by the observance of either tribal norms, or the norms that are valid in large, anonymous societies.

Recapitulation

In this and the preceding chapters, a cognitive modelling of norms has been attempted. It has been argued that the normative choice has to be clearly distinguished from behaviour simply corresponding to norms, and such a difference is shown to be allowed only thanks to a theory that views norms as a two-fold object (internal, or mental, and external, or societal).

Some instruments, still rather tentative, have been proposed for a formal treatment of the internal side of norms. In particular, a view of norms as a complex mental object has been attempted. This object has been shown to consist of other more specific ingredients, namely goals and beliefs. The notions of normative belief and goal have been provided and discussed, and aspects of the process of norm adoption examined and confronted with the process of adopting another agent's goals.

Some distinctions among various types of normative reasoning have been introduced. In particular, the differences in the minds of the Observers, Addressees, and Defenders of norms are explored.

Aspects of normative decision-making, that is the process leading to normative actions, are explored, namely the expected costs of transgression and obedience. Transgressions by other Addressees of the norms one has already observed have been argued to clash with a principle of normative equity. Consequently, observers of norms are argued to pursue a norm-defending goal in one of its possible forms (directly preventing transgressions, punishment, reporting on others' normative reputation, normative influencing). The norm-defending goals are responsible for a fundamental mechanism of norm spreading: the spreading of normative requests.

Indeed, behavioural regularities may spread over a population of agents out of conformity. But if we wish to make room for the spreading of a genuinely normative mechanism, we need to refer to the mental ingredients or correlates of such a phenomenon. If we limit ourselves to recording the frequencies of behavioural regularities, without exploring the minds of the agents involved, we cannot truly speak of norm spreading, unless, once again, we are simply referring to a purely conventional notion of norms. The spreading of the normative behaviour is also explained through the spreading of normative influencing. The mechanism of normative influencing seen above is merely an attempt to account for behavioural regularities in terms of the spreading of normative requests.

Finally, some non-unanimous functionalities of norms, to use Jasay's terms, have been discussed, and some relations holding among norms and the interests of their Addressees have been examined briefly.

At the cognitive level, the normative mechanism is made possible by an artificial type of utility. In line with cultural evolutionary theories of moral systems, it could be argued that, in some species, the cognitive endowment required by norm adoption evolved as a means for enabling autonomous agents to observe even non-unanimous, collective–rational norms.

From the diverse external inputs so far examined (structural pre-conditions, others' goals/interests, and the norms), a general notion of external goal may be drawn. In the next chapter, we will endeavour to show that such a notion displays extraordinary similarities with the notion of finality (function), often used in biology and in the social sciences.

Thanks to the notion of external goal, the circular nature of the micro–macro link is accounted for. As there are inputs to the micro, cognitive level of action, so there are also macro-social effects of cognitive action (finalities, collectives). In turn, these macro-social effects feed back to the cognitive action, selecting and reproducing it. This is what we will turn our attention to in the final part of the book.

PART FOUR

Closing the micro–macro circle: macro-level effects as emergent inputs to micro-level action

CHAPTER EIGHT

Towards a unified theory of goals and finalities

Introduction

For many years, teleological concepts such as goal and its appendages were banned from psychology by behaviourists, who accused them of being shamefully metaphysical. With cognitive science these concepts have re-entered the field with full status by virtue of the cybernetic models. In a number of still separate domains (decision theory, AI, etc.), these models have seen increasing development. An attempt to rethink the field of psychology as a whole with a goal-governed approach, as we call it, was made by Miller et al. in 1960; so far, their ideas do not seem to have been fully developed.

Current goal-governed models, though, still seem limited. In particular, they focus mainly on the self-regulation of the various systems. They always define a goal in terms of something internal to the system that regulates the system's behaviour.

In this chapter, instead, we try to develop the idea that there may be goals that are external to the system and that determine such a system from without, and in varying ways.

We illustrate the notion of "external goal" as a crucial connection between systems and phenomena of different levels of complexity. In this sense, the theory of the link between external and internal goals may contribute to the solution of the problematic micro–macro link.

As mentioned in the Introduction, a social system works mainly thanks to the behaviours of its members, and then through their goals and their capacity to pursue them. These are the main questions that we have raised in the Introduction:

(a) *How do social systems regulate the behaviours of their members?* How do these behaviours happen to respond to the goals of the social system?

(b) Could we answer the previous questions by stating that *the members are able to represent the social system's goals explicitly in their minds?* Or, do the members' goals and plans happily coincide with those of the social system? Our answer to both these questions is: Not necessarily!

(c) What, then, is, *the relation existing between the social system's goals and the goals internal to its members*, which directly and actually regulate the latters' actions?

This chapter is devoted to a pre-formal treatment of a theory of this relation.

As you will see, this general theory does not only apply to the relations holding among the goals of one agent and those of another agent, which was the topic of the preceding chapters. It also applies to some relations between one agent and inert physical objects. Physical objects are often selected and shaped so as to reflect their use, destination, **function**; in a word, the goals of the agents using them. This is an example of a **teleological** phenomenon. In the following we will provide a definition of *goal-oriented* vs. *goal-governed systems*. Here, let us say that a phenomenon, or entity, is teleological when at least part of its characteristics reflect someone's goal. On one side, we will endeavour to show the underlying and abstract similarities among diverse teleological phenomena, and, on the other, we will attempt to account for the differences among the various layers of goal-governed systems' complexity.

The basic unifying questions are as follows:

(a) *many features, behaviours, and goals of micro-systems serve and derive from* others' requests, advantages or needs. As inert objects are shaped by users, goal-governed systems may be shaped by *external requirements* of any sort. These requirements may be either imposed on those systems by some designer, educator, authority, or may not be imposed by anyone but simply result from an adaptive pressure or a social practice. But how can agents' features and goals be derived from external requirements and pressures?

(b) *Many natural and social behaviours exhibit a teleological character; nevertheless, they could not be defined as goal-governed*: we do not want to attribute represented goals – e.g. intentions – to all kinds of animals; consider the functional effects of social action (e.g. technical division of labour) as necessarily deliberate, nor attribute goals to society as a whole. Is there a concept that accounts for the teleological character of (social) behaviour without postulating internal goals ?

Once we have introduced the distinction among teleological, goal-oriented and goal-governed systems, we will:

1. *examine the role of external goals on goal-governed vs. goal-oriented systems*, starting with the various types of external goals imposed on objects (teleological systems): use, destination, function;

2. *consider the relation between external and internal goals* in simple non-human goal-governed systems: a boiler with a thermostat, and a horse. We try to show that *external goals* may be imposed on people as well, and examine the case of a traffic policeman, the commands he gives to the drivers, the commands of the traffic light, the rules of the traffic code.

Once the concept of external goal has been introduced and illustrated, we use it as a *bridge* to reach a more *radical unification of the concept of goal and all functional concepts up to and embracing biological finalities*. In essence, we assume that there may be goals external to a goal-governed system that are not internal to that of any other (i.e. goals that are simply external). We call these goals finalities. This requires a reformulation of the very concept of goal.

Systems and goals

In this section, we will introduce our notions of purely teleological vs. goal-oriented vs. goal-governed systems; a preliminary definition of external goals, and their application to teleological phenomena, namely use, destination, function.

Goal-governed vs. goal-oriented systems

As we saw in the Introduction, we call goal-governed a system or behaviour that is controlled and regulated purposively by a goal internally represented, a *set point* or *goal state* (cf. Rosenblueth & Wiener 1968, Rosenblueth et al. 1968). The simplest example is a boiler-thermostat system. As we will show, a goal-governed system responds to external goals through its internal goals.

What we call **goal oriented,** in a narrow sense, is a system or behaviour whose underlying mechanism is just a releaser, a reflex, a rule, not a deliberate device (McFarland 1983).

In a broad sense, any goal-governed behaviour is also goal oriented (see

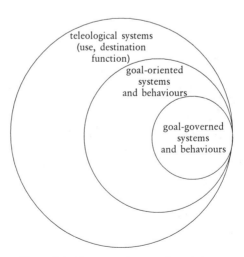

Figure 8.1 Systems and types of regulation.

Fig. 8.1): it is oriented towards a goal thanks to an internal device that determines its behaviour.

Finally, both types of systems are also teleological. More generally, teleological systems may not *behave* at all, but their characteristics and properties are at least in part determined by their use or function.

The notion of external goal: a first approximation

We could synthesize the current definitions of goal shared within the cognitive sciences as follows: a goal is a representation of a world state within a system, that regulates the behaviour of the system, selecting and monitoring its actions, trying to adapt the world to that representation.

Now, the concept of external goal may appear incompatible with this definition, or at least peculiar. In order to stay within the limits of this definition we shall use a narrow notion of external goal, leaving aside biological goals or adaptive functions and, in general, what we shall subsequently call, finalities. For the moment, we will relinquish one of the great conceptual advantages that the term goal and its synonyms (and their equivalents in other languages) provide, that is, the effective unification of the two categories.

When we speak of external goal we will refer to a goal-governed system x whose goals are internal regulatory states governing its actions. But what we are examining here is a particular relation between system x and the external world. More precisely, we are focusing on the effects that the existence of such a regulatory state within x has on external systems, both goal-governed and non-goal-governed.

One of the relationships that comes about between system x and system y, which is different from x, as a result of x's regulatory state g_x, is the emergence of an external goal placed on y.

A goal mentions entities (agents, actions, and states). If we formulate a goal in terms of predicates that describe the states of the world to be realized, these predicates concern certain entities (agents, places, things, events, etc.). For example, if x's goal is "that the chair be out of the room" his goal mentions two entities, a given chair and a given room.

Let us imagine that a goal of system x mentions an entity y. Suppose y's lot is somehow influenced or determined not only by chance but by the fact that it is mentioned in one of x's goals. In this case, we say that y has an external goal, or that x has placed an external goal on y.

Use

The simplest type of external goal is use. Let us consider a non-goal-oriented system, for example, a stone. A stone *per se* does not have and cannot have any kind of goal. But let us suppose that system stone, y, comes into contact with system x in a field of grass, that x comes up with a goal g_x that mentions the stone, for example, the stone cracks the walnut. In this case there is an external goal on the stone, a goal that resides in x.

Now let us suppose that x begins to operate to achieve g_x: he picks up the stone and, holding it in his hand, starts to pound some walnuts with it. x uses the stone as a means to the goal of cracking the walnuts by pounding them. The stone that was lying inert on the ground has undergone a change in position and is now involved in some type of movement; it receives blows, etc.; all this has occurred because it has fallen prey not to chance forces but to forces that respond to a design.

Its physical properties – size, shape, weight, hardness, cleanness – have been considered before and during the action with regard to their respondence or aptness to the goal placed on the stone. When the stone is chosen for use or is used, it possesses – for x and with respect to the goal g_x – a *use value*. It is judged by x as having the power to achieve the required goals, that is, its *external goals*. In connection with this, we notice that the stone has had two external goals placed on it by x; one a condition for the other. One goal is precisely that the stone have the power to (achieve) g_x – to have g_x achieved by x. The other goal that is going to be pursued only if the former is achieved, is precisely g_x. The former goal controls the actions of checking and choosing or discarding that x performs on y; the latter goal controls the employment of y once the choice has been made. The first goal is called *goal of use*, the second, *goal of use value* (see Fig. 8.2).

G1: goal of use
(to crack a walnut)

G2: goal of use value
(to be apt to . . .)

object

Figure 8.2 External goals on objects.

In this case, x does nothing to the stone itself to achieve the *use value goal* – the goal that it should possess the necessary properties, that it be suitable (except the possibilities that x might wish to clean it). x simply discards it or chooses it. What happens to the walnut is a different story. It has to be rendered edible by shelling. If it is not shelled by x, the walnut does not possess the power to be eaten in a satisfying way. In order to achieve its external goal of use value, the walnut must therefore be *transformed*. This is the first external goal placed on the walnut (a condition for other goals) and its first use. But there will be others.

It may certainly seem a little odd to speak of the *use* of the walnut when breaking it. Language here is more subtle, though; it distinguishes the *means of the action* (stone) from the *object* of the action (walnut). And the walnut seems to be the object of the action in the sense that the state resulting from the entire action is its change, whereas some possible change that the stone may undergo, for example if it breaks, is not important.

Destination

Now let us suppose that x notices that the above-mentioned stone could also make a good paperweight, because of its shape, dimension and weight, and also because of its decorative red veining. x will then take it home to use it as a paperweight. The stone, however, is not continually used this way: sometimes there are no papers to hold down so it just sits there, in display on a shelf or on a desk: sometimes, just for a change, it is replaced by other paperweights. Yet it is now destined to be a paperweight, it has become a paperweight, and it will remain a paperweight even when it is not holding down papers. This case, then, is different from the case in which x might have just used it once as a paper-weight, for example, in the same field of grass to keep his newspaper from flying away. But how did this transformation, which has given the stone a second nature, occur without any physical transformation occurring in the stone (except maybe a good polishing)? This transformation is due to another type of external goal. The stone was simply mentioned in such a goal – not the goal of one single use, but what we might call a nomic goal that deals with several unspecified events. That is to say it was mentioned in the intention of x to use it at various unforeseen times for that goal.

This external goal of destination determines a transformation of the functional properties of the object because it has made it a functional object (very similar, as we shall see, to artefacts or utensils) which, owing to the fact that it has this kind of function, may be recognized as belonging to a new class, that of paperweights. Even if the stone is not being used at the moment to hold papers down, it sounds sensible to say that "it has the goal of holding paper down", that "its goal is to . . . ".

Function

We call function an external goal placed on a system that results in a transformation of the structural properties of the system. In order for the system to satisfy its goal, to be apt for its use, the system, for example an object, undergoes a transformation. The external goal in question is the goal of the use value: to obtain a given use value, the initial properties of the object are altered. The higher-level goal is the goal of use or of destination. The characteristics the object acquires are determined by its function (and show it). Later, we will examine a more complete and general definition of finalities. Here, we intend to refer essentially to the functions of artefacts and tools. However, interestingly there are similarities between these notions, and this is precisely what we are after in this chapter.

A function is an external goal that seems to be inherent in the object even more than in the case of use or destination. In fact, in this case the same physical or mechanical characteristics the object possesses have been caused by the goal, and not vice versa. A chair is "made for", "has the goal of" being sat upon. A knife "has the goal of" cutting. We have here an artefact, a teleological or, better, a functional product of human activity. And if its function is to serve as a means and not as an object (in the above-mentioned sense) when it is used, it is also a tool.

The function of a thing, as in the case of destination, results in uses. For example, the function of a chair (that one single person may sit down and lean back on) is realized every time someone sits on it. Yet, an object is not always used or destined in a manner that corresponds to its function. For example, I may use the chair to stand on and take a book from the shelf. I use the chair as a step-ladder or a stool (exactly like x used a stone as a hammer) but the function of the chair remains that of a particular type of seat.

External goals on goal-governed systems

Let use now examine the case in which also y is a goal-governed system and is treated as such. y is not just mentioned in x's goal but x's goal includes y doing something, not simply to cause something, or to change its state – as in the cases of the walnut and the stone respectively, which are involved in the action of x – but to act on its own. To say that an action of y is mentioned in g_x is like saying that y is mentioned as having and pursuing an internal goal.

A simple goal-governed system: a boiler thermostat

To gradually introduce our claims, and to formulate the theory in a general way, let us start from the case in which y is a boiler-thermostat system, the simplest kind of goal-governed system, in which the internal representation of the goal is just a *cybernetic set-point*. x is the owner of the apartment who installed y, or the person who is to use it now. x's goal is that the temperature in the house where he resides and where he is cold (13°C) reach 25°C; to this end, he turns up the thermostat to 25°C. x has a goal that must be reached by making use of another system's internal goal and capacity to achieve it. Note that the boiler thermostat's (its regulatory state) and x's goals are not one and the same, even if reaching the former permits the latter. In fact, x's goal is to feel warm, or, we might say, that the house be warm (at 25°C), while the goal of the boiler thermostat is not that the house be warm, nor that it be 25°C, but that the index that varies with the actual room temperature (thermometer) coincides with the index showing the objective desired. Moreover, this goal is always the same no matter what temperature x selects.

y has an external goal (warm house), which corresponds to the goal of x's, and furthermore, y has an internal goal (coinciding indexes), and there is a particular relationship between them; the internal goal is a subgoal, a means for the external one (see Fig. 8.3).

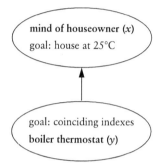

Figure 8.3   External goals on simple minds.

The system has a function (and not simply of a use or destination) because its external goal has selected and shaped its structural and functioning characteristics, including its internal goal, namely a set-point.

We call **respondent internal goal** an internal goal of system y, by means of which that system is able (use value) to respond to the external goal placed on it by another system, but that is not identical to this external goal.

A more complex goal-governed system: a horse

Let us now examine the case where y is a rather more complex goal-governed system, for example a horse. Suppose that this horse has the destination (and it would not be wrong to say the function) of a mount. To have this use value, that is, to be adequate for this kind of external goal, the horse must be adapted and, more precisely, it must be broken and trained. But a horse is also an animal and, as such, it is a system that follows its goals autonomously, on its own initiative. What it needs to become a mount is precisely to learn to have internal (that is, its own) goals respondent or identical to the external ones placed on it by x.

For the horse-breaking and training consist of exactly this: learning to obey x's commands and to tolerate him on its back. To obey really means to give oneself an internal goal, equal or respondent to the external one to allow the latter to be achieved. Let us examine the relation between external and internal goals during the use of the horse. *x* mounts and wants *y* to stand still while he mounts. *y* stands still; *x* wants *y* not to throw him, and *y* does not throw him; *x* wants *y* to walk, so he kicks the flanks of *y* with his heels, and *y* starts walking; he wants *y* to turn right and *y* turns right; he wants *y* to jump, and *y* jumps; etc. *x*'s goals on *y* (that is *y*'s external goals) somehow generate goals in the mind of *y*. In our terminology, *x* is influencing *y*.

This relation between *x* and *y* poses a host of interesting problems; we shall examine two.

(a) First, *are the goals in y's head the same as the goals in x's?* There are three cases:

(i) We hold that certain goals are common to both. For example, *x* may have the goal "*y* jump the hurdle" and *y* the goal "*y* jump the hurdle". Naturally these goals are identical in the observer's meta-language; but they will be represented in different ways in the minds of *x* and *y*, since one is a person and the other is a horse. Even if they had the same system for representing goals, there would still be a difference between the goal formulated in *x*'s mind and in *y*'s mind. *y*, to *x*'s mind, is an individual that *x* has certain knowledge about, whereas *y*, in *y*'s mind, is a particularly special individual: itself.

(ii) On the other hand, certain other goals are present only in *x*'s mind and never enter *y*'s. For example, for *x*, the goal "*y* jump the hurdle", may have a supergoal, "*x* win the horse show" and it is possible that *y* will either ignore, will not have, cannot have or even cannot understand, this particular goal of *x*'s.

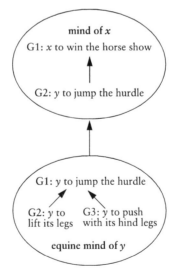

Figure 8.4 External goals on more complex minds.

(iii) Finally, there are still other goals that are present only in y's head. To reach the goal "y jump the hurdle", y must pursue a series of subgoals: "y lift and bend its forelegs", "y push with its hind legs", etc (see Fig. 8.4). All these are goals that need not be in x's mind. Just as y is a goal-governed system, capable and trained to regulate itself in reaching goals such as jumping, x entrusts y with the pursuit of such goals. These goals are derived respondent internal goals of y, with respect to the external goal of jumping, and are normal subgoals with respect to the same goal that has become internal. The internal goal of jumping is just a respondent one that regards winning the horse show.

This shows that y's internal goals may have at least two distinct origins: they may be borne in a merely endogenous way, as means of y's internal goals, or they may be borne as translations of external goals.

(b) How can the goals of x (external to y) be translated into goals within the mind of y? Does y always adopt x's goals? In other words, does y understand (is there a representation in its mind of) x's goal (for example, "x wants y to jump the hurdle") and adopt it? y may not understand x's goals at all, x's signals may not mean anything to it, but a certain sensation (a blow on the flanks, a pulling of the reins, etc.) may reactively provoke the desired response.

From external to internal goals

From all the examples examined, we can conclude that an external goal can be implemented in, or better translated into, a goal-governed system in two different ways:

(a) As a **copy goal**: an internal goal identical to the external goal and derived from it. The external goal is explicitly represented within the mind. This mind may both be aware of the fact that its goal p is also an external goal (somebody's will, a norm, a biological finality) or it may ignore this. We will call this type of translation **internalization**. External goals may be internalized thanks to a number of different processes and mechanisms (goal adoption, selection, training).

(b) As a respondent **internal** goal: a goal which is functional to and derived from an external goal, but which is not identical to it. The external goal is not represented within that mind, but, in a certain sense, is implicit in it.

"As-if" goals

We stressed the above two ways of implementing external goals within the impinged mind, because we were mainly interested in the relations between external and internal goals in goal-governed systems.

However, now it is important to add a third relevant kind of implementation through which external goals succeed in controlling the behaviour of goal-oriented systems. This we will call as-if goals: in fact, they are behavioural mechanisms (for example, a reactive device) that do not imply an explicitly represented goal. However, the system is oriented towards the production of certain results, *as if* it were regulated by an explicit internal goal; but, in fact, the goal is neither explicitly represented, nor has it been planned, decided upon, or reasoned about.

An implicit goal means that there is an external goal towards which the system behaviour is oriented, but this goal is not explicitly represented within the system.

We will shortly analyze two crucial examples of non-respondent implicit goals calling them *as-if* goals (it will become clear why): reflexes, and the principle of utility.

Reflexes as "as-if" goals

Let us take the example of the flight reflex. The case of a bird that, as soon as it recognizes the silhouette of a falcon behind it, reacts by immediate escape. Or, the case of a robot provided with sensors and reactive motor behaviours, which in presence of a certain acid immediately reacts by abandoning the room.

We are speaking of stimulus–response mechanisms, or, at least in the bird case, of releasers: a key stimulus elicits a more or less fixed motor pattern. We can suppose that, in the case of the bird, the adaptive finality that selected its flight behaviour is that of not being preyed upon. As for the robot, we may suppose that the designer's intention was that of avoiding a massive contact with a disruptive acid, and therefore avoiding disruption. The goal that both reactive systems pursue is avoidance of danger, or safety. It is *as-if* the two systems were internally regulated by the goal of avoiding a specific danger and be safe. But, we know that in fact this goal is not represented explicitly in either system. These goals are merely the (non-casual) outcome of the behaviour activated or elicited by a determined stimulus. As regards the robot, the true goal is represented within the designer's mind; as regards the bird, it is only a biological finality. In both examples, any true internal goal regulating, governing (through a feedback mechanism) a *deliberate* behaviour (Rosenblueth & Wiener 1968) should be excluded. The usual goal-governed mechanism in which a set-point or regulatory state is matched with the current world state and an action modifying the current world state is activated (as in the TOTE model of Miller et al. 1960), is replaced by a simple match between the condition of the action (like the left part of a production rule) and the world stimuli: this match (rather than a match between the current state and the desired one) can elicit the action.

Utility and profit as "as-if" goals

Reflexes like those seen above are low-level mechanisms that represent implicit goals. Also some higher-level mechanisms may seem to play the same role. Some meta-goals (goals about the internal explicit goals, as found in Wilensky (1983)) may work as *as-if* goals, apparently regulating the behaviour, but in fact only indirectly impinging on it.

We believe that the goal of ensuring the best resource allocation, achieving the greatest number of most valuable goals with the minimum cost, is not a true *internal goal* of the layman. In our view, individuals act in view of concrete and specific goals (like being loved, eating, having a book published, making money), which are heterogeneous: i.e. they are not the means for a unique, totalitarian, top-level goal (pleasure, or utility).

Nevertheless, it is absolutely true that agents habitually choose the most convenient goal (given their limited cognitive capacities) to achieve out of a set of goals possibly in conflict with one another. Our claim is that this result may be allowed not necessarily by a goal, but by a mere mechanism or procedure of rational balance and choice. Agents have but the implicit goal of choosing the most convenient goal. They operate *as-if* they had such an internal goal. In fact, it is only an external goal that shaped this mechanism of choice.

External goals, social goals and the goal of influencing

An external goal placed on a goal-governed system and referring not to a trait of this system but to its mental states is a *social goal* (as we defined in Chapter 2): an external goal placed on system y is a social goal of another system x when it mentions a mental state of y's. In particular, an external goal implies an influencing goal, when it mentions an action, or better, a goal, of y's.

If x wants y to perform an action a_1 that is an initial subsequence of action a ($a_1 < a$), and succeeds in influencing her, y will have a respondent internal goal. *If x wants y to perform a* and succeeds, y will have an identical goal.

Functions of people

People are subject to use and destination by other people and higher-level systems (group, organization). For example, if, among a group of boys who set off to steal apples there is one who cannot climb the fence very quickly but who can whistle, he will be chosen as a lookout. In this case, a *use* is being made of the boy. If, having succeeded, they repeat the action, the group becomes a gang, and the boy is given the job of being a lookout each time they make a hit; then we can say that he has been *selected* to be a lookout.

However we are here mainly interested in analyzing people functions. In social sciences, people uses, destinations, and especially functions are called *roles*.

Let us consider a traffic policeman. We can compare him to an object provided with a function, traffic lights. To a large extent, their functions may be considered to be one and the same. This will permit a detailed examination of the similarities and differences that occur when these two systems carry out that function – one is goal-governed and the other is not. We speak of the traffic lights function because they have been chosen, built and installed to regulate traffic at intersections and this goal has determined all (or almost all) of their construction and installation characteristics: lights of three well-defined colours, in a particular position and arranged in a particular way, with subshades and water-proofing materials. As for the policeman, he too, owing to his job as traffic policeman, has acquired a whole set of characteristics that (a) he did not have before becoming a traffic policeman; (b) that he does not have when he is off-duty; or (c) that he would not have were he not a policeman at all.

These characteristics are strictly functional to his task (external goal). In this, he is different from an ordinary driver who, exasperated by a traffic jam, gets out of his car and starts controlling the traffic by himself, just like a policeman. The driver acts *like* a policeman but is not a policeman, just like the rock that serves as a hammer but is not a hammer, or the chair that serves as a step-ladder but is not a step-ladder. The driver *uses* himself as a traffic policeman but has not acquired the function of traffic policeman. Functional characteristics may be: (a) transitory (in the case of traffic policeman, a uniform, an armlet and gloves, a whistle, etc.) and (b) permanent, (in the same example, knowledge of the traffic code, licence plates, procedures relating to fines and penalties, signals, etc.). In short, permanent characteristics are all those things the traffic policeman must acquire when training to become a good traffic policeman.

Yet what we want to draw attention to here is neither the knowledge nor the abilities but the *goal* that a traffic policeman must have. In fact, of all things that have a function, a policeman is more like a boiler thermostat than a chair or, as we shall see, traffic lights, for he achieves (responds to) his external goals by pursuing an *internal goal*, that is, through certain goal-governed actions.

From the very act of acquisition of his function (that is of the functional characteristics), she (y) starts with a common internal and external goal: the goal of being a traffic policeman. Naturally, she has this goal not because she shares the supergoal of x, that is, of society or, more modestly, of the local council (that needs a certain number of new traffic policemen to improve traffic flow). On the contrary, y has her own higher-level goals: to have a job within local government, to earn money, to have a uniform, to show that women can do male jobs. Even though the higher-level goals are different, at least one of the external goals of y coincides with one of y's internal goals. Note that it is y who adopted x's goal by responding to the announcement of the competition for a job.

Therefore, x and y have the same goal: that y be a traffic policeman; and to this end they have the same subgoals: that y learn certain things, wear certain things, etc. The reason why y should have the goal of wearing the uniform or knowing the regulations is that x has the goal, and x has established the conditions that y, in order to be a traffic policeman, must wear the uniform, know the regulations, etc. These goals become internal goals of y's fundamentally because they are external goals that x has placed on her, and that y adopts. We may suppose, however, that y also understands the utility of these goals, and may, in a sense, agree with them. x's and y's principal goal then, is that y performs certain actions, that at the proper moment she pursues certain goals, such as to punish whoever has broken the law, or to keep the traffic flowing smoothly. These are the goals that become the function of traffic policeman and that y must adopt.

These goals will also have to be specified by y and put into effect on every new occasion. This means that a series of subgoals that y pursues to fulfil the function of traffic policeman are left up to her. They are not merely copies of *external goals*. Once y has adopted the basic goals of the function of traffic policeman, it is left up to her to reach them in a way appropriate to varying circumstances, that is, to formulate contingent subgoals. Once she has adopted x's main goal, y is allowed to autonomously pursue it (she is allowed a special kind of autonomy, or plan autonomy, which we discussed in Ch. 3). If system x were in total control of the way y must carry out the external goals placed on her, it would be senseless to use an intelligent and autonomous system y, that is capable of regulating itself and solving problems, like a person.

The comparison with the traffic lights is interesting. The traffic lights are a non-goal-governed system that are nonetheless capable of replacing a goal-governed system in some of their functions. The traffic lights are not run by goals. They are a purely mechanical object. Their signals are transmitted at regular time intervals, with no other considerations.

The traffic lights' *disadvantages* compared with the policeman's are evident: the traffic lights might send out messages even if no one were present, they might stop a long row of cars even if no one were approaching from the other direction: they cannot give the right of way to the Red Cross, the Fire Brigade etc.; they cannot deal with subgroups of cars or single individuals. But there are *advantages* as well. Autonomy has also some negative effects. A traffic policeman may start pursuing his own *extra-function goals* (leaving his post, chatting, relating, fooling around, etc.).

To sum up, even people may have functions and these functions shape not only these people's physical characteristics, knowledge, and abilities, but, most important, give rise to internal goals. People adopt their functions, which are therefore self-governed and fulfilled through the normal mechanisms used for the pursuit of internal goals. The obvious main difference between policeman and boiler thermostat is that the former had adopted (for his own prior and independent goals) x's request (x's external goal), thereby translating the external goal into a *like* internal goal: whereas the boiler thermostat has no ability to adopt anything (a boiler thermostat cannot be given orders, instructions, rules, regulations) and the internal goal corresponding to its function has been built into it by its designers. It is the designer who has adopted the request of the possible buyer to have his heat regulated.

External goals and finalities

We have considered a goal as a state that is always represented in at least one goal-governed system, provided with a series of controls and actions in order to achieve that state in the world. In doing so, we have been using a definition of goal that omits biological (adaptive) finalities, or philogenetic goals, and social finalities However, these notions are not unrelated. There must be a concept which provides a bridge between them.

Biological and social finalities

Let us try to show the advantages of an abstract theory of goal. In Chapter 9 we will try to prove that the concept of finality is also necessary in order to account for certain social phenomena that are not reducible either to the goals of a single individual or to the goals of social systems (such as communities, institutions, etc.) and whose somewhat teleonomic (Mayr 1982) character has always been acknowledged without ever having been adequately explained (social finalities). Our claim is that all we will illustrate about biological finalities holds good also for social finalities.

Biological finalities are certainly not goals in the above-mentioned sense: neither nature, nor species, nor selection nor any other analogous entity are goal-governed systems in our sense.

Nevertheless, it may be possible and useful to have a more abstract notion of goal and define it as a selecting mechanism. This notion includes both regulatory states of goal-governed systems and what we call finalities. The bridge between the two concepts is provided by the concept of external goal. In fact, finalities work on organisms in a way analogous to external goals operating on objects or goal-governed systems. They modify an organism's characteristics not in a purely chance fashion, but in a way that will render it more *apt*. A goal in the strictest sense is an internal representation that selects a given behaviour. A finality *is a selecting effect*.

134

A goal selects one out of a set of potential behaviours; a finality selects one out of a set of actual behaviours.

More explicitly, we (Castelfranchi & Conte 1992) defined finality as follows:

(a) *Let x* be an entity which is instantiated in a sequence of distinct repetitions $(x_1, x_2 \ldots x_n)$. A sequence of repetitions is defined as a set of occurrences or instances (if any) of the same entity all genetically linked to one another, that is, linked in such a way that each is produced by the preceding, and produces the following occurrence (if any) in the sequence, thanks to any mechanism of reproduction whatsoever.

(b) Also let *Bx* be a set of behaviours and characters of *x*, and

(c) some items in *Bx* produce effects (states of the world) unintended by, and unknown to, *x*;

(d) we can say that any item in *x* that produces unintended effect is functional, if that effect acts through a causal feedback loop on the mechanism of reproduction, favouring *x*'s reproduction, and as a consequence that of the item itself. The effect is no longer a simple one among others, but is a finality of the behaviour or character in question. It selected and shaped that behaviour to be as it is.

Artificial selection and natural selection

In this regard the comparison between artificial selection of animals or plants and natural selection is enlightening.

We have defined a function as that external goal which not only determines the employment of something but its characteristics as well. Therefore, on the one hand, there are philogenetic or adaptive functions that are produced by natural selection; on the other hand, there are artificial functions, that are produced by teleological activity of a goal-governed system.

The variety of shapes of the beaks of aquatic birds is determined by the kind of food the birds eat and by the way they must find it (whether digging, fishing, dredging, etc.). Beaks are indeed real natural utensils that must perform efficiently when used: they would not have the characteristics they have if they did not serve this purpose.

Likewise, the function of chairs, say, has determined their structural characteristics. As a matter of fact there is an important difference between chairs and beaks: a chair acquires its characteristics through a series of direct actions on its components' properties; it is the product of a teleological activity, whereas a beak is not moulded by any designer through the application of forces to its matter. Biological finalities operate through a process of random trials and errors, of tests and rejections. The beak of the various members of a species must be considered as the result of a series of random tests.

Procedures of pure selection recur in human production as well, not only with respect to finalities but also to internal goals. Where it is not possible to intervene directly to predetermine an outcome, there is no choice but resort to an *a posteriori* sifting out process. Consider the size of oranges. Ever since oranges became commodities, size has acquired a function because the bigger the orange, the bigger the value. Size has a function because it is deliberately given to oranges; work is devoted to this goal for the use value it has. Obviously, size is not really *given* to the oranges (if we disregard selection of breeds, grafts, planting and growing techniques) through direct modifying actions (as is done, for example, with bread) but by sifting out. For example, when oranges are graded, they are rolled on planes with holes. Each plane has smaller calibre holes than the previous one. This is how oranges of different sizes are separated and the desired product is obtained: big oranges. So we begin with oranges of different and random sizes and we reject the unwanted ones.

The differences between selection and action are, in reality, less marked than they appear. Selection is a necessary part of any process of regulation and it represents, we think, its most abstract essence and its unifying concept. In fact, a goal in its strict sense (internal representation) acts, in the process of regulation, exactly like a sieve for: the existing world states (satisfying or not); the actions' effects (created states) – both partial and final; the expected and potential results, concerning each action. In essence, it is a sieve for the actual actions to be carried out.

A more general notion of goal

Another facet worth emphasizing for achieving conceptual unification of the philogenetic goals or finalities and the regulatory states represented within the system is the following: if the operations or properties of a system are caused by their effect then they have a goal. Obviously, this always presupposes a particular history of such operations or properties aiming to the effect of having chronologically preceded its operations or property. This is possible in at least two ways:

   (a) *a repetition in time of a property or operation*; the effect of a given *occurrence* influences the appearance or non-appearance of the subsequent occurrences (then when a given property or operation does or does not repeat itself, we may say that this depends on the effects it has had);

   (b) *a possibility of representing the effects within the system*; it is actually that representation that precedes the operation or property.

On the basis of the previous considerations we can envisage the following very general definition of *goal*: a goal is the sieve used to select the properties of a system (whether they be morphological or behavioural properties, actions) so that we may say that at the time T_1 such a system's properties are not the result of chance, but its preceding history (T_0) that consists of the rejection created as a result of the sieve's sifting the alternatives (actual or symbolic) of a given property.

Given this general concept of goal, we may distinguish between goals in the strict sense, or internal, or represented goals, and finalities, that are exclusively external goals, that is, not internal to some goal-governed system that placed them on some other system.

Advantages of a general theory of goal

Now let us examine various advantages that come from considering biological finalities as goals (Williams 1978, Mayr 1982), more precisely external goals.

Similarities among types of adaptive characteristics

We made a comparison earlier between chairs and beaks: in both, the external goal is translated into a function (in our technical sense), that is, into structural characteristics. But in biological organisms it is not just the somatic characteristics that are adaptive. Behavioural characteristics, actions they are capable of, are adaptive as well. For example, the kinds of movements necessary for the use of the different kinds of beaks, are apt as well. But when we speak of behaviour, of actions, we are normally really speaking of internal goals. So when we say that the behaviour of biological organisms responds to external goals (biological finalities), we are saying that within these organisms there are internal goals that respond to external goals. We are in a situation that is analogous to the boiler-thermostat system.

The biological organism responds to its own finalities (external goals) through its own regulation, and not just by physical means. The external goal has *translated* itself not only into somatic characteristics but into goals as well. Nearly always, this means the appearance of goals that are subgoals (respondent goals) of the adaptive finalities, and almost never does it consist in the adoption of the finality itself, that is, in goals identical to the external ones. For example, not even the goal of reproduction, which is probably the main external goal on organisms, ever seems to be an internal goal (except in human beings); it is only a consequence (and a finality) of the sexual goal. It is just implicitly operating within the organism to regulate its behaviour.

In sum, by likening adaptive finalities to goals, one brings to light both,
  (a) the *similarities between different types of adaptive characteristics*, and therefore:
  (b) the relationship between *internal goals and philogenetic goals*.

Hierarchical organization among finalities

Another advantage is that the concepts of goal hierarchy, of means–end relation, of supergoal, plan, etc. can be applied to adaptive finalities. We said previously that the most fundamental biological goal is an organism's reproductive advantage, a greater probability of replicating its own genetic heritage, or better what biologists call *inclusive fitness*; but we also talked freely about other biological goals: to reproduce, to mimic, to avoid being preyed upon, to feed. Many more, of course, could be added to the list.

Now, the general principle of hierarchical structure and organization has the same value for finalities as for any other goal. The principle may be formulated as follows: a goal g to be achieved under different circumstances must be specialised into goal $g_1, g_2 \ldots g_n$ (subgoals). g is the top-level goal, while $g_1, g_2 \ldots g_n$ are separate, non-sequential, but being specialized means achieving g in those specific circumstances. Different biological species are but different solutions to the same problem, each found under different circumstances. To say that biological species have mainly adapted to their environment is just like saying that each of them has accidentally found within its environment a sufficient way of guaranteeing its biological finality (inclusive fitness). Furthermore, a given species does not have only one way open to it but has various ways that may converge and, vice versa, one single characteristic (somatic or behavioural) may respond to several finalities. For every species, and for every organism, there is a complex hierarchy of external goals, namely biological finalities, that all converge on g.

The highest goal in every hierarchy is the same for all species, while the means to achieve them differ (and this is what species consist of). Naturally, there are overlaps in other parts of the hierarchy as well, that is, on other finalities, namely *analogies* and *homologies*.

While we believe that in biological finalities there is only one aim or final goal and there may be no conflict among final goals, we nonetheless think that there may be conflicts among lower biological external goals (and their internal representatives). Two finalities under certain circumstances push the organism towards opposite adaptations: if it responds optimally to one of them the other is jeopardized and vice versa. Here, a goal-governed balance is needed, a balance that can only be regulated (like the balances of internal goals) by an economy or rationality principle: to obtain the maximum benefit with the minimum cost among the existing alternatives. Without this principle, it is senseless to speak of balance.

There is a difference between balance among finalities on the one hand, and balance among internal goals on the other hand. In the former, as there is no mind to evaluate and compare them, each finality is measured solely in terms of how much it contributes to inclusive fitness. The balance of internal goals is of a different sort. Not all internal goals are means of achieving one and the same internal higher-level goal (pleasure or utility) and not all are evaluated on their capability of achieving it. There are various final goals, and a balance is possible only because the mind allots them some value coefficient.

Final internal goals converge only externally and within the converging finalities they adopt. The value of internal goals cannot but find its source in the sort of value that the corresponding finalities have, and which consists only of the importance that each finality has in ensuring the achievement of the primary and most important finality, fitness.

How can one account for the hierarchical structure of biological finalities (hierarchies, plans, conflicts, balances) without a theory of external goals and a unified notion of goal (and consequently of plan, conflict, etc.)?

We believe that a very interesting way to analyze the evolutionary process may be through observing goals: both hierarchies of finalities and repertoires of internal goals.

Three evolutionary tendencies appear to be emerging:

(a) *an ever-more complex hierarchy of finalities*;
(b) *an increase in the number of internal goals* that regulate organisms;
(c) *the development of goal-governed systems* capable of solving problems, of generating (also on the basis of prior experience) internal goals to achieve. In the higher species, natural selection does not specify *low* goals, goals that directly govern behaviour. On the contrary, it builds into the organisms some final goals, and provides them with the capacity to pursue them autonomously, generating the lower-level ones. The same holds for society and the social finalities impinging on its members. Society too relies on agents' *self-regulation*. Agents are allowed to decide whether, and when, to respect or not respect the social norms (and bear the consequences of their decisions), how to fulfil the assigned tasks, how to achieve the objectives of their roles, etc.

A unified notion of goal can help explain the similarities between human behaviour and animal behaviour, and in general allows similarities among many layers of evolutionary systems to be accounted for.

Between deliberate and accidental

In the Introduction we have seen various ways to connect the micro- and macro-levels. *Inter alia*, we have proposed the development of abstract unifying concepts applicable at different evolutionary levels and to systems of varying complexity.

The notion of external goal allows many forms and types of teleological behaviours or structures (at the biological or social level) to be accounted for that cannot be explained by postulating deliberate action and planning. How to explain behavioural phenomena that cannot be intentional, but are certainly not accidental either? This is one of the most crucial questions in social, behavioural and cognitive sciences.

To state it differently, to understand social phenomena, the study of the mind is insufficient.

Let us consider two crucial examples, the notion of social action and the notion of goal adoption.

A general notion of social action

In our terms, an action is social when its goal mentions some other agent as a goal-governed system (endowed with an intentional stance; cf. Dennet 1983) and the action is rated on a sociality scale. One may wonder if the behaviour of inferior animals (e.g. the courtship of the stickleback fish) is really social from the standpoint of internal goals, that is to say if, for example, the internal regulatory states governing the behaviour of the stickleback mention the female. They probably do not. The internal set points probably mention only some of the stickleback's somatic alterations and some of its movements (what they control), and not the effects on the female. Nonetheless, there is no doubt that the stickleback's behaviour is rightly defined as social. Not only cognitive agents have social behaviours. This is because at the level of the external goals (or, selecting effects, finalities), another individual is mentioned. That specific behaviour has evolved and specialized precisely for the purpose of inducing specific reactions in the female. It is neither intentional nor accidental. It is a social behaviour selected by an external goal.

A general notion of goal adoption

When do we find a prosocial, helping, or co-operative behaviour in animals (or in general in non-goal-governed systems)? An immediate answer could be when the behaviour of an individual x favours the achievement of an individual y.

In defining goal adoption among goal-governed systems we say that x must want y to achieve y's goal. This definition seems inadequate for non-goal-governed systems. Now we know that there is an important alternative, a third possibility between wants and chance, namely finalities, external goals.

In our view, goal adoption is the basis of all prosocial behaviour, including altruism, co-operation, exchange, and so forth. We have got to apply these conceptual categories to describe the behaviour of lower species and other non-goal-governed systems. A general notion of goal adoption would be as follows: x does something which favours y's achievement because x has the goal of favouring y, where x's goal is either an internal goal or a finality that has selected his internal goals (consider, for example, birds' parental care and nurturing of offspring).

Of course, in the case of goal-governed systems, the notion of goal adoption must be specialized and enriched. Any level of agency may have its specific notions of goal, goal adoption, co-operation, and so forth.

140

Recapitulation

In this chapter we have attempted to work out a unifying notion of goal, allowing the similarities among different types of teleological phenomena to be shown and investigated.

The notion of external goal has been proposed as a connection between the internal mechanism of regulation of systems and the process of (natural or artificial) selection and design of systems.

First, we have defined different types of systems (goal-governed, goal-oriented and merely teleological) according to their different mechanisms of regulation; hence, we have examined the role of external goals on each type of system, starting with the various types of external goals imposed on objects (teleological systems): use, destination, function.

We have also analyzed the relation between external and internal goals in simple non-human goal-governed systems (e.g. a boiler thermostat). Subsequently, the same type of analysis has been applied to more complex goal-governed systems. People have been shown to acquire functions (usually called roles). As an example, we have examined the case of a traffic policeman, his characteristics, tasks, and the advantages such a complex type of system has over non-autonomous functional objects (such as traffic lights).

After introducing and illustrating the concept of external goal, we have used it as a bridge to reach a more radical unification of the concept of goal and all teleological concepts up to and embracing biological finalities. Essentially, our main claim is that there are goals external to a goal-governed system that are not internal to anyone else's (i.e. goals that are simply external). We call these goals finalities. This requires a reformulation of the very concept of a goal. An attempt to reformulate in more general terms the notion of goal has also been made.

Finally, the advantages of a general theory of goals have been discussed.

CHAPTER NINE
Emergent social finalities among cognitive systems: the case of co-operation

Emergent effects of deliberate social action

Current literature on emergent functionalities, as they are called, is usually about systems that we call subcognitive. By *subcognitive* we mean either goal-oriented systems (Agre & Chapman 1987, Agre 1989, Brooks 1989) that do not have a representation of the goals they achieve, nor actually plan, *sensu stricto*, to obtain what they realize; or, *subsymbolic* agents, acting on a neural network base.

In our view, it is misleading to propose two alternative models of intelligence (Steels 1990), one pointing to emergent functional properties of dynamic systems, where problem-solving and social behaviours are wholly extramental, and the other pointing to a cognitive agent with far-reaching predictions and fully rational calculations and decision-making. This is rather a hypercognitive view of agenthood, a view which favours, but is also derived from, the theoretical opposition set out above.

The association between emergent finality and subcognitive systems is restrictive: even the actions of cognitive agents give rise to unpredicted effects, which sometimes prove to be finalities. This is a truism if one considers routines and other reactive actions that all systems share to some extent. Less obvious is the fact that deliberately planned actions may produce outcomes far beyond any agent's prediction and understanding.

We have claimed that, for a general and explanatory theory of social action, it is necessary to study extracognitive social relations, which allow social interactions to be predicted and explained, and provide premises and evolutionary steps of cognitive social relationships. In Chapters 1 and 2 we have analyzed some precognitive bases of social interaction, such as the relations of dependence and interest, and their role in predicting future social action. In this chapter, we will focus on *emergent (extracognitive) finalities* of actions intended and planned by *cognitive* agents. In particular, we will apply this notion to some forms of co-operation. Obviously, not all emergent properties, or macro-level effects, are co-operative and useful for the agents involved.

Levels of social action

The effects of action may be:
  (a) *accidental*, like the interference relations seen in Chapter 1; action is not truly social.
  (b) *deliberate*, the social effect is represented as a goal (internal goal) in a goal-governed system (he knows and wants to produce it). Action is social.
  (c) *functional*, that is directed toward a given finality; the effect of action is not deliberate, but is not accidental either; the action is undertaken precisely because it produces that effect (external goal). The effect is thus a finality and the action is functional to the effect produced.

After decades of indiscriminate utilization, the notion of *finality* (often called *function*; in our vocabulary, finalities also cover social functions) has undergone a great deal of criticism and manipulation especially in the social sciences, and has now come up once again in many different fields (system theory, AI, sociology, etc.).

In dealing with cognitive agents, it *must* be assumed that this effect remains unknown to the agent itself. Even if the effect rewards the agent's goals and needs, reinforces the agent's behaviour, and consequently reproduces itself, the agent must be unaware of such a link between its actions and the obtained reward (van Parijs 1982). Otherwise, that effect will be pursued deliberately; the agent will reproduce its behaviour *in order to* obtain that result.

A general theory of social interaction (human, animal, and artificial) could and should be worked out, such that it includes both intentional and **functional actions** and relations, internal and external social goals. To be fully adequate, in sum, such a theory should account not only for biological finalities but also for cultural and social finalities (such as those studied by anthropologists and sociologists). We claim that functional co-operation among cognitive agents is due to the selective pressure of social systems rather than to the role of biological finalities.

From accidental to functional co-operation

The AI view of co-operation is fundamentally hypercognitive. This precludes a unified theory of co-operation. If society is exclusively located in the mind, it is not possible to unify intentional and functional co-operation.

Indeed, functional co-operation is not only relevant to comparison with other species, but is also of extreme importance within human societies. Besides, co-operation in complex differentiated systems (human–computer and human–human via computer), is largely functional: it is a co-operation among social roles rather than one decided and negotiated by agents.

There are several models of functional co-operation in DAI: from market-like models (Malone et al. 1988), to models of negotiation (Rosenschein & Genesereth 1988) sometimes enriched by an intermediary (see, von Martial 1990), and from blackboard architectures (Fennell & Lesser 1977) to CSCW (Greif 1988). Many of these approaches do not necessarily attribute to the agents involved any mental representation of the joint plan, the common goals, the other's beliefs, and mutual dependence.

Other formal approaches to social action, such as the game-theoretic one, provided a view of co-operation as an emergent property of strategic choice (Kreps et al. 1982, Axelrod 1984, Axelrod & Dion 1988, and many others).

Theoretical unification of models of objective co-operation and models of co-operative agents fully aware of highly rational deals is possible only if one works out a theory of plans and goals so general as to embrace both deliberate and functional actions.

In the following we will address co-operation as an example of social interaction evolving from precognitive, accidental co-operation to extracognitive, functional co-operation.

Plans inside and outside minds

In the following, we will use the notions defined in Chapter 8, relative to internal and external goals and their hierarchical structure, to analyze four types, or levels, of co-operation that must be a prerequisite to any understanding of functional co-operation.

Accidental co-operation

Accidental co-operation occurs when *two agents are mutually dependent on each other and, even if unaware of the fact, perform the actions required*:

$$(A \text{-} COOP \, x \, y \, p) \stackrel{def}{=}$$

$$\exists a_x \exists a_y \big[(M \text{-} DEP \, x \, y \, p) \wedge (DONE \text{-} BY \, x \, a_x) \wedge (DONE \text{-} BY \, y \, a_y) \big]$$

Consider a variation of Power's (1984) example of what he calls *accidental co-ordination*: two vandals independently arrive at an art gallery with the goal of destroying a particular picture. One, who is intercepted by a guard, diverts her attention. In doing so, he enables the other to succeed in tearing the picture.

This is not true co-operation, although we name it as such; it is a useful milestone for a theory of co-operation and an evolutionary forerunner of functional co-operation. Indeed, no goal or finality is involved. Both actions

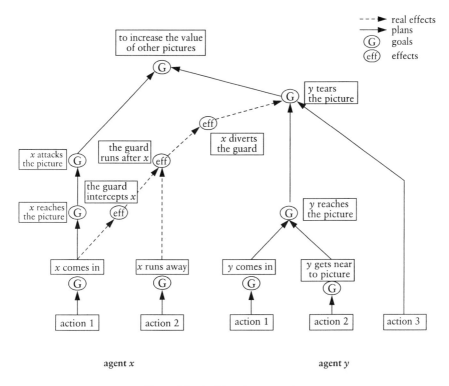

Figure 9.1 Accidental co-operation.

have favouring effects, which are neither wanted nor believed by the agents involved (cf. Fig. 9.1).

Deliberate co-operation

In our terms, full co-operation does not only imply mutual belief of mutual dependence, but also two identical goals, that each does his/her own share of the common plan (Ch. 3). We have also shown (Ch. 6) that, thanks to mutual commitment, one wanting the partner to do what she has promised is a legitimate goal, while one wanting to do what one has committed oneself to do is a normative goal.

In Figure 9.2, a co-operative cognitive **plan** – a plan being defined as a set of actions which converge on at least one and the same goal – is shown, as it is represented in both agents' minds.

Orchestrated co-operation

Suppose, now, that some of the mental attitudes attributed to x and y in Figure 9.2, which allow them to fully co-operate, are no longer represented in

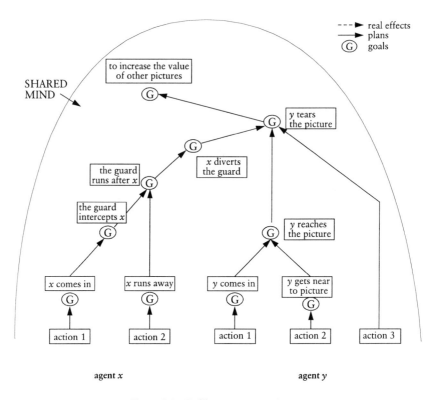

Figure 9.2 Deliberate co-operation.

their minds, but in some third agent's, that of a boss, who acts as an orchestrator.

The third agent knows what goal is realized by x and y, and also knows that agents are mutually dependent. She is the one who plans the goal's achievement in view of, say, increasing the value of some other pictures of the same artist that she owns. It is even possible that the agents ignore both each other's (as in accidental co-operation) and the chairman's existence. The co-operative plan outlined in Figure 9.2 is this time in a single mind: the chairman's (see Fig. 9.3).

Co-operation here is not intentional, but is not accidental either, for it is wanted by the boss. If we look at it from the third agent's point of view, it is a cognitive phenomenon, but if we take the agents' perspective it is in a certain sense functional: to co-operate is a goal external to their minds. It is an effect unintended by agents which selects their behaviours.

As will be shown in the next chapter, this external structure of co-operation plays a relevant role for understanding collective agents and teamwork. It is typical of group leadership as well as of many organizations: here a structure of *roles* is worked out by the boss. This situation presents interesting

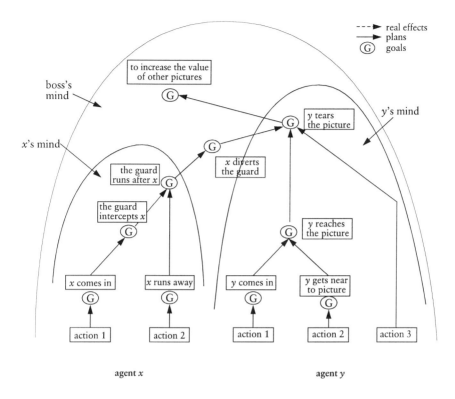

Figure 9.3 Orchestrated co-operation.

similarities with the acquisition of one's role examined in Chapter 8 with regard to the traffic policeman. In this case, the *as-if* co-operating agents adopt the goal of the boss, while the traffic policeman adopts the goals of society. In both situations the agents are used as *tools* for someone else's goals. But while the traffic policeman works out the whole plan on her own, the criminal plan worked out by our criminal mind requires two **complementary agents**. The two agents are complementary with regard to that plan:

$$(COMPL\text{-}AGT\ x\,y\,p) \stackrel{def}{=} \exists z \exists a_x \exists a_y \big[(S\text{-}DEP\ z\,x\,a_x\ p) \wedge (S\text{-}DEP\ z\,y\,a_y\ p)\big]$$

In general we can say that *two agents or more are complementary with regard to a given goal, when there is a third agent who is* AND-*dependent on all of them to achieve that goal*. The relation of AND-dependence is expressed as follows:

$$\big(\Lambda_i = 1, n(AND - DEP\ xy_i a_i p)\big) \stackrel{def}{=}$$
$$\big[(S - DEP\ xy_1 a_1 p) \wedge (S - DEP\ xy_2 a_2 p) \wedge \ldots \wedge (S - DEP\ xy_n a_n p)\big]$$

147

Orchestrated co-operation occurs when two complementary agents are led to do the actions they are competent for. Of course, hybrid situations are frequent, where agents know and share some or all of the plan worked out by the orchestrator. Finally, the chairman might also be one of the executors of the plan. We will see an interesting application of this notion in the next chapter.

Functional co-operation

Let us replace the boss of the criminal plan with natural or cultural selection. The final goal of the plan is now a finality, and is not represented as a goal in any mind (although it is known to the observer–scientist).

Let us consider the classical example of the division of social labour into skilled and unskilled labour. It appears to perfectly match the role of biological finalities. Division of labour may come about naturally and impose itself, with no authority or collective mind rationally deciding how to divide up the tasks (external goals) among the complementary agents, or establishing the various fields of production, etc. The process is only ratiomorphic and it takes place, we may say, *through selection*. No one decides that a certain number of people, in a predetermined quantity, must make shoes, that others must manufacture bowls, that still others must farm, etc. A general dynamic equilibrium and a sort of common plan in which the actions of all agents are complementary is ensured by local-level decisions. Single members (individuals or small groups) make decisions in a deliberate and intentional way, only with regard to their own narrow and known interest. They do not make their decisions in view of the global equilibrium or plan.

If x's activity becomes increasingly less useful, the amount of labour invested in this activity and its products does not translate into an exchange value equal to the amount of labour invested in other fields of production: in exchange, x will not receive from others as much labour as he is providing them with. As a result, on the one hand, x will probably drop his earlier superfluous activity and set out to do something more useful, thereby ensuring *his own* social usefulness and, at the same time, ensuring that no share of the available labour force will be wasted. On the other hand, by making his decision, x by no means aims at being useful to others or worries about how society's resources can be best employed.

This model has also been assumed by classical economists as the general model of economic relationships: single individuals' selfish choices ensure the best possible organization; and it is easy to understand why Hegel could perceive the *cunning of reason* within this paradox.

In such a case, again, co-operation is neither deliberate nor accidental. The actions are functional to, and selected by, the effect that they have produced. If, rather than x's mind, we consider the community, we find a set of trials and errors: some trials are successful (and society rewards them), others are discarded (with no explicitly collective decision to discard them). It is more or less through this process that labour is divided according to needs and complementarity. In this case, the selecting mechanism, the *sieve* consists of satisfying a need, or better, an *anonymous demand*. If we synchronically consider some stages in the division of labour we will observe that all different types of activities respond to a given need of society as a whole, as well as to the need for increasing the productivity of labour. These activities are functional; they have been positively selected. That some fellow pursues the intention of making bowls is not sufficient. Bowlmakers can thrive only if their goals found correspondence in an external finality (the social need for bowls). More probably, their goals were caused by such finality.

To sum up:

(a) *There are forms of merely emergent or functional co-operation even among cognitive and intentional agents.* Examples can be found in human sociality and the organization of social labour; often, we work together in a common plan although ignoring one another.

(b) We tried to show that *the concept of finality is necessary in order to account for* certain *social phenomena that are neither reducible to the goals of a single individual* – since an internal goal is conceived of as necessarily immanent – *nor to the goals of* another individual (e.g. a boss) or *superindividual organisms* (such as communities, institutions, etc.). The teleonomic character of those social phenomena has already been acknowledged, as in social structural–funtionalism, without its ever having been adequately explained.

Recapitulation

In this chapter we have attempted to show that some consequences of social actions are socially relevant, although unintended, and some of these unintended consequences are not accidental. There are emergent finalities set up by intentional actions of cognitive agents: many social relationships are functional, non-deliberate. Social roles, for instance, are the result of functional mechanisms, even though they are played by agents for personal reasons.

To this end, we have illustrated different types of co-operation: accidental, deliberate, orchestrated and functional. A general notion of objective agent complementarity has been worked out to account for the last two types of co-operation. A theory of action, where goals are allowed to exist outside the mind of agents is called for, for functional co-operation to be integrated with the other levels of social action. This form of co-operation, as well as other types of goals and plans at the same level of analysis, may be seen as emergent finalities.

CHAPTER TEN

Objective and normative foundations of collective agents

Collective intentionality

The notion of collective intentionality is a controversial one. In the last few years, it has been debated by philosophers of mind (Tuomela & Miller 1988, Tuomela 1989, 1991, 1993, 1994, Searle 1990) and AI scientists (Hobbs 1990). Furthermore, several formal and computational models of joint intentions, teamwork and *togetherness* are currently being developed within computational theories of rational action and MAS research (Grosz & Sidner 1990, Levesque et al. 1990, Cohen & Levesque 1991, Rao et al. 1992 etc.); see also the computational models of *coalition* framed in a rational action approach (e.g. Ephrati & Rosenschein, Ketchpel, Shechory & Kraus, Zlotkin & Rosenschein, all in press).

We will examine the aspects of the existing work on joint intentions and togetherness that we consider of special interest for the modelling of agents' social capacities. Hobbs (1990: 449), who evaluates the "talk about group minds, the collective unconscious, and so on" from a "hard-core AI point of view", raised the important question: "What work does it do for us?" Likewise, we will ask what work existing models of collective intentionality do for the *construction* of autonomous social agents.

The classical view of *We-intentions* first proposed by Tuomela & Miller (1988) is still the most influential within AI theories (Cohen & Levesque 1990b, Levesque et al. 1990, Cohen & Levesque 1991, Rao et al. 1992 etc.). Such a view shares a methodological individualistic assumption: collective intentionality, relative to a given set of agents, is assumed to be essentially a summation of, and hence reducible to, the intentions and beliefs of the members of the set.

On the other hand, the view of collective intentionality suggested by Searle (1990), who firmly rejects the Tuomela–Miller model and the associated methodological individualistic assumption, is not completely satisfactory either. What is lacking is a theory of the formation of collective intentionality, and of the reasons *why people form groups and remain in them*.

In this chapter, we will propose a dependency-based notion of common goals and collective agents. This hypothesis is meant to suggest a way out from the view of joint intentions as individual intentions plus mutual beliefs, on one hand, and the idea, suggested by Searle, that collective intentions are non-derivable, primitive mental objects that individual agents are likely to form. As we shall see, this way out consists of finding the external inputs of collectives and coalitions, in terms of objective pre-conditions and social constraints. More specifically, objective pre-conditions are necessary in order to account for why collectives *are formed*, but they are not sufficient to explain why collectives are not deserted by the individual agents once they have reached their goals. This is precisely why another type of external input, namely the normative constraint, is demanded: norms are necessary in order to explain why collectives *survive* the achievements of (a part of) their members. This is an additional, fundamental step in the micro–macro circle: external conditions provide inputs not only to the individual agents' goals, but also to the collective ones. But in order to make such a step, one must disentangle social from collective actions and goals. The social dimension indeed represents a fundamental bridge between individual and collective action. Let us see why.

The individual–collective gap

First, we will examine a well-known model of teamwork (Levesque et al. 1990, Cohen & Levesque 1991), which essentially traces back to Tuomela & Miller's (1988) analysis of collective intentions. Some criticisms, a number of which were first made by Searle (1990), will be addressed.

Furthermore, Searle's analysis itself will be criticized.

Descriptive vs. prescriptive

Let us start with a problem of meta-level. In Levesque et al. (1990) the natural concept of joint activity is said to be irrelevant:

> The account of joint action presented here should probably not be regarded as a descriptive theory. We are primarily concerned with the design of artificial agents . . . what we seek are reasonable design specifications . . . that would then lead to desirable behaviour. (Cohen & Levesque 1991: 2).

We do not fully agree with this claim. Rather, we believe that natural facts should be taken into account and different social situations should be compared in order to be able to rule out situations that we by no means want to equate with *teamwork*. We do *not* mean to provide a comparative analysis of various kinds of social co-operation and interaction for the sake of a social–psychological description. We are more interested in discussing the matter from within a (D)AI perspective, focusing on the internal purposes of this discipline. In our opinion, concepts that do not get a hold of reality will have also an undesirable impact on the design of artificial systems. In order both to provide a good notion of teamwork and to design an artificial agent capable of co-operating, it is necessary to work out a theory of the agents' reasons for participating in teamwork; of the process through which co-operation is formed out of the individual needs and desires; of the rewards that are expected and obtained through co-operation. In other words, not only should the way down the micro–macro link be accounted for, but also the way up, i.e. not only should the direction from the group to the individual be studied, but also that from the individual to the group. If agents do not take into account and look after their own interests, they will behave irrationally, that is, inefficiently.

Individual intentions plus mutual beliefs

The analysis of Cohen & Levesque proceeds from the following questions:

> What is involved when a group of agents decide to do something together? . . . what motivates agents to form teams and act together? . . . What benefits do agents expect to derive from their participation in a group effort? (1991: 2)

However, in fact, Cohen & Levesque immediately restrict their inquiry to some subquestions, such as: How does a team work? What is a joint intention? How is it translated into an individual one? These questions differ considerably from the initial ones. Many problems relevant to social theory are consequently disregarded.

In Cohen & Levesque's (1991) terms, x and y *jointly intend* to do some action if, and only if, x and y are jointly aware that:

(a) they *each want collective action to be taken*,

(b) they *each intend to do their share* (as long as the other does it),

(c) *mutual knowledge persists until it is mutually known that the activity is over* (successful, unachievable, etc.)[1].

The final definition proposed by Cohen & Levesque is somewhat different from this, because this is considered "too strong". Therefore, the present definition will be refined only in order to be weakened! On the contrary, with Searle (1990), we find it is all too broad, and will show why in the next section.

In general, a team, a *social agent* (Rao et al. 1992) is defined in terms of *joint persistent goals* (Cohen & Levesque 1991). More specifically:

A team of agents have a joint persistent goal relative to q to achieve p (a belief from which, intuitively, the goal originates) precisely whenever:

(1) they mutually believe that p is currently false;
(2) they mutually know they all want p to be true eventually;
(3) it is true (and mutually known) that until they come to believe either that p is true, that p will never be true, or that q is false, they will continue to mutually believe that they each have p as a weak achievement goal relative to q and with respect to the team. (Cohen & Levesque 1991: 11),

where a weak achievement goal with respect to a team has been defined as "a goal that the status of p be mutually believed by all the team members" (Cohen & Levesque 1991: 10–11).

In short, the notion of togetherness, of group and teamwork is based upon the notion of joint persistent goals, which are but individual goals associated with social, namely mutual, beliefs.

What should be ruled out

In line with Searle (1990), we believe that this notion of joint action and teamwork is too broad. To see why, we will examine the most insightful among Searle's examples in order to show one aspect of it that perhaps the author himself did not perceive, and which bears interesting consequences for the purpose of the present discussion.

The example refers to a group of businessmen, all subscribing to the hidden hand theory: each strongly believes that, by pursuing his own self-interest, he will help humanity, and all have a mutual belief that, while attending to his own interests, each one will produce the same effect. Finally, each agent intends to help humanity, and believes his selfish efforts will be successful. Suppose also that the moral code of the school prescribes that each keeps the others informed about his own achievements. As Searle observes, the group of businessmen satisfies the Tuomela–Miller conditions, and for that matter also those of Cohen–Levesque, but has no collective intentionality.

Searle provides a necessary but insufficient explanation of this example. He says that if the businessmen had formed a *pact* to help humanity, their successive intentions would be collective. The question is *why* a pact should be formed. Indeed, why should the businessman co-operate? In the Tuomela–Miller definition, as well as in the Cohen–Levesque one, the reasons why agents adopt (and hence share) others' goals are ignored. And so they are in Searle's analysis (1990). However, motivations are part of the notion of group, or of co-operation, or of joint activity, and allow, for example, exchange to be clearly distinguished from co-operation. Such reasons fill the gap, provide the connection between the individual intentions and the collective ones. As Hobbs (1990: 446) remarks, from a hard-core AI viewpoint, the agent is essentially a *planning* system. Its plans consist of a top-level goal, such as "I thrive", and breakdowns of this ultimate goal into one or more (layers of) subgoals. Therefore, in order for the notions suggested by other disciplines or frameworks to be recast in the terms of an AI framework, continues Hobbs, these notions ought to be tied ultimately to the goal of "I thrive". Without such a connection, an AI theory is essentially unfeasible. Without an explicit representation of the link between collective intentions and individual ones, an AI theory of collective intentions is useless.

To sum up, as defined, the notion of joint persistent goal cannot account for any truly co-operative work, because two further conditions are missing:

(1) *mutual obligations*, or, in Searle's terms, a pact;
(2) *mutual dependence*: without this, the commitment to participate, to do one's own share is unmotivated, irrational. An agent's belief that he depends on others to achieve his goals or, in other words, his belief in a *necessity to collaborate* is a fundamental condition for truly co-operative work (Conte et al. 1991, Jennings 1992). We will come back to this point in "An objective view" (p. 157).

What should be included

The above definition is not only too broad (lacking necessary conditions for teamwork), but also too narrow. It seems[2] to rule out a fundamental case of teamwork that is not only a natural phenomenon but also a useful form of co-ordination among natural or artificial agents and may have important applications. What we have in mind is *orchestrated co-operation* among cognitive systems (see Ch. 9).

In Chapter 9, we saw an example of orchestrated co-operation, where it is *indifferent* whether complementary agents are aware or not of the actual purpose of their activity. Let us now consider those cases in which it is *required* that the members of a team be *not* aware of the overall plan (for example, the members of an army commando during an attack); nor are they always informed about the existence of other participants (think of partisans, guerrillas, or comrades of a terrorist organization). Their actions are part of one and the same plan, they are co-ordinated with one other, necessary to one other, and act deliberately. However, no mutual belief about the plan and its executors can exist.

How can the Cohen–Levesque conditions for joint intentions and teamwork be extended to such examples of collective action?

Individual collective intentions

AI theories of collective intentionality essentially boil down to the Tuomela–Miller conditions. However, these conditions have been shown to be neither necessary nor sufficient for collective intentionality.

Hence, Searle draws the *intermediate conclusion*: "We-intentions cannot be analyzed into sets of I-intentions, even *I-intentions supplemented with* beliefs, including *mutual beliefs*, about the intentions of other members of a group."(1990: 404; our italics).

That is to say, collective intentions are different from a mere summation of individual intentions. However, any theory of collective intentions, says the author: "*must be consistent with the fact that society consists of nothing but individuals.*"(1990: 406; our italics).

Searle's final conclusion, therefore, which is believed to be the only possible solution consistent with the fact that society consists of nothing but individuals, is to conceive of collective intentionality as a primitive form of intentionality, not reducible to I-intentions plus mutual beliefs. Where does such a type of intentionality come from? It presupposes, says the author: a "*background sense of the other* as a candidate for co-operative agency" (1990: 414; our italics).

We take Searle's intermediate conclusion to mean that collective intentions are not derivable directly from an individual intention, that is, one mentioning only the individual agent in whom the intention is represented, plus the individuals' mutual beliefs. If this is what is meant by *I-intention³*, then Searle's intermediate conclusion seems reasonable.

What instead we disagree with is the final conclusion claiming that collective intentionality cannot be derived from any other mental state, and should be taken as a primitive notion. This does not appear as a solution to the problem of collective intentionality because:

(a) *it is not a true explanation*: it does not explain the reasons why collective intentionality is formed, other than as a generic background for co-operative agency;

(b) it is not altogether clear *how collective phenomena* that are in fact *derived from individual intentions* should be categorized (e.g. a rogue plots a collective robbery to seize a fortune, which he could not have done on his own).

To sum up, Searle's reasoning is as follows:

(a) collective intentions cannot be reduced to *I-intentions* plus mutual beliefs;

(b) society consists of nothing but individuals;

(c) collective intentions are irreducible individual *We-intentions*.

Both the second premise and the conclusion are unwarranted for two distinct but related reasons, which will be examined in the following sections.

A bridge between individual and collective: social goals

In both the AI and the philosophical literature examined so far, the term *social* is used in a confused and ambiguous way, and is equated to either:
  (a) *distributed*, or shared: the notion of social intention or goal (e.g. Werner 1988) is used to characterize a goal or intention shared by many agents; the notion of social commitment and social plan is used to denote the idea of reciprocal commitments within a team of agents; or
  (b) *collective*: the notion of *social agent* (e.g. Rao et al. 1992) is used to designate a unitary entity, although formed by distinguishable subcomponents, i.e. a group or a team.

However, a further important meaning of social action, social agent, and social mind, which has been defined in Chapter 2, and referred to throughout the book, has been essentially disregarded by philosophers and AI people. By this, we mean a mind or action being directed toward another social entity while at the same time remaining individual. This also points to a further level of analysis, between the individual and the collective. This is what we consider the fundamental level of sociality. Autonomous, self-interested agents in a multi-agent context are and must be seen also as social agents precisely in this sense. Let us specify some fundamental properties of this notion:
  (a) unlike Searle's collective intentionality, it implies *no built-in co-operativeness* but can be applied to competition as well; moreover, it is thoroughly compatible with self-interested action;
  (b) unlike Cohen & Levesque's (1991) notion, *it can be applied to goals* and intentions and not only to beliefs.

Indeed, it is precisely because an intermediate notion of sociality is lacking in the field that social (that is, shared) goals are either reduced to individual goals plus mutual beliefs, or defined as irreducible individual drives to co-operate. A collective goal as such cannot be tied to an "I thrive" goal, to use Hobbs' (1990) terminology, without the connection provided by social goals. In the car convoy example, Bob and Alice will have the same goal if at least one of them adopts the other's initial goal, and both adopt each other's goal in order not to be cheated. If a collective goal is derived from an individual goal (i.e. it is not a primitive goal, in Searle's sense), it necessarily implies some goal or interest adoption. Therefore, a collective goal can be reduced, and unless it is a primitive, must be reduced to individual goals by means of some sort of social goal. While collective goals cannot be directly reduced to I-intentions plus mutual beliefs, they can be reduced to individual social goals. The social goals fill the gap between individual and collective goals. Collective goals need not be built into the agents. They may be formed out of the agents' self-interest by means of goal adoption. This explains why collective action may be derived from personal interest, as in the rogue example, and even from anti-social motivations. Let us reverse the businessmen example. Consider a spy joining the military command of an enemy country. In order to be accepted and to learn his enemy's secrets, the spy needs to adopt some of their goals. He must even participate in some of their military undertakings, maybe against his own native land. All the same the spy can hardly be said to have an irreducible intention to co-operate with his enemies!

However, saying that social goals may fill the gap between collective and individual minds is insufficient. When does this happen? When do agents resort to collective action? Let us turn to this question, which is fundamental for an AI planning view. In the following, we will claim that social dependence provides the fundamental reason for individual agents to engage in teamwork and participate in collective action.

An objective view

In this section, we will provide a definition of common goals and a preliminary model of a *collective agent* x_i, which is based upon an objective condition of interdependence, or mutual dependence, among the members of x_i.

Indeed, while agreeing with Searle's thesis that collective intentionality cannot be reduced to *I-intentions* plus mutual beliefs, we do not agree with his version of the classical methodological individualistic assumption, according to which society would consist of nothing but individuals. Society consists of individuals and the pattern of structural, objective relations that hold among them, to say nothing of the existing norms and mutual commitments which concur to rule the behaviours of social members.

Social dependence

Let us recall the definition of social dependence provided in Chapter 1: x depends on y with regard to an act useful for realizing a state p when p is a goal of x's and x is unable to realize p while y is able to do so.

As we know (see Ch. 2), many important consequences can derive from x and y's (either unilaterally or mutually) becoming aware of social dependence. Let the reader be reminded that an objective relation of mutual dependence holds among two agents x and y when they depend on each other to implement an identical goal p, and p can be achieved by means of a plan including at least two different acts such that x depends on y doing a_y, and y depends on x doing a_x (for a more formal definition see Ch. 1). As observed in Chapter 3, co-operation is a function of mutual dependence: there is no co-operation in the strict sense without mutual dependence.

Two notions of collective agents

According to our analysis, there are at least two fundamental notions of collective agents: a minimal one, which does not imply any mutual belief on the part of the agents involved, and a higher-level one implying, but not reduced to, mutual beliefs and shared intentions among the agents involved.

Low-level collective agent

A minimal notion is that of a multi-agent plan, or co-operation, among *complementary agents*. Agents are complementary when there is a third agent socially dependent on all of them with regard to a given goal of his (cf. the notion defined in the previous chapter). Two or more agents are complementary with regard to someone's goal when they each ought to accomplish one out of a set (or sequence) of actions in order for that goal to be attained. In other words, agents are complementary with regard to a given *plan* for achieving someone's goal. The question is, who designed this plan? In what agent's mind is this plan represented? Take the example of the criminal mind described in the preceding chapter. The professional criminals adopt the goals of the central co-ordinator in order to achieve their own personal interest, which may have nothing to do with the final end of the crime (increasing the value of the other pictures owned by the orchestrator). Indeed, they accept to *exchange* their service against money (see Fig. 9.3). However, they objectively participate in a multi-agent plan, co-operating (without knowing it) with one another.

In any case, the minimal conditions for a collective agent are the following:
(a) a sequence of actions a_i achieves a given agent's goal p,
(b) a set of agents x_i are complementary with regard to a set of actions a_i, which achieves p (whether they are planned by someone or not),
(c) the set of agents x_i does a_i.

More formally:

$$(COLL - AGT\, x_i a_i p) \stackrel{def}{=}$$
$$(COMPL - AGT\, x_i a_i p) \wedge (DOES\, x_i a_i)$$

that is: *a set of agents x_i is said to be a minimal collective agent of a sequence of actions a_i relative to a goal p, if and only if, x_i are complementary relative to that sequence of actions with regard to someone's goal p.* Therefore, orchestrated co-operation, seen in the preceding chapter, is a form of collective action: were a given agent z pursuing p, z would be depending on the set of agents x_i with regard to p. The set of agents x_i forms a collective agent with regard to goal p when x_i must perform a given plan, or sequence of actions, for any agent to achieve goal p.

High-level collective agent

More often, the notion of collective agent is not meant to imply a central co-ordinator, a designer of a multi-agent plan, but rather a distributed, decentralized form of co-operation. We believe that this higher-level notion of collective agent should be based upon mutual dependence. In the sequel, we will limit ourselves to providing what we view as necessary conditions for drawing up such a definition, rather than a proper definition.

A relation of mutual dependence relative to a set of agents can be defined as a conjunction of unilateral dependence relations between each agent and all other members of the set. Hence, a set of agents x_i can be said to be mutually dependent when all agents included in the set have an identical goal p, and each agent depends on all others to achieve it.

Therefore, a decentralized form of collective agent (see Fig. 10.1) occurs when at least the following conditions hold:

(a) all agents *have the goal that a given set of actions be done* by a given set of agents, *relativized to*

(b) *their shared belief that they are mutually dependent*, that is, that each agent in the set depends on all the others to achieve a given goal p, and

(c) *all agents commit themselves* (see Ch. 6) before
  – one another, and
  – the group authority, if any
    to do each action he is competent for.

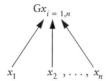

Figure 10.1 High-level collective agent.

What is interesting about these conditions is that although the agents' beliefs about their mutual dependence is necessary for them to be motivated in order *to join* in collective action, these beliefs are no longer necessary for the agents *to remain* in the team. The decision to resort to teamwork may not coincide with the decision to stick to it. Indeed, the two decisions do *not* overlap perfectly even when the agents *hold* the belief that they are mutually dependent throughout their joint action. The latter decision, in fact, is based not only upon this belief, but also upon the agents' commitments, and therefore, upon a pertinence normative belief.

Let us consider the following example. A bunch of crooks decide to band together and rob a bank vault, a job that none of them would be able to accomplish alone (cf. Castelfranchi et al. 1989). Each offers to carry out part of the job. Once the tasks have been assigned, each agent wants both to do his own job and also the others to do theirs. Correspondingly, each agent will adopt the others' goal that he does his part in the common plan. To see this, suppose that, during the enterprise, the lookout finds an easier way to make good money (a badly-guarded jewellery shop next door). Were he alone, he would simply abandon his previous goal. As things are, however, he cannot do so without betraying his friends. Unlike what Cohen & Levesque (1991) seem to imply, the fact of him informing his comrades about his change of mind would not make things any better: the pact does not terminate when beliefs diverge, but when goals do! As Bond (1991) has observed, a pact can be loosened only through negotiation. Communication is insufficient.

Advantages of the notion proposed

The present notion of a collective agent ultimately relies upon the objective structure of interdependence among individual agents.

This view seems to have several advantages over pre-existing notions of collective agent and joint intentions:

(a) it includes some minimal conditions for collective action, which do not imply mutual belief in the overall plan, *it is* therefore *applicable to orchestrated co-operation*;

(b) thanks to mutual dependence, our stronger notion of collective agents *allows for collective goals to be tied to individual ones*; in other words, it contributes to explaining how collective agents are formed, why autonomous, self-interested agents should participate in teamwork, and form part of collective agents;

(c) *it accounts for the normative aspect of joint action* and teamwork; therefore, it can help explain why it is *not* rational to abandon teamwork even when one has reached the conclusion that he no longer depends on the other agents.

From collective agents to collective minds: some speculation

In the preceding section, we proposed two diverse notions of collective agent, a minimal, or broader, notion, and a narrower one. In either case, there is no need for deliberate planning. As conventions gradually emerge from interference, multi-agent plans may gradually emerge from the pattern of dependences and complementarities existing in a given community of agents. The division of labour is certainly one example of emerging multi-agent plans determined by heterogeneity and complementarity. Stable co-operative effects should be seen not only as a function of a wide differentiation of interactional strategies, as evolutionary models (Lomborg 1994) seem to indicate. A highly co-operative answer should also, and moreover, be expected in communities with a high degree of complementarity among the agents.

However, the two views of collective agenthood so far described may be attributed to two different types of intelligence. Orchestrated co-operation is but an individual intelligent solution which takes advantage of social resources. Decentralized co-operation, instead, implies a distributed intelligence, an *iteration* of the same multi-agent plan in the minds of a number of interdependent agents. This is true in a broad constructivist sense, according to which institutions and organizations are *constructed by* the same people who are ruled by, or participate in, them (for an overview, cf. Douglas 1986 and also Conte 1989). Consequently, institutions and organizations are also said to be made up of the mental constructs of those agents. Institutions, in particular, are modelled in such a way as to consist of the shared mental constructs of the agents involved. This is what is usually meant by stating that institutions do some sort of cognitive activity, such as categorizing (Douglas 1986); decision-making (Schotter 1981); problem-solving (Ullman-Margalit 1977), etc.

In short, collective agenthood may be achieved, although not necessarily, by means of some sort of collective mind. But what is exactly meant by a collective mind? Does it necessarily imply the aforesaid iteration? We do not think so.

Indeed, several intermediate phenomena, which we have not explicitly addressed, seem to exist between orchestrated and mutually believed co-operation. In social life, people are neither entirely manipulated nor fully conscious of the reasons and effects of their actions. More often people are only partially aware of what is going on, of the global effect they are contributing to bringing about, etc. When they become aware of this global effect, on the other hand, they may have only a confused perception and understanding of the causal and means–end links embedded in the activity they are participating in. In such a case, complementary agents, although aware of participating in a collective action and of co-operating to bring about what is believed to be a common goal, need to be assigned some tasks. Here, the collective action is to some extent orchestrated, although the goal is common. In this case, the complementary agents comply with the requests of someone, to whom they entrust the organization and co-ordination of their activity, in order to achieve one of their own goal. The situation is illustrated in Figure 10.2.

This leads to a further more interesting notion of collective mind which implies a deliberate, as opposed to emergent, multi-agent ideation of plans and subplans, a plan broken down, as opposed to iterated, in the minds of a number of complementary agents. Indeed, there is no clear-cut difference between the ideation and the execution of a multi-agent plan. Often, multi-agent plans require complementary mental actions (in a football game, each

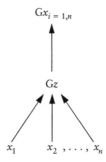

$$Gx_{i\,=\,1,n}$$

$$Gz$$

$$x_1 \qquad x_2\,,\,\ldots,\,x_n$$

FIgure 10.2   Middle-level collective agent.

player's task implies a rather complex mental work). Sometimes, not only the execution, but also the plan's ideation and design may require a complementary mental effort. Organization theorists have pointed out that not all organizational procedures are explicitly instituted. Often, only some meta-rules are issued. More detailed procedures are either informally established (Fikes 1982) by convention and negotiation, or prescribed by the agents who occupy the intermediate levels of the organizational hierarchy, and may vary with staff turnover. This may be due to several reasons. First, it may be due to the specialization of roles and responsibilities. Secondly, it may be due to complementarity of the agents' viewpoints. An example of the latter is the ideation of a plan for a prisoner's escape. Suppose the prisoner, the boss of a criminal organization, works out an escape plan with the aid of his fellows. Indeed, the latter will take care of the subplans that ought to be designed and accomplished from outside the jail and will provide the prisoner with the resources he could not obtain from within. Analogously, the boss will develop and carry out the subplans which require experience and familiarity with the prison, its habits, rules, and routines.

To sum up, a collective agent, defined here as a set of complementary agents performing a multi-agent plan, can be said to form a *collective mind* when either:

- *a multi-agent plan is iterated* in the minds of all the complementary agents which are needed to execute the plan (decentralized co-operation);
- *a multi-agent plan is broken down* in the minds of some complementary agents who are needed for the plan to be fully detailed; the mental activity implied by the plan ideation and execution requires in turn a set of complementary individual minds.

However, a collective action does not necessarily imply a collective mind. As we have endeavoured to show in this and the preceding chapter, some forms of co-operation may occur without necessarily implying that either a centralized or a decentralized intelligence designed and co-ordinated it.

Recapitulation

In this chapter we have discussed at some length both the notion of joint intentions largely prevailing in the social AI literature, and Searle's (1990) theory of *collective intentionality*.

Both views have been found unsatisfactory, especially since both lack a theory of the individuals' reasons for joining teams and remaining in them.

Furthermore, two preliminary notions of collective agents based upon mutual dependence and complementarity have been proposed, and some preliminary ideas about the concept of collective minds have been put forward.

In our view, an AI study of the *individual social mind* is badly needed. Even in order to account for collective agents and activities, individual motivations ought to be accounted for, since they have an impact on the nature and quality of groups and interaction. A social perspective on agenthood does not mean that "the whole [society] precedes the part [the individual], . . . and the part is explained in terms of the whole . . . " (Mead 1934 as quoted by Gasser 1991a: 3). In our terms, a social perspective is but a theory of action and knowledge of the agents situated in a social world. The agents can reach their goals if they have the capacities to control and co-ordinate with (predict, exploit) the actions of other agents.

That of collective agents is an issue of vital importance. However, the cement of a collective agent, at least if made up of cognitive members, is the social mind of its members. We share Gasser's view that most social relations pre-exist interactions and commitments among the individuals, but social relations and organizations are not held or created by the (mutual, social) commitments of the individuals. Autonomous agents in a multi-agent world (to recall the title of the European DAI workshop) find themselves as *socially situated agents*. They find themselves in a network of relations (interference, dependence, concurrence, power, etc.) that are independent of their awareness and choices. But, of course, this uncommitted structure presupposes individuals, their goals, needs, capabilities, and resources. Especially their social goals and capabilities.

CHAPTER ELEVEN
Computational applications: conclusions and perspectives

Abstract

In this chapter, the potential of the approach presented in the book for the computational study of social action is discussed. Various potential and current applications are examined in the following areas:

(a) *Distributed intelligent systems.* So far, distributed problem-solving has been characterized by pre-compiled co-operation, and MAS rely essentially upon the benevolence assumption. In the last few years, however, the question of autonomy has been receiving a great deal of attention from systems designers and DAI researchers. In distributed systems, there is a growing demand for autonomous self-interested co-operation. For this to be realized, agents should have the capability to select the requests received and reason about how to use others as resources for their own goals. In other words, they should rely upon information about objective social interference, both positive and negative, obtaining in their world. As an example of this application of our model, a system now under implementation for the purpose of computing a dependence network is described.

(b) *Social simulation.* The field of social simulation is proving interesting and heuristic. However, this is a new area of research, and has a number of drawbacks (coarse-grained modelling of agents simulated; behavioural characterization of the macro-social phenomena of study, etc.). Examples of application of our model to a simulation-based understanding of norm functionalities are provided.

Towards the social sciences

In this book, an integrated view of social action has been proposed, that is to say, a model of social action as a multi-level phenomenon.

Throughout the book, social action has been shown to be built up gradually through the action of several forces and factors, both external and internal to the agent. On the one hand, social action is induced and constrained, layer after layer, by the structuring effect of inert, objective pre-conditions; it undergoes the influence of other agents' desires and interests; it is modelled by explicit requests and prescriptions; finally, it is reinforced by its own effects by means of functional feedback mechanisms. On the other hand, social action does the shaping and reproducing of the macro-social structures and allows the macro-social system to achieve its goals.

The causes and functions of social action are certainly not revealed in this book. The main effort made here consists of constructing an integrated model of these causes and functions, linking them to one another, and reconstructing the process leading from one level of analysis to another. The reconstruction of this process was made possible by assuming cognition as a fundamental medium between external inputs and social action. To see how external factors of any sort structure and constrain action, one would need to look inside the head of the agent, and search for the mental trace, the footprints, so to speak, of those factors.

More specifically, a number of interesting social facts have been pointed out and, to some extent, accounted for:

- *objective foundations of sociality* and their role in *predicting social action*;
- a *unifying notion of goal*, that may be used at different levels of analysis, and which is indispensable for understanding how entities of various nature (agents and physical objects) may be controlled by external agents and factors;
- various *forms of positive social action* (exchange, co-operation, etc.);
- *helping beyond requests and goals* (interest adoption):
- *a mental notion of norm* as a hybrid configuration of beliefs and goals; and
- feedback on social action: *how norms enter exchange and co-operation*;
- a model of some forms of social action as *emergent effects of the interaction among intelligent agents*;
- a specific notion of *social action and goals as distinct from shared and collective actions or goals*;
- a notion of *collective agents as based upon complementarity and dependence* relations;
- a distinction between *joining a collective agent* and *keeping to it*, and the role of norms in the latter.

To account for these facts is relevant for social theory, especially for the purpose of relating the micro- and macro-level. But what is the relevance of this account to (D)AI and computer science? What work, a (D)AI scientist might ask, does such theorizing do for us?

Towards AI

The analysis of social interaction that we have so far proposed may contribute to many AI applicative domains, especially those domains that imply a model of interaction, such as HCI, MAS, CSCW, collaborative design, organizational re-engineering.

Here, we will mention only a few ideas as to how research in these fields could profit from a study of the issues discussed in this book, especially:

(a) *dependence relations and rational interaction,*
(b) *various forms of positive social action,*
(c) *helpfulness, over-answering and paternalism,*
(d) *norms and robust co-operation.*

We will now briefly examine the last three issues, while in the following section we will turn to the first one and describe at some length both a computational model (*CogAgent*) and a system (*DEPNET*) that apply the model of dependence differently as well as several other ideas presented in this book.

Various forms of positive social action

AI applications to organizations, co-operative work, group activity, are mainly aimed at optimizing only one basic form of relation among the agents, i.e. co-operation.

In Fikes' (1982) classic analysis of organization, for example, all the helping, the exchanges and the co-operative interactions that take place within an institutional setting are reduced to just one fundamental relation between a *client* and a *contractor* linked by a pact. Spontaneous adoption (without request) is not allowed and role commitments (that is, commitments required by one's role) are not distinguished from personal commitment. The variety of possible forms of and reasons for collaboration are ignored.

An analogous consideration should be made with regard to Medina-Mora et al.'s model of collaborative work as *action work flow* (Medina-Mora et el. 1992). The authors identify and support only one elementary form of collaborative interaction which should cover hierarchical commands, free agreement, help, obligation, exchange, and co-operation. However, we know that obligations upon agents and their expectations vary according to the kind of collaboration rational agents are involved in. For example, in truly co-operative activity the agents can be expected to be more reliable since they are co-interested in the final result, while agents are not interested in results useful to each other (cf. Chs 3 and 10).

Uniformity and a narrow set of types of interaction provide no good grounds for collaborative work. Conversely, variability and differentiation are said to be fundamental resources of natural systems. Why should it be otherwise with artificial systems? As Lomborg (1994) pointed out in his computer-based experiment on multi-agent co-operation, a stable co-operative answer emerges only in conditions of very high strategic variability. Analogously, autonomous, rational agenthood implies the capacity to choose the most convenient form of interaction from a number of possible options. Therefore, an artificial agent should be allowed to establish, and should be supported in managing, the different kinds of formal and informal, obligatory or free, co-operative or exchange activities. It should be supported in managing the very different consequences (e.g. normative prescriptions) implicit in the different kinds of social relations it is involved in.

Helpfulness, over-answering and paternalism

If we are interested in truly helpful, co-operative, interactive systems, both in HCI (with helping systems), and in MAS (with intelligent agents, intermediary agents, and so forth), we should work out:
  (a) a *notion of adoption which goes beyond the actions requested* by the users, and embraces also their goals and plans, and
  (b) *which allows* the helper to take initiatives, *to give help spontaneously*;
  (c) also *a model of the user's*, or any other agent's, *interests*.
  A narrow notion of adoption (as confined within the limits of the requests received) reduces the benevolent agent to a mere executor of actions with no autonomy, rather than model it as a truly helpful and co-operative system (let us recall the example illustrated at the beginning of Chapter 3, of a solicitous robot hurrying to get a beer to its owner while the latter is dying of a heart attack).
  Help giving does not involve only the actions that the recipient wants the helper to carry out. Adoption must refer also to the recipient's goals above and beyond her requests. If the recipient stops short at wanting actions performed by the helper and the helper is duty-bound to carry out only the actions wanted by the recipient, the helper's intelligence, knowledge and problem-solving capacity are being set aside! If help is defined as *performing a required action* (Cohen & Levesque 1990b), the agent becomes a mindless executive (Castelfranchi 1992).
  Obviously, there is a delicate *boundary around helpfulness*. A truly helpful system may be bent on adopting not only the goals currently contained in y's (tacit) plans but also other important goals, which may be temporarily inactive, or even some of her interests (advantageous situations which y may not be aware of and which have not lead her to form any corresponding goal). As defined earlier in the book, x may have a *tutorial* goal *vis-à-vis* y. Tutorial goals are helpful at the extreme. However, they jeopardize both human relations and artificial *friendly* systems (recall the example given in Chapter 4 of an expert system that is asked to book a table in a given restaurant and re-

plies: "Are you sure you can afford it? It is very expensive.").

Clearly helpfulness must somehow be restrained, so that it does not become intrusive. In natural interaction there are supplementary courtesy rules, which tell you when you are entitled to intrude upon someone else's wishes. In artificial interaction, instead, a conventional constraint ought to be established. For example, x could be allowed to adopt y's interests and inactive goals only when they are compatible with y's current goal; conversely, x is not allowed to adopt any of y's interests that clash with the goals she is autonomously pursuing.

Norms and robust co-operation

Even when publicly known and shared, an intention remains only an intention. You can always change your mind and give it up if you wish.

This truism has fundamental social consequences, which ought to be taken into account in implementing systems supporting co-operation among autonomous agents.

Co-operation among autonomous agents is intrinsically fragile. It is always liable to be abandoned by one or other of the agents involved, since any one of them might find a more convenient solution to its necessities. Co-operation is fragile because intentions also are. The need for an increased degree of *robustness of system performance* was quickly perceived by DAI scientists (think of Hewitt's (1991) notion of commitment). To this end, stronger co-operative constraints, such as *conventions* (Jennings 1993) and *responsibility* (Jennings & Mandami 1992), are currently being proposed and implemented. Jennings & Mandami took the most correct and most direct way to solve the problem at hand, since responsibility is the key notion for ensuring robust performances. However, as it is treated by these authors, responsibility is still fundamentally based upon the notion of joint persistent goal worked out by Cohen & Levesque (1991) and discussed in the preceding chapter. As has been said, this notion includes, *inter alia*, that it should be true and mutually believed by the agents involved in a teamwork that each has the *weak achievement goal* that the status of the common goal (whether fulfilled, or unachievable) be known to each of them.

All these solutions, conventions, responsibilities, weak achievement goals, are insufficient, because they do not account for the normative decision-making and *choice*. The relative advantages of these different ways of including norms in an agent architecture have been analyzed elsewhere (Conte 1994). Here, we draw attention at least to the following:

(a) Unlike the other solutions, *norms can be modified when the system is on-line*; in other words, if the agents are endowed with a mechanism for goal and norm adoption (as described in Ch. 7) they can adopt or learn norms anew.

(b) Constraints, if automatically followed, are in *contrast with the postulate of rationality and self-interest* of autonomous agents. Why should an autonomous, self-interested agent spend time and resources in publicly declaring his intention to drop a joint goal?

The solution consisting of giving notice of one's intention to abandon the joint action merely allows the damage caused by defection to be reduced by notifying it, rather than preventing defection and making the agent more reliable. In Cohen & Levesque's (1991) analysis, as in Jennings' (1993), the agent is allowed to drop his joint intention with costs no higher than those encountered when he drops his personal intentions. Consequently, the analysis does not provide sufficient tools for supporting and reinforcing (artificial or heterogeneous) co-operative environments. Conversely, the truly normative mechanism is wholly compatible with the self-interest postulate; indeed, as shown in Chapter 7, the normative mechanism takes advantage of it. Norm adoption is based upon the rule of goal adoption, which is a fundamental rule of autonomous agenthood. Following such a rule, truly autonomous agents are allowed to adopt a norm only if they see some advantage in doing so.

Let us examine this aspect more concretely and roughly compare the consequences of dropping an individual vs. a joint intention. With individual intentions, there are essentially two consequences,

(a) the *goal utility*, if any, *is abandoned*:

(b) the *invested resources*, energies, time, etc. *are wasted*.

Of course, if the positive outcome of abandoning a given goal is greater than (a) plus (b), then dropping that goal is rational.

With joint intentions, there are also consequences for the other partners. One's dropping a joint action will jeopardize the others' achievements and/or cause them to incur additional costs (do your job). But, who cares? Neither in Cohen & Levesque's (1991), nor in Jennings' (1993) analysis of joint intention is the goal of *not cheating* or not damaging your fellows included. Hence, the agent is not bound to take this difference into account.

Only *by including norms and normative goals in joint intentions* does the difference between dropping a personal vs. a joint intention become apparent. With joint intentions, there are additional consequences besides those mentioned in (a) and (b):

(c) a *legitimate* (for a definition of this notion, see Ch. 6) *protest* and *retaliation* by the partners;

(d) two sorts of *sanctions*;
  – internal, or moral;
  – external, by the witnesses, the group, or any other authority;

(e) **bad reputation** (cheater, free-rider, etc.), which will jeopardize the cheater's future co-operation and search for help.

That is why we said that normative goals are a more cogent kind of goals. There will be a greater resistance on the part of an agent to drop out of a normative goal than out of a desire-based goal.

Dependence relations and rational interaction

As mentioned in the Introduction, one of the major inadequacies of current distributed systems (for an overview cf. Reddy & O'Hare 1991) is the *explosion of communications* among co-operative agents with the consequent huge *co-ordination costs*.

On the other hand, a representation of a given dependence network, preceding conversation and commitment and simply implying the agents' tasks and capacities, may facilitate their communications and commitments.

The theory of social dependence is a fundamental instrument for analyzing *objective rationality* of communication and interaction and improving the efficiency of MAS communication and co-ordination.

In current models and systems, the agents' rationality is only *subjective*, that is, actions are rational if consistent with the agents' beliefs and preferences.

However, since knowledge is limited, such a notion of rationality by no means prevents a rational choice from leading to counter-productive or ineffective consequences. An action based upon an adequate, *realistic* model of the objective conditions in which it will take place would be much more effective.

Dependence is an objective notion, defined from the observer's point of view, without necessarily implying any awareness of the agents involved. From such an external point of view, it is possible to evaluate the effectiveness of a given agent's beliefs, choices, and interactions on the grounds of their objective conditions, and compare different options on a scale of adaptiveness and convenience. It is possible, for example, to establish when communication is superfluous or ineffective, and when it is necessary; which coalitions are convenient for any given agent and which are not, etc.

Objective rationality *per se* is not relevant in DAI or MAS. It is useful only for an external evaluation. To be useful, the dependence relations must become known to the agents.

However, if we consider co-operative systems mediated by intelligent agents, the idea that the system embodies knowledge about the dependence relations among co-operating agents, even beyond what the participants are known for, may be of great interest and utility. The system could usefully direct the agents' requests and their acceptance, their exchanges and commitments, optimizing their interactions with respect to their objective needs. One possible use of the dependence relations among the agents is to provide co-operation support systems with objective knowledge.

Indeed, the utility of dependency-based knowledge is even more evident when one considers how likely some undesirable events are; consider at least the following:

(a) a user or system may *seek help*:
  – in order to do something it is able to accomplish on its own;

  - blindly, or address the wrong agents, that is, those who do not possess the required skills or are not playing the expected roles;
  - in an unsuitable way, asking for benevolence where it could find co-operation and gratitude, collect its credits, and vice versa;
  - when it could more easily influence certain agents to do what it needs;
(b) accept to *give help*, when:
  - it is not able to fulfil it;
  - its interests clash with the recipient's;
  - it is not economical, for example, because it could not get any remuneration from the recipient, etc.

Given these and other inadequacies, it is evident that a support system endowed with some capacity for reasoning about objective dependencies can considerably improve the efficacy and optimality of its interactions.

From the theory of dependence, which we have described in several chapters, two types of computational models have so far been developed, one oriented toward providing an autonomous artificial agent *(CogAgent)* with *heuristics for social reasoning* (Cesta & Miceli 1993, Miceli & Cesta 1993), the other oriented toward observing the performance of a *dependence network simulator*, called DEPNET, in an open MAS for several applications (Sichman et al. 1994a).

Dependency-based heuristics for social reasoning: the CogAgent *approach*

A crucial problem to be clarified concerns how this kind of analysis of social interaction can actually be used to improve the performance of intelligent systems. The authors' claim is that as long as applications in which both human beings and machines interact in the same environment are going to be developed, the issue of cognitive plausibility of the intelligent machines at the interaction level will become more and more important.

To test this issue, Miceli & Cesta (1993) have set up a simplified scenario aimed at showing the possible inclusion of knowledge about dependence relations in an agent architecture in order for an artificial autonomous agent to achieve cognitively plausible behaviour. Suppose an artificial agent is dealing with a problem and builds up a preliminary plan to solve it. It turns out it is not able to perform an action, and in order to achieve its goal it must resort to some other agent's help. Identifying the (hopefully) right agent is a knowledge-intensive planning activity.

Two aspects are critical in any such planning:
(a) the need to produce a *social subplan by using well-founded heuristics to analyze the agent's social knowledge* (i.e. its knowledge about others). Agent x should come to know not only which other agents it depends upon and why, but also some other relevant information about the oth-

ers' mental states, including their goals as well as their beliefs about x's goals, about their own duties and roles, and about their own dependence relations;

(b) the need to *avoid producing a plan which is in conflict with other general (or personal) goals* of the agent.

In *CogAgent* architecture the planning component is given as input a number of goals the system wants to achieve, and works to produce a plan for *CogAgent*. A number of specialists contribute to the creation of the plan guiding the agent's behavior: a *memory-based planner* builds up initial plans for achieving the goals; a *resource analysis and allocation module*, once a plan has been built, is called into play to identify any problem related to future execution of the action. In particular, for each plan action, this module tests whether it is included in the action repertoire, and whether all the resources involved in action execution are accessible to the agent. After resource analysis has identified the need for other resources, two specialists are called into play:

(a) A *social knowledge specialist* responsible for searching social resources, that is any other agent in the world at large who might give x some help to get the work done.

(b) A *social goal-conflict analyzer* responsible for scrutinizing social plans provided by other modules, in particular by the previous specialist, in order to check for negative interactions between such a plan and other goals (this module performs a task similar to conflict analysis in classical planning).

The problem-solving is based on the use of dependence-based criteria for seeking agents both useful and willing. Two major criteria were found: the CANDO criterion, for selecting, through different strategies, those agents who are able to perform the needed action, and the WILL criteria, for selecting those agents who are likely to perform it. The CANDO search is prior to the WILL search, because while agents can act upon the willingness of others (through influencing), they are not able to modify others' skills. So the CANDO is a filter condition.

CANDO criterion: search for a capable agent

A first problem agent x will have to face is thus: How to find out those ys who CANDO a, or what should x know in order to know if y can do a? Given a certain y, x may search for either one or the other of two general kinds of information in order to assess whether y CANDO a. The first is called a bottom-up or performance criterion for CANDOs' detection, while the second might be called a top-down criterion.

(a) *Bottom-up criterion.* Agent x may search his memory for a belief such that action a has been done by y:

$$\left(BEL\, x \left(DONE \text{-} BY\, y_1\, a \right) \right)$$

because, for the assumption of action ability (AAA):

$$\left(DONE \text{-} BY\, y_1\, a \right) \supset \left(CANDO\, y_1\, a \right)$$

if y has done a, she must be able to do it. Such a belief may either derive from x's direct observation of y_1's behavior (x has already seen y_1 doing a), or from someone else's communication (see also Ch. 2).

(b) *Top-down criterion.* However reasonable, the former subcriterion sounds rather unlikely to occur. More exactly, we believe it is applied when no other information is available, i.e. when the top-down criterion is not applicable. Consider an office environment, agent x (let us call him John) is not likely to wonder for each of his colleagues whether he saw them resetting the e-mail server. John already knows that a class of people – say, computer scientists and technicians, and in particular system managers – are endowed with the CANDO in question. So, when faced with a particular colleague, Carol, John is likely to see whether Carol belongs to that class.

This implies that when the top-down criterion is applied, the first query x should make is about the kind of action a required: does a belong to a class a_i of actions which can be performed by a certain class y_i of agents? If so, x will look for those specific ys he knows to belong to that class. Suppose John knows Carol is a computer scientist: this allows him to infer that she can reset the e-mail server. To put things in a formal style:

$$\left(BEL\, x \left(\left(\left(CANDO\, y_i\, a_j \right) \wedge \left(V_{i=1,n} \left(y = y_i \right) \right) \wedge \left(V_{j=1,n} \left(a = a_j \right) \right) \right) \supset \left(CANDO\, y\, a \right) \right) \right)$$

that is: *x believes that if a given y belongs to the set y_i and a given a belongs to the set a_j, and the set y_i is able to do a_j, then any member y of the former set is able to perform any member a of the latter set*. This amounts to saying that, when faced with a particular y_1, an agent x who follows the top-down criterion will not ask himself whether DONE-BY y a, but whether $y = i$, in order to assess whether CANDO y a.

The CANDO criterion, be it either a top-down or a bottom-up one, will be recursively applied by x to each of the agents in his world until he finds one agent y that CANDO a. If x does not find any, of course he will end his search and probably give up his goal p. In this case, application of the criterion has just prevented x from embarking upon useless and effort-consuming requests for help from people who would not be able to satisfy them. However, if x's search is successful, that is, if he finds that CANDO y a, what will he do? Will x automatically turn to y for help?

WILL criteria: search for a willing agent

Cesta & Miceli (1993) propose three *WILL* criteria to be applied by x in his search for an agent. The ordering of application of such criteria may depend on some priorities established by the specific agent x in question according to his own preferences, biases or character.

Search for an exploitable y

Agent x can see whether y already has the goal to perform a, in order to take advantage of y's performance. Suppose John knows that Carol will need to use the e-mail and, being able to reset the server, is likely to do the job: John will just wait for her to do so.

Now, how can x assess whether y has the goal to do action a?

Again, we can assume both a top-down and a bottom-up criterion to be applicable. In the former case, x can see whether y belongs to a set y_i of agents with the goal that a_j be done. For instance, John can see whether Carol belongs to the class of (competent) users of the e-mail server. In the case of the performance criterion x should either actually see y performing a or carry out some plan recognition according to which x can believe y is going to perform a.

Search for a benevolent y

In Chapter 3, we said goal adoption is terminal when it is sufficient that an agent believes that p is a goal of another agent for the former agent to adopt such a goal. So, if y believes that x has the goal p then also y comes to have the same goal p. This phenomenon is also known as *benevolence*. Now, there exist at least two possible types of benevolence (terminal goal adoption): individualized, (or personal) and non-individualized benevolence. Let us see them in turn.

(a) *Individualized benevolence.* This type of benevolence occurs whenever a given agent y exists such that y wants the goal(s) of a given agent x to be achieved. In other words, y is likely to adopt the goals of a specific agent. It is reasonable to believe that when benevolence is individualized it usually applies to any goal of the recipient's: if y is benevolent with regard to x as a specific agent (as opposed to an element of a set), y usually wants x to be contented and well adapted. On the contrary, when benevolence is not individualized, it usually applies to a well-defined set of goals of the recipients.

(b) *Non-individualized benevolence.* This type of benevolence occurs when y (usually a given set of ys) adopts the goals of a given set of xs. In the general form of non- individualized benevolence three sets of objects are mentioned: the recipients, their goals, and the benevolent agents. So, the recipient may believe that if he belongs to a set which receives benevolence with regard to a given set of goals from a set y_i of agents, and if y belongs to that set, he will receive benevolence from y:

$$\left(BEL\,x\left(\left(G\text{-}ADOPT\,y_i\,x_j\,p\right)\wedge\left(V_{i=1,n}(y=y_i)\right)\wedge V_{j=1,n}(x=x_i)\right)\right)\supset$$

$$\left(BEL\,x\left(G\text{-}ADOPT\,y\,x\,p\right)\right)$$

Non-individualized benevolence seems to have two general sources:

(i) *Role tasks:* non-individualized benevolence is generally set up by the structure of social roles existing in a given domain. We say that agent x may be a recipient of non-individualized benevolence, when x is mentioned as a beneficiary in the role of some y_s. In such cases, x is due benevolence, and y is held to give help to x relative to some specified set of goals. In our example, the agent y might be held by role to reset the e-mail facility. This implies that agent x should have knowledge about roles and role tasks. He should then be able to see whether the action he needs matches the role task of some other (class of) agents, as well as if his own role repertoire includes him as a beneficiary of such a role task.

(ii) *General norms:* sometimes norms control when adoption should be given to whom, independently of the structure of roles. In some contexts, some agents might be expected to adopt some goals of other agents: on the bus, people are expected to give up and leave their seats to the disabled; car drivers are supposed to give way to cars coming from the right. A special case is represented by the norm of reciprocation: y is held to reciprocate, that is, to adopt some goals of those agents who have intentionally benefited her in the past without being obliged to do so. If Carol asks John, who can write Spanish, to write to some Spanish-speaking colleague, Carol will probably be expected to return the favour somehow. This implies that x will check his domain knowledge for any norm mentioning a set of beneficiaries and that the agent architecture is endowed with a memory of past interactions. Either the agent knowledge should contain indexes of debts and credits of the last interactions occurred, or an interaction buffer should be checked every time other agents are screened.

Search for a dependent y

This criterion implies the search for an agent who, besides being able to perform a, is in turn dependent on x for some other action. In other words, x should try to move from assumed unilateral dependence of x himself on y to assumed bilateral dependence of each one on the other. Bilateral dependence would obviously allow for a more powerful position of x: in fact, on the grounds of his assumed dependence on y, x has the goal of influencing y to perform a_1; now, also y, on the grounds of her assumed dependence on x, should have the goal of influencing x to perform some other action a_x. So, x might offer his own performance of a_x in exchange for y's performance of a_y. This offer of exchange is in fact a form of negotiation based on assumed dependence. Going back to our example, suppose that while Carol is able to

175

reset the e-mail server, John knows ancient Greek very well and he knows that Carol doesn't and is in need of a translation from English into ancient Greek.

As one can see, situations of this sort are the basis for a great part of social interaction. However, this aspect has received a stronger emphasis in the *DEPNET* system, presented below.

This is one way to use dependence and goal-adoption theory for modelling rational search of help. However, one can use the same basic notion for modelling *the complementary problem* and perspective in a multi-agent co-operative environment, when and why help others? Consider two application examples (Rizzo et al. 1994):

(a) *In a work environment* (e.g. an office) several people are performing their tasks, and are committed to particular goals that allow them to obtain a desired reward; one of the agents could require some help because he has run out of resources or is temporarily unable to perform an action. Other agents could help him because all of them are part of the same organization and could apply a default co-operation rule. But, even when not considering cases of competitive behaviour, it is plausible that agents waste time while helping and eventually may lose their own rewards. In such a case, they should apply some decision criteria to assess whether to help or not.

(b) *In a completely artificial scenario*, some software agents perform their own tasks in a distributed environment. If we suppose that agents have knowledge about each other's capabilities, it may happen that one asks another to do something, but each agent is reasonably built so as to maximize some expected utility function, and, reasonably enough, helping others does not increase that utility. If, in the meantime, agents are also built in such a way as not to harm others, how can they distinguish when it is the case to help?

Rizzo et al. (1994) stress how in order to account for such a behaviour one should refer to both autonomous self-interest strategic reasoning, and to *normative factors*. In particular, two general norms appear to regulate helping behaviour:

– *a norm of social responsibility*, which prescribes helping those people who are dependent on us;
– *a norm of reciprocity*, which imposes reciprocation of an agent who has previously helped us.

DEPNET

Sichman and others have implemented a simulator known as *DEPNET* (cf. Sichman et al. 1994a,b) to calculate the dependence relations among agents and construct the dependence networks of a given agent. This simulator is composed of the following facilities:

Agent edition module

The user can dynamically create new agents and edit their goals, actions, resources, and plans, (see below) or modify those of an existing agent; for the sake of example, consider Table 11.1.

Once *DEPNET* is integrated into a multi-agent platform, each time a new agent enters the agency, he broadcasts a message informing of his goals, actions, resources and plans. Automatically, the agent edition module updates the agent description to include this information (see Table 11.1). What is the philosophy underlying the system?

In order to be really autonomous (in the broad sense), an agent ought to be endowed with a social reasoning mechanism, based upon knowledge about others. In Sichman et al. (1994a,b) a social reasoning mechanism is defined as a mechanism that uses information about others in order to infer some conclusions. Therefore, any agent (despite the possible different internal models an agent may have) must have a data structure where this information about the others is stored. Such data structure is called an *external description* and is composed of the following elements:

(a) *goals*: the goals an agent wants to achieve. An agent may have more than one goal, and in this point we do not make any reference if a goal is currently active or not: this discussion is outside the scope of this work's current stage;

(b) *actions*: the actions an agent is able to perform;

(c) *resources*: the resources an agent has control over;

(d) *plans*: the plans an agent has, using any actions and resources, in order to achieve a certain goal. These actions and resources do not necessarily belong to his own set of actions and resources, and therefore an agent may depend on others in order to carry on a certain plan.

Therefore, an agent ag_i will be action-autonomous for a given goal g_k, according to a set of plans P_k, if there is a plan that achieves this goal in this set

Table 11.1   Output of the DEPNET agent editor.

name:	x		name:	y
goals:	g_1 g_2 g_3 g_4		goals:	g_5
actions:	a_1		actions:	a_3
resources:	r_1		resources:	r_3
plans:	$g_1 = a_3(r_1)$		plans:	$g_5 = a_3(r_3)$
	$g_3 = a_1(r_1), a_2(r_3)$			
	$g_4 = a_1(r_1), a_4(r_5), a_5(r_4)$			
	$g_2 = a_6(r_1), a_7(r_2)$			
name:	z		name:	w
goals:	g_4		goals:	g_3
actions:	a_5		actions:	a_7
resources:	r_5		resources:	r_7
plans:	$g_4 = a_1(r_1), a_5(r_7)$		plans	$g_3 = a_1(r_2), a_7(r_3)$

and every action appearing in this plan belongs to the set of actions ag_i is competent in.

Analogously, an agent ag_i will be resource-autonomous for a given goal g_k, according to a set of plans P_k if such a set contains at least one plan achieving g_k, and all resources used by that plan are controlled by ag_i. Finally, an agent ag_i will be socially-autonomous for a given goal g_k, according to a set of plans P_k if he is both action-autonomous and resource-autonomous for this goal. The major contribution of this work is the fact that this notion of autonomy is closely related to the set of plans used in the reasoning mechanism. In other words, an agent can use either his own set of plans or those of the others in order to infer his own autonomy. In doing so, an agent can simulate the reasoning of the others, by using their knowledge (in our case, their plans). This may be done by explicit communication whenever an agent enters the agency (for instance, using an introduction protocol as described in Sichman et al. 1994a) or by the agent's perception mechanisms. The important point is that this information corresponds to the beliefs an agent has regarding the others, and that these beliefs may be neither necessarily true nor complete.

Dependence network constructor

If an agent is not autonomous for a given goal, he will depend on others to achieve it. An agent ag_i action-depends on another agent ag_j for a given goal g_k, according to a set of plans P_k, if he has g_k in his set of goals, he is not action-autonomous for g_k and there is a plan in P_k that achieves g_k and at least one action used in this plan is in ag_j's set of actions. Analogously, an agent ag_i resource-depends on another agent ag_j with regard to a given goal g_k if ag_i is not resource-autonomous with regard to such a goal and there is at least one resource used in the plan contained in the set P_k that is controlled by ag_j.

Once these dependence relations have been defined, an agent can construct a dependence network to represent all of his action/resource[1] dependencies regarding the others in one and the same structure. These networks can be used later in the agent's social reasoning mechanism, in particular to detect the dependence situations regarding two agents for a given goal, as described in the next section. A dependence network is defined as a directed graph where all dependencies of a given agent are presented; a dependence network

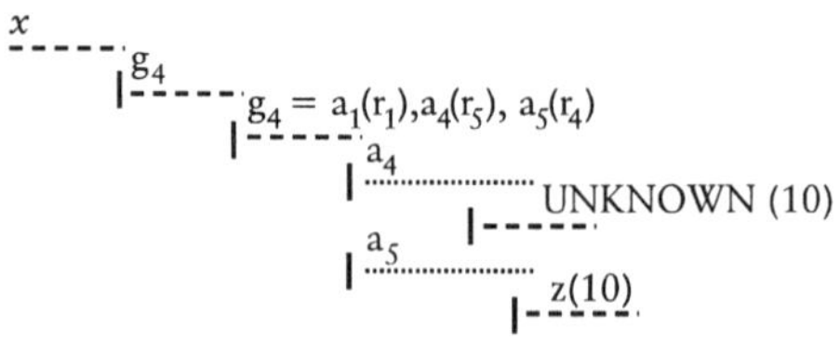

Figure 11.1 Dependence network constructor.

may be related either to a specific goal or to all of an agent's goals. For example, the dependence network of agent x with regard to its goal $g4$ is as in Figure 11.1.

This dependence network includes an *AND* dependence link (the starred lines). To achieve its goal, x depends on both z and an unknown agent. Enclosed figures express the degree of dependence for each action, which is determined by the value of the action, here assigned by default. Information about dependence on unknown agents tells you what action you need. In an open system, this may be relevant because, if a self-presentation message from a newcomer includes that action, the dependence network is automatically updated.

Dependence situation constructor

This module calculates the *type* of dependence situations regarding a given agent and one of his goals. A dependence situation is defined as the particular type of dependence relation holding between any two agents (unilateral, reciprocal, or mutual). The user must specify the actual type of dependence situation he is interested in. Since an agent has constructed his dependence networks, he can use this information when reasoning about the others. In other words, for a given goal g_k, an agent ag_i can calculate for each other agent ag_j which the dependence situation relates to for this goal. As formally defined in Chapter 2, mutual dependence is a situation where an agent ag_i infers that he and another agent ag_j action-depend on each other for the same goal g_k, according to a set of plans P_k. Reciprocal dependence is a situation where an agent ag_i infers that he and another agent ag_j action-depend on each other, but for different goals g_k and g_l, according to the sets of plans P_k and P_l (both sets belonging to the same external description entry).

In the case of mutual dependence, a possible co-operation regarding this goal can occur. On the other hand, in the case of reciprocal dependence, one of them will have to adopt the other's goal first in order to achieve his own in the future. This mechanism is called social exchange. By adding a mechanism for social choice to *DEPNET*, it ought to be possible to show whether the most rational social choice in a situation of reciprocal dependence is social exchange, while the best option in a situation of mutual dependence is co-operation.

Furthermore, an agent locally believes a given dependence (either mutual or reciprocal) if he uses his own plans exclusively when reasoning about the others. If he uses both his own plans and those of the others to reach such a conclusion, it will be said that there is a mutual believed dependence between them.

The difference between the locally and the mutually believed situations (either in mutual or reciprocal dependence) is very subtle: in the first case, one of the agents may not be aware of this dependence (for instance, when one of them has a different set of plans to achieve the considered goal and in neither of these plans does he action-depend on the other). In this case, a plan negotiation will have to be made in order to achieve the desired goal.

The situation dependence menu is illustrated in Figure 11.2.

DEPENDENCE SITUATION MENU

Type 1 (calculate mutual dependence)
2 (calculate reciprocal dependence)
3 (calculate unilateral dependence
4 (print the external description)
5 (return to dependence network menu)
6 (return to main menu)
7 (quit)

Suppose we choose 1. We want to know whether x is in a relation of mutual dependence with someone with regard to a given goal.

****calculate_mutual_dep function****

Type the name of the agent to calculate the dependence: x

Type the goal of the network: g4

Regarding agent: (z)

```
x
-----g4
    |-----g4  = a1(r1),a4(r5), a5(r4)
          |-----a5
                |-----  z(10)
                      |-----
```

```
z
-----g4
    |-----g4  = a1(r1),a5(r7)
          |-----a1
                |-----  x(10)
                      |-----
```

Figure 11.2 Dependence situation constructor.

The simulator constructs the above dependence situation. *x* is in a situation of mutual dependence with regard to its goal *g4*: *x* and *z* are mutually dependent in order to achieve that goal; *x* depends on *z* for action *a5*, while *z* depends on *x* for action *a1*.

The utility of *DEPNET* is intuitive; in particular, it may be used for:

(a) *decreasing the communication flow.* Even if every agent sends a broadcasting message to introduce itself, this is done only once, when it enters the system. Since the others can take this information into account, there is no longer any need to send a broadcasting message every time an agent needs a given action or resource, as it can know *a priori* whom it should address;

(b) *selecting the help-givers* on the grounds of the most convenient dependence situation. Two factors may be involved in this selection – the amount of dependence and the dependence situation. In the case of the former, it is reasonable to assume that an agent will ask those on whom it is least dependent. But, other things being equal, how would it choose between a plan with regard to which it AND-depends on two or more agents, and a plan for which it depends on one agent? A module for calculating the amount of dependence which takes into account the dependence network and the dependence situations is being implemented. However, disregarding the quantification of dependence, dependence situations may help choose the most convenient help givers. Hypothetically, a situation of mutual dependence should be preferred to a situation of reciprocal dependence, and the latter should be preferred to unilateral dependence;

(c) **social simulation**. Using the *DEPNET* simulator, we can investigate and validate some theoretical hypotheses concerning the choice of a given social action, the relative convenience of exchange and co-operation, as well as the creation of collective agents, etc.

The potential of the model in social simulation research

Social simulation is a most promising research field at the intersection between Computer Science and social sciences. Research in this field is on the increase (cf. Gilbert & Doran 1994).

What has a model of social action, such as the present one, to offer to research into social simulation?

One possible answer emerges from the need for a more sophisticated cognitive modelling approach that is now being expressed in the field (see the Introduction to Gilbert & Doran 1994). Indeed, so far, the computer-based simulation of social processes has implied a rather crude oversimplification of the agents' make-up.

However, this is neither the only, nor the principal contribution that the present model can offer in this field of research. There are two possible directions of development of the present model in the field of social simulation, (a) the emergence of social action from objective pre-conditions (dependence, concurrence, etc.; see Ch. 1 and 2); (b) norm functionalities and the spreading of the normative requests (see Ch. 7).

The first direction is related to the progress achieved by *DEPNET* (see above). The second one was undertaken recently and has produced some preliminary results, which we summarize below.

Towards the computer simulation of normative requests

A simulation experiment was carried out for the purpose of exploring the role of norms in the control of aggression in a population of agents. At this stage, agents are allowed little autonomy, if any: they perform some elementary routines for the purpose of surviving in a situation of food scarcity. An experimental situation in which the agents followed a norm (not to attack an agent who is eating the food which happened to be located in its own territory) were compared with identical situations where players followed some sort of utilitarian rule. In other words, a *normative* routine was compared with one in which the agents did not attack stronger eaters. Of course, given the extreme *naïveté* of the agents' modelling, norms cannot be architecturally distinguished from other rules. At this stage, the difference is only factual: *a normative strategy is one which may be disadvantageous to the agent that applies it,* and would therefore be discarded if the agent could make his decision on a strictly utilitarian basis. The differences among the experimental conditions (control, utilitarian, normative) have been observed and measured along some indicators (number of aggressions, average strength, and its variance; for a detailed report see Conte & Castelfranchi 1995). Essentially, the findings show that at least one particular type of normative strategy, which can be likened to the *finders-keepers* norm, produced:

(a) an *average strength significantly higher* than both that of the control condition and the utilitarian strategy;

(b) a variance, or *polarization, of such strength significantly lower* than in both the other conditions.

These results seem to indicate that, while reducing aggressions, *some type* of norm distributes the social costs of aggression control in a *more equitable* way than a merely utilitarian strategy.

Further studies

That computer simulation is a feasible and useful method of investigation of social processes is no news. Traditionally, this approach has been applied to the study of the emergent properties of micro-interactions. In particular, such things as conventions, norms of co-operation, etc. are seen as emergent properties of micro-social *behaviours*. Conventions and norms are seen as spreading behavioural uniformities.

In future developments of the simulation study of norms described above, we intend to observe the spreading of normative reputation and even of normative requests.

Several experimental phases are planned, aimed at:

1. observing the relative *frequencies of different strategies* (utilitarian and normative) *of aggression control* within the same population of agents;

2. observing their *relative spreading* (by allowing stronger agents to be cloned);

3. *introducing some level of choice* (by assigning costs and benefits to each strategy);

4. *implementing a norm of reciprocation*, and the accompanying normative reputation (a memory of past interactions);

5. *allowing some cheating* and observing whether the normative reputation has any impact on the control of cheating;

6. *implementing a gossip mechanism* (the spreading of normative reputation) and observing its effects on the average strength of those who have a bad reputation and those who spread the news.

The general hypothesis underlying these studies is that some norms, or other macro-social phenomena, cannot be explained merely as *emergent properties of rational behaviour*. So far our study seems to have shown – but of course, it needs refinement and replication – that a specific effect (aggression control with low polarization of strength) is produced as long as the agents do *not* pursue their individual utilities. Indeed, it looks almost as if collective interests, if any, sometimes select a non-utilitarian behaviour. How is this possible? What is the use of norms of this sort for the stronger agents? We do not have any convincing answer to these questions. However, we think that they are important ones, and that computer simulation may make a substantial contribution to highlighting them.

Apologies and hopes

In this book we embarked upon a doubly ambitious enterprise. On the one hand, we endeavoured to get AI and the social sciences, with their different languages, traditions, theoretical and methodological tools, and especially their reciprocal mistrust, to confront each other on some common ground. On the other hand, we claimed to have something new to say about the micro–macro link problem. Both objectives are challenging, but the second is also not novel. We apologise in particular for being convinced that cognitive modelling, in the sense intended in this book, is in fact a *new* way of approaching the micro-macro link problem and at the same time provides a *common ground* for a productive interplay between AI and the social sciences. Most probably, the specific solutions we have provided, our notions and hypotheses will be found unsatisfactory, naïve, incomplete. And in many cases, we suspect they are. We apologize for such incompleteness and *naïveté*. Nonetheless, we think that our fundamental suggestion is correct and relevant, namely that *cognition ought to be viewed as something different from rationality in the game-theoretic sense, and from the hypercognitive models worked out by many social and AI scientists*. We think that our view of cognition is preferable because it is compatible with a theory of the structuring effect of macro-social agents and factors, that is, more compatible than both other views are.

We reject a view of the micro–macro link which is reduced to the emergent properties of micro-interactions. We think social scientists are right when they say that social agents, their minds, volitions and beliefs are in turn structured by society. The problem is how to break out of what may appear as a vicious circle, an acrobatic speculation, a dialectic escape. In our view, it is none of these things, but this view needs to be proved. And here is where AI and computational methodology can help us. We have got to build minds and get them to interact with one another and with humans to see what properties are needed for an agent to survive in a social world, and for a social world to survive and reproduce itself.

We hope we have been successful in achieving two things: to have convinced our readers of the utility of this approach, and to have avoided placing too great a burden on their attention and patience.

Appendix

Syntax and semantics

The formalism used is a simplified version of Cohen & Levesque's (1990a,b) language for describing their theory of rational action. Consequently, it has the usual connectives of a first-order language, plus operators for mental attitudes, obligations, and actions.

In the following, x and y denote agent variables with $x \neq y$ always implicitly stated, a denotes an action variable, e a sequence of events, r a resource, and p and q well-formed formulae representing states of the world (with $p \neq q$).

(*HAPPENS a*) and (*DONE a*)	an action will happen next or has just happened
(*BEL x p*) and (*GOAL x p*)	x has a belief or goal
(*OUGHT p*)	there is an obligation on proposition p
(*AGT x e*)	x is the only agent of the sequence e
(*RESOURCE r a*)	r is needed in order to perform a
(*CANDO x a*)	x has a in his action repertoire, i.e., he is able to perform a by himself
$e_1 \leq e_2$	e_1 occurs before e_2
p?	test action
$\Diamond p$	p will be true at some point in the future

Beliefs and goals are given the usual possible world interpretation, and consistency and realism are ensured in the same vein as in Cohen & Levesque. As for consistency, the Hintikka-style axioms for beliefs apply to this model (see Halpern & Moses 1985). As for realism, goals are a subset of beliefs. (The accessibility relation G, which defines the set of worlds in which goals are achieved is a subset of the accessibility relation B, which defines the set of worlds belief-accessible to a given agent.)

In our approach, a goal is a regulatory representation. While a belief is a representation which the agent *tries to liken to the world*, a *goal* is a representation which the agent tries *to liken the world to*.

Therefore, our notion of goal is slightly weaker than that allowed by Cohen & Levesque. We propose to treat goals as *realistic* desires, rather than *chosen* ones. In our terms, a goal is but a regulatory mental attitude which calls for a series of operations, including some preliminaries, involved in planned action.

In other words, along the lines of classical AI planning systems, we define a goal as a device which activates planning and action. In our terms, a goal may be abandoned not only when it is believed to be fulfilled or unachievable, but also when it is found incompatible with another more important goal.

The predicate *OUGHT* intuitively means that there is some sort of **obligation** on proposition *p*. For the time being, we take it as an atomic one-place predicate, although it seems possible to further analyze it as some sort of external reason which forces a given goal, namely the adoption of a given goal. However, we will assume obligation as a primitive, which defines a set of worlds in which *p* follows from obligations. The relation of accessibility *O* is a subset of *B*.

Cohen & Levesque's language has raised a number of criticisms, some of which (Rao & Georgeff 1991, Rao et al. 1992, Zamparelli 1993) are quite interesting and insightful[1]. Nonetheless, thanks to its degree of explicitness and its intuitive foundations, the model worked out by Cohen & Levesque is more suitable for cognitive modelling than other languages are. (For example, the linear treatment of time, its drawbacks notwithstanding, is rather more intuitive than the branching time model. In the agents' minds, time is usually represented as a succession of events, rather than a set of parallel scenarios.)

Molecular predicates

In the following, we present a number of definitions grounded upon the above atomic predicates that are necessary to understand the formulae provided throughout the book. Most of them are drawn from Cohen & Levesque's model, and we present them here for the convenience of the reader unacquainted with that model. Some have been introduced by the authors and other collaborators in earlier works (Conte et al. 1991, Castelfranchi et al. 1992b).

$$(DOES \, x \, a) \stackrel{def}{=} (HAPPENS \, a) \wedge (AGT \, x \, a)$$

saying that *x is the only agent of action a, which will happen next.* We need an analogous predicate for past actions,

$$(DONE\text{-}BY \, x \, a) \stackrel{def}{=} (DONE \, a) \wedge (ACT \, x \, a)$$

saying that *x is the only agent of action a, which has just happened.*

In this work, Cohen & Levesque's **assumption of action competence** is valid; in other words, the performance of a given primitive action implies that the agent believes he has performed it.

Assumption of action competence:

$$\forall x \forall a (DONE\text{-}BY\ x\ a) \equiv (BEL\ x(DONE\text{-}BY\ x\ a))$$

Cohen & Levesque have also introduced the following predicate to refer to sequences of world states:

$$(BEFORE\ q\ p) \overset{def}{=} \forall c(HAPPENS\ c;p?) \supset \exists a(a \leq c) \wedge (HAPPENS\ a;q?)$$

in words: *q comes before p when, for all events c after which p is true, there has been at least one event a preceding c, after which q was true.*

As for goals, Cohen & Levesque have introduced the notion of **achievement goal**, which is defined as follows:

$$(A\text{-}GOAL\ x\ p) \overset{def}{=} (BEL\ x\ \neg p) \wedge (GOAL\ x\ \Diamond p)$$

that is: *x has an achievement goal p if x believes that p is not true now but will eventually become true.* Throughout the book, whenever the notion of goal is used, it will be meant as an achievement goal in the above sense, unless otherwise specified.

Indeed, in our model (as well as in Cohen & Levesque's), an achievement goal is not yet an intention.

The process of transforming a goal into an intention has been modelled only partially. For example, Cohen & Levesque's theory of *persistent* goals is an account of a relevant aspect of this process; persistent goals are those that the agents believe to be neither realized nor unachievable:

$$(P\text{-}GOAL\ x\ p) \overset{def}{=} (GOAL\ x\ p) \wedge$$
$$(BEFORE((BEL\ x\ p) \vee (BEL\ x\ \neg\Diamond p)) \neg(A\text{-}GOAL\ x\ p))$$

in words: *x has a **persistent** goal p if before giving up trying to achieve it, x believes that p is true or will never be true.*

However, since goals are defined by the authors as both *chosen* desires and primitives, the process of their choice has not been addressed so far by the authors.

It should be noted that there are several factors which contribute to transforming an *achievement goal* into an intention. In Cohen & Levesque's model, persistent goals are *unachieved* but *realizable* goals, in the sense that they are belief-compatible. In the present view, however, realizability is meant to be stronger, more restrictive than mere belief-compatibility. Rational balance is a further requirement. Reasonably, the costs of any goal pursuit ought not to exceed those of not pursuing it. In other words, a goal is always confronted with other existing goals (including that of avoiding a waste of resources) of the agent's, and possible conflicts are detected and solved. In line with other authors (cf. Bell 1993), we believe that the evaluation of goal persistence or abandonment is a *goal-driven* process, and not simply constrained by belief-compatibility. An *achievement goal* may or not be executed, depending whether it is compatible with other goals of the agent's or not. Therefore, if our notion of goal is weaker than Cohen & Levesque's, our notion of intention is stronger. In formal terms, however, this part of our model has not yet been developed. This is why we will never speak of intentions in the proper sense. We will limit ourselves to speaking of persistent goals in the sense defined above, warning the reader that the tests for persistence included in that definition are necessary but not sufficient. This will be especially relevant for the treatment of normative goals (Ch. 8). A normative goal may be persistent in the sense defined by Cohen & Levesque but can be abandoned all the same simply because it is not convenient for the agent to implement it.

Finally, to speak of subgoals, that is, decomposed goals, Cohen & Levesque have proposed the notion of **relativized goal**:

$$(R\text{-}GOAL\ x\ p\ q) \stackrel{def}{=} (A\text{-}GOAL\ x\ p) \wedge$$

$$\Big(BEFORE\big((BEL\ x\ \neg q) \vee (BEL\ x\ p) \vee (BEL\ x\ \neg\Diamond p)\big) \neg(A\text{-}GOAL\ x\ p)\Big)$$

or: *x has a goal p relativized to q, when x has an achievement goal p, and before ceasing to have p as an achievement goal, x believes either that p is realized or unachievable or that the escape condition q does not hold.* Essentially, this means that *x* has *p* as long as and because he believes that *q*.

Since we will also need to speak of **mutual beliefs**, we define a **mutual belief** in the usual way, with three levels of nesting:

$$(BMBxyp) \stackrel{def}{=} \Big((BEL\ x\ p) \wedge (BEL\ x(BEL\ y\ p)) \wedge \big(BEL\ x(BEL\ y(BEL\ x\ p))\big)\Big) \wedge$$

$$(BEL\ y\ p) \wedge (BEL\ y(BEL\ x\ p)) \wedge \big(BEL\ y(BEL\ x(BEL\ y\ p))\big)\Big)$$

that is: *x believes p and believes that y believes p, and believes that y believes that x believes p, and so does y.*

As there are achievement goals, we will need to speak of achieved goals. To do so, we have introduced the following notion (Conte et al. 1991):

$$(OBTAIN\ x\ p) \stackrel{def}{=} p \wedge \big(BEFORE(A\text{-}GOAL\ x\ p)\ p\big)$$

that is: *x achieves p if p is true and beforehand x had p as an achievement goal.*

Finally, we need to be able to distinguish an intended effect from an unintentionally caused effect. Therefore, we have introduced the following notion:

$$(DOES\text{-}FOR\ x\ a\ p) \overset{def}{=} (DOES\ x\ a) \wedge$$

$$\left(R\text{-}GOAL\ x(DOES\ x\ a)\bigl(BEL\ x((DONE\ a) \supset p)\bigr)\right) \wedge (A\text{-}GOAL\ x\ p)$$

or: *x does an action a for p, when he has p as an achievement goal, and has the goal to do a relativized to its belief that if a is done, p becomes true.* The same distinction is valid in the past:

$$(DONE\text{-}FOR\ x\ a\ p) \overset{def}{=} (DONE\text{-}BY\ x\ a) \wedge \left(BEFORE\bigl[(A\text{-}GOAL\ x\ p) \wedge\right.$$

$$\left.\left(R\text{-}GOAL\ x(DOES\ x\ a)\bigl(BEL\ x((DONE\ a) \supset p)\bigr)\right)\bigr](DONE\text{-}BY\ x\ a)\right)$$

which means that *agent x has done a for p, if he has done a and before doing it x had p as an achievement goal and a goal to do a relativized to its belief that once a was done, p would become true.* This will have some important consequences for the present discussion.

Some rules

Below, a number of rules and assumptions are presented. Some of them clarify our agent model.

The following, denoted as a goal-generation rule (GGR), is a fundamental rule for deriving subgoals. It plays a crucial role in the definition of autonomous agenthood.

$$((BEL\ x\ q \supset p) \wedge (A\text{-}GOAL\ x\ p)) \supset (GOAL\ x\ q)$$

in words: *if x believes that p follows from q and x has p as an achievement goal, then x will also have q as a goal.* The latter does not need to be an achievement goal, since, if q is already true, x will want q to continue to be true.

This is a generalization of a planning rule. Actually, it goes back to Aristotle. One version of it is called a *rule of pragmatic inference* (see, for example, Pearl 1993). Like the action-pre-condition rule (Cohen & Perrault 1979), it is recursive: if x believes that a_1 is a condition for intended (or target) action a_2, a_1 in turn becomes a target action, and so forth. Analogously, if x believes that if it rains he will find mushrooms to gather, x will keep wanting it to rain. Indeed, such a rule is necessary for relativized goals, which would remain too abstract a notion without a rule of this sort. An agent x's goal p being relativized essentially means that this goal exists as long as and because x believes the goal to be useful or convenient. The **goal-generation rule** (GGR) provides grounds for relativized goals.

In our model, an **assumption of action ability** holds:
Assumption of action ability

$$(DOES\ x\ a) \supset (CANDO\ x\ a)$$

which means *that if an agent performs an action, it has that action in its repertoire.*

As in Cohen & Levesque, action is always intentional:
Assumption of action intentionality

$$(DOES\ x\ a) \supset \exists p \big[(P\text{-}GOAL\ x\ p) \wedge (DOES\text{-}FOR\ x\ a\ p)\big]$$

that is: *if an agent performs an action whatsoever he has a given p as a persistent goal and performs that action to achieve p.*

However, not all the consequences of one's actions are desired, that is:

$$\neg\big(((DONE\text{-}BY\ x\ a) \supset p) \supset (DONE\text{-}FOR\ x\ a\ p)\big)$$

As we know from the definition of (*done–for x a p*), two further conditions would have to be true for the above conclusion to be allowed: namely, that agent x has the goal p, and that he believes that the action done implies next p.

Glossary

Note: Italics denote that the term is defined in the glossary. The first instance of a defined term in the body of the text is indicated by bold type.

achievement goal, a *goal* that is not true now but will eventually become true.

action, a relation holding among *agent*(s), *goal*(s), and, possibly, *resource*(s). An *agent* acts when it causes an *achievement goal* to become true.

adaptive cognition, a set of mental states (*beliefs*, *goals*, etc.), and some basic principles and rules to manipulate them, that allow a system to behave adaptively.

adoption rule (AR), a corollary of the *GGR*; if an *agent* believes that adopting a *goal* of a given *agent* is a means for his obtaining one of his own *goals*, he will adopt that *goal*.

agent, a system, either *goal-governed* or *goal-oriented*, that has the capacity to produce some effects in the world thanks to a regulatory mechanism whatsoever (be it based upon some internal *goal* or simply appearing as such).

aggressive goal, an *agent* wants to attack another *agent*, when the former *agent* wants the latter not to achieve one of her *goals*.

as-if goal, a regulatory mechanism (for example, a reactive device) that does not imply an explicitly represented *goal* within the concerned system, but all the same allows it to produce certain results, *as if* the system were regulated by an explicit *internal goal*.

assumption of action ability, if an *agent* performs an *action*, it has that *action* in its repertoire.

assumption of action competence, if an *agent* performs a primitive *action*, it believes it has done so, and vice versa.

assumption of action intentionality, if an *agent* performs an *action* it must have a *persistent goal* for which it performs that *action*.

assumption of failure-competence, when an *agent* performs a given *action* for achieving a given *goal* and fails, it will then believe it has not obtained its *goal*.

autonomous agent, endowed with the capacity to generate and pursue its own *goals*.

belief is a representation which the *agent* tries to liken to the world.

bilateral dependence, two *agents* depending upon each other.

cognitive agent, a goal-governed *agent* endowed with a cognitive regulatory apparatus, also called *mind*, consisting of symbolic representations of *goals* and *beliefs*, and the capacity to manipulate (confront, modify, etc.) them.

cognitive modelling, an explicit account of the symbolic representations and the operations performed upon them, which are involved in mental activities, including understanding, problem-solving, reasoning, planning, communicating, and many forms of learning.

collective agent, a set of complementary *agents* executing the *actions* they are competent upon. In a stronger sense, a collective *agent* is a set of mutually co-operating agents.

collective mind, when either a multi-agent plan is iterated in the *minds* of all the *complementary agents* needed to execute the *plan* (decentralized co-operation); or a multi-agent *plan* is broken down in the *minds* of some *complementary agents* needed for the *plan* to be fully detailed; in the latter case, not only the execution of the *plan*, but also the mental activity implied by the *plan* ideation requires a set of complementary individual *minds*.

common world, a multi-agent world where the agents' mental states and skills bear consequences on one another's achievements.

complementary agents, with regard to a given *goal*, when there is a third *agent* who is dependent on all of them to achieve that *goal*.

concurrence, when two or more *agents* depend on one and the same *resource*, and the *resource* cannot be used by both at once.

contracting, a communication module where any contractor unit that needs *co-operation* can send out requests, and bidding units, if any, will send messages of acceptance in return.

co-operation, occurs when two or more *agents* intentionally achieve a common *goal*, that is, a *goal* with regard to which the *agents* depend on one another.

copy goal, an *internal goal* identical to an *external goal* and derived from it. The *external goal* is explicitly represented within the *mind*.

decentralized (or distributed) control, a AI-based method for designing systems – mainly used for more or less complex performances, from perception to problem-solving – whose overall performance is distributed over a number of interacting units and where the co-ordination of the tasks accomplished by these units is achieved, at least to some extent, without resorting to a central co-ordinating unit.

emergent properties, properties of a phenomenon that can neither be attributed to its elements or aspects nor be derived by a one-to-one correspondence from the properties of such elements or aspects. Emergent properties consist of either a synchronic differentiation of the phenomenon into levels of complexity, or a diachronic differentiation of the phenomenon into stages evolutionarily, historically, or developmentally linked to one another.

exchange, *x* and *y* engage in exchange when each adopts the other's *goal* on condition that the other will reciprocate.

external goal, an entity has an external goal when it is somehow influenced or determined not only by chance but by the fact that it is mentioned in one agent's *goal*.

extracognitive causes include the objective, structural relationships holding among *agents* situated in a common world and the functional mechanisms, such as those underlying the spreading of conventions and the formation of elementary forms of *co-operation*.

favour, factual help; an agent benefits another when at least one of the accidental consequences of an *action* done by the former coincides with a *goal* of the latter.

finality, a selecting effect; an effect produced by an entity that modifies the characteristics of that entity in a way that will render it more apt (to achieve its *goals* or *functions* to survive etc.). Social finalities work on social systems and structures in a way analogous to biological finalities operating on organisms: as external goals operating on objects or goal-governed systems.

formal (model) is meant here in a more general sense than is implied by the use of a mathematical or logic-based language. By this term, we mean something very similar to Ullman-Margalit's notion of *formal* (1977: 6–7) and Weber's notion of *ideal-type*, that is to say, as referring to the abstract and structural aspects of the situations of study. As a consequence, concrete, idiosyncratic aspects of the phenomena will be ignored.

function, an *external* goal placed on an entity that has resulted in a modification of the system; function is a special case of *finality*, because it is a selecting mechanism. It differs from a *finality* because, while a *finality* is a selecting effect and does not presuppose any *goal-governed system*, a function is attributed by a *goal-governed system* (e.g., a human being) to an entity (e.g., an artefact).

functional action, an *action* oriented toward a given *finality*; the *action's* effect is neither deliberate nor accidental; the *action* is undertaken precisely because it produces that effect. The effect is thus a *finality* and the *action* is functional to the effect produced.

goal, a sieve that selects the properties of a system (whether they be morphological or behavioural properties, *actions*) so that we may say that at the time T_1 such a system's properties are not the result of chance, but the result of a preceding history (T_0) that consists of the rejection created as a result of the sieve's sifting the alternatives (actual or symbolic) of a given property. In a stronger sense, a *goal* is internally represented in a system (see *internal goal*).

goal adoption, an *agent* adopts another *agent's* goal when he wants the latter to achieve that *goal*.

goal-autonomous, whatever new *goal* such an *agent* comes to have, there is at least another *goal* of its own to which the *agent* believes the new *goal* is instrumental.

goal-generation rule (GGR), an *agent* will have as a *goal* any state that implies that another of its *goals* will be achieved.

goal-governed (or deliberate) **system**, an entity, not necessarily autonomous, that has the capacity to achieve a *goal* that is internally represented in it. A *goal-governed system* is not necessarily cognitive either: it is not cognitive when the representation of the *goal* is not symbolic and does not allow any mental manipulation (comparison, modification, reasoning, etc.).

goal-oriented system, a system or behaviour directed towards implementing a specific state of the world that is not internally represented in it, and whose underlying regulatory mechanism is often based upon a mere reflex, or releaser. *Goal-oriented systems* act as if they were *goal-governed systems*. [In a broad sense, they also cover goal-directed systems, i.e. systems, or behaviour, directed towards implementing a specific state of the world through an internal regulatory mechanism]

goal of influencing, an *agent x* has the *goal* of influencing another *agent* when he wants that *agent* to have a new *goal*.

interest, an objective world state facilitating a given *goal's* achievement. An interest relation holds between one *agent* with his mental states and some external state of affairs when a given state of the world implies another world state, and the latter is a *goal* or subgoal of the *agent's*.

interest conflict, the same world state is an *interest* with regard to one given *goal* while it is a counter-interest with regard to another.

interference, when a given *agent's* action implies another *agent's* pursuing, and then achieving, her *goal*.

internal goal, a regulatory representation of the world internal to a *goal-governed system* that, if possible and necessary, the system endeavours, through its actions, to liken the world to.

internalization, the process through which an *external goal* gives rise to a copy goal within the agent upon which the *external goal* is placed thanks to a number of different processes and mechanisms (goal adoption, selection, training).

legitimate goal, a norm-protected *goal*; a legitimate goal is such that, if it clashes with another *goal*, it is obligatory for the latter to yield.

micro–macro link, connections between the macro-social systems and their members.

mind, see *cognitive agent*.

multi-agent system (MAS), also called social system or macro-system, a special type of *goal-oriented system*; an aggregate of *agents* (be they individuals or multi-agent subsystems) that produce given effects in the world by means of a more or less complex and formal organization, acting as if their behaviour were goal-governed.

mutual belief, two or more *agents* sharing (a) a given *belief*; (b) the *belief* that each believes it; (c) the *belief* that each believes that they all believe it.

mutual dependence, when *agents* depend on one another to achieve one and the same *goal*.

negative interference, when an *agent's* reaching his *goal* prevents another from reaching one of hers.

norm adoption, the formation of a *normative goal* from a *normative belief*, thanks to some intervening rules (GGR and AR).

norm-defending goal, having the *goal* that what is required by a given norm will happen.

norm-governed system, a *goal-governed system* with norms internally represented in such a way that they can be reasoned about, decided upon, etc.

normative belief, a belief that there is an *obligation* on a given set of *agents* to do a given *action*; it implies the *belief* that a legitimate authority has a *normative influencing goal* that the set of *agents* forms a normative belief and *goal* in the *interest* of some superset of *agents*. The authority is included in this superset and may coincide with it.

normative belief of pertinence, an *agent* has a *normative belief* relative to a set of *agents*, and believes that he is included in the set.

normative decision-making, the process leading from a *normative goal* to compliance or transgression of a norm.

normative equity principle, *agents* want their normative costs to be no higher than those of other *agents* subject to the same norms.

normative goal, an internal goal relativized to a *normative belief*.

normative influencing goal, a *goal* to generate an *obligation* for a set of *agents* to do a given *action*.

normative reasoning, mental operation upon the internal representation of a given norm, which may lead to that norm being adopted, thereby forming a *normative goal*.

objective pre-conditions of social interaction. Any relation occurring either between two (or more) *agents* or between one single *agent* and the external physical world is defined as objective. To assess whether a relation is objective we must take the stance of a non-participant observer (namely, the scientist's point of view): objective relations are those relations that are described at least in the observer's *mind* and that may or may not be described also in the *minds* of the *agents* involved.

obligation, a mental object that represents a necessity on propositions that describe the results or the performance of *actions*.

persistent goal, a *goal* that the *agent* believes to be neither realized nor unachievable.

plan, a set of *actions* which converge on at least one and the same *goal*.

plan-autonomous help-giver; can only have *goals* as means to achieve *goals* of others (that can be either adopted by, or built into the *agent*).

pragmatic learning rule, if a primitive action is done for a *goal* and the *goal* is not achieved, the *agent* will believe that its causal belief concerning the link between the *action* and the *goal* is false.

precognitive relations, objective relations which are neither wanted nor believed by the involved *agents.*

prevailing interest, relative to a given agent the world state that comparatively favours the highest number of *goals* of that *agent's* with the highest probability.

rational choice principle, principle of maximum expected utility: between two options, that which ensures the maximum outcome compared with the relative probability of occurrence will be chosen by a rational *agent.*

reciprocal dependence when *agents* depend on each other for realizing different *goals.*

reciprocation, an *agent's* adopting someone's *goal* relativized to the belief that the latter has adopted one or more of the agent's *goals.*

relativized goal, a *goal* that can be abandoned either because it is found already realized or unachievable or if a given condition is believed to hold no longer. Essentially, this means that the *agent* has that *goal* as long as and because he has a given *belief.*

reputation, set of evaluations that interacting social agents make about one another.

resource, anything that is involved in the *action*, except the *agent.*

resource dependence, an *agent* depends on a *resource* relative to a given *goal* of its own, when that *resource* is involved in doing an *action* that achieves that *goal.*

respondent internal goal, an *internal goal* of a system by means of which the system is able to respond to the *external goal* placed on it, but which is not identical to the *external goal.*

self-interested agents, *agents* who adopt other *agents'* goals as long as and because these are means for the former *agents* to achieve their own *goals.*

social action, an *action* achieving a *goal* that mentions another *agent's* mental state.

social commitment, an *agent* commits himself to do a given *action* before another *agent* when they agree that the former *agent* adopts one of the latter agent's *goals*; the former *agent* thereby deliberately creates the condition for a norm to concern him, and a *legitimate goal* in the latter *agent* to expect and control that he does that *action.*

social dependence, a resource dependence where *resources* are filled in by social *agents*; an *agent* depends on another with regard to an act useful for realizing a given state when that state is a *goal* of the former *agent* and it is unable to realize it, while the latter *agent* is able to do so.

social simulation, the computer-based reproduction of social processes and phenomena.

social structures or phenomena, inert objective social conditions, such as resources of various kinds, that affect the agents' behaviours. An example at the macro-level is the division of labour.

subcognitive systems, *goal-governed systems* that are not endowed with a cognitive regulatory apparatus, e.g. reactive systems that do not calculate the utility of their *actions*, nor plan, *sensu stricto*, to achieve what they obtain; or subsymbolic systems, acting on a neural network base.

teleological, a phenomenon, or entity, the characteristics of which reflect someone's *goal*.

tutorial goal, an influencing *goal vis-à-vis* another *agent* that, once achieved, is believed to realize a given interest of the influenced agent.

unilateral dependence, one agent depends on another to achieve one of his goals.

Notes

Introduction

1. Also called agents; in line with Rao et al. (1992), we will maintain the term agent even when referring to multi-agent subsystems.
2. By these is meant a more general notion than that of social system; social structures include inert objective conditions, such as resources of various kinds, that affect the agents' behaviour. For example, the division of labour is a social structure which affects social agents, but can hardly be defined as an agent. Some organizations, e.g. a firm or institution, such as a Parliament, can be viewed as agents, or even as goal-governed systems.
3. In our terms, a social goal is defined as a goal that is *directed towards* another agent; in particular, a truly social goal aims at modifying some mental state of another agent (cf. Ch. 2).

Chapter 1

1. From now on, the following convention will be used: the pronoun "it" will be used for isolated agents, in dyads, the male pronoun will be used to refer to agent x (often, speaker or help giver), while the female pronoun will be applied to y (listener or recipient). This convention will be maintained throughout the book, unless otherwise specified.
2. For example, our notion of favour differs from von Martial's (1990), since the latter is a cognitive and intentional relationship of help.
3. Since an interest is referred to as an achievement goal and an achievement goal is a state that the agent wants to be achieved sometime in the future, a conflict of interest may occur only when there is a temporal do-reference between the considered interests. We thank Phil Cohen for this suggestion.

Chapter 2

1. If x believes there is an interest-conflict between his goal p and y's goal z, and x also believes that p is true, he will next have the goal to either influence y not to

pursue her goal or prevent her from assuming that p is true.

2. One could ask why a simple request should be considered aggressive. For example, Adam might ask Eve: "Please, do not put your cube on the one I need!" Now, this may be ineffective but is not aggressive. However, what remains aggressive is Adam's higher-level goal: if Adam does *not* want Eve to achieve her goal, his goal is aggressive even though, to obtain it, Adam resorts to a non-aggressive strategy.

Chapter 3

1. For example, in his proposal for a commitment-based analysis of co-operative work, Fikes (1982) suggested that the basic criterion for successful task completion and commitment fulfilment was the *satisfaction of the client*.

2. This is not at all obvious. Consider the case in which *y's point of view differs from both x's and the observer's*: y believes that glass is more valuable than gold (it is brighter, can be looked through, etc.). From the observer's point of view, y is poorer than he was before the so-called exchange took place. However, from y's point of view, he is richer. He enjoyed the exchange and feels he has been rewarded. Indeed, evaluative criteria are considered as necessarily subjective and variable. Typically, zelators of free negotiation bring this argument into play when they claim that exchange is fair as long as it is *perceived* as such by the partners. However, such a conclusion seems unwarranted: that evaluative criteria necessarily differ among agents does not mean that they are necessarily *adaptive* for each agent. Since interests are not necessarily believed, it follows that even evaluative beliefs can contrast with the agent's prevailing interest. Assuming that glass is more valuable than gold is a standard which clashes with one's own interests. Consequently, if an explorer gives natives glass and takes gold, is he socially culpable or not? This is a rather complicated question that has kept moral philosophers busy for ages, and we are not going to disentangle it here!

Chapter 4

1. We do not introduce a quantitative definition of this notion since it presents evident similarities with the current notion of utility (see Luce & Raiffa 1989/1990); see also Savage (1990) for a re-formulation of von Neumann and Morgenstern's (1953) notion of utility. However, two important differences should be kept in mind:

   (a) in our view, a *prevailing interest* is not necessarily expected by the agent. The theory of interests presented here requires an external observer, one that has sufficient information to evaluate world states in the light of one agent's goals and to predict relevant changes in the latter.

   (b) Consequently, our theory of interests is *prescriptive*, in the sense that it allows us to state which goals agents should have. However, like any other prescriptive theory, it needs to be integrated with a *descriptive* theory of the agents' behaviours. Agents are not primarily motivated to act by their interests. They are driven by their goals. One of the functions fulfilled by social interaction is pushing agents to realize their own interests.

2. Obviously, if x is wrong about y's interests, he may harm her interests considerably. What is more, x may pretend to know y's interests, and deceitfully persuade her to implement something that is not in y's, but in x's own interest.

3. One interesting answer that is peripheral to the present discussion is that agents do not like to achieve useless goals, whether their own or others'.

4. Of course, this reward also includes personal prestige and social reputation. As argued so far, however, none of them can justify the adoption of the beneficiaries' interests.

Chapter 5

1. We owe the careful reading of this passage to Ullman-Margalit (1977: 68–69).

2. Transgressors resort to a variety of self-justifying arguments, such as: "if this norm had been applied equitably, I would be eager to observe it; but as things are . . . ". Indeed, this line of reasoning apparently implies that norms should be in fact observed more (or better) than they are.

3. Ullman-Margalit finds that a definition of norms according to which a norm is "an entity which has causal power and which interacts with and directs people and groups" (Morgenbesser 1967: 161) is in danger of reification. We wonder, however, in what respect the above definition essentially differs from Hart's (1961) characterization of norms as prescribed conducts, which instead Ullman-Margalit agrees with.

4. Sidgwick's (1962) famous dilemma between *selfish rationality* and *co-operative rationality* (cf. Magri 1986) is a subcase of the present dilemma: the question is not really how selfish agents can co-operate, but rather how autonomous agents (be they selfish or not) accept requests from an external source.

5. In line with Rao et al.'s (1992) recursive notion of social agent, we propose a recursive notion of autonomous agent that may be referred to both the individual and the multi-agent levels of complexity (see Ch. 10).

Chapter 6

1 . By a cognitive approach we here mean something radically different from what is referred to as *cognitivistic analysis* by moral philosophers (such as Ayer 1936, Stevenson 1937, Hare 1952) dealing with norms and normative judgement (for a recent formulation, cf. Gibbard 1990). While the philosophical sense of cognitivistic analysis seems to refer to the truth value of propositions, here *explicit, symbolic representations and operations required by a cognitive system's activity* will be referred to as cognitive. A cognitive approach to norms and obligations, although formal, does not necessarily coincide with the semantic study of normative utterances known as deontic logic, which, to use Ullman-Margalit's (1977: 6) definition, investigates "the validity of arguments in which" [terms such as] "obligatory", "permissible", and "forbidden" occur. In a cognitive study

of norms, the focus is not on the semantic value of propositions about obligations, but on the status that obligations have in the agents' minds, the possible interrelationships among obligations and other mental states, and, hence, the role that obligations have in controlling the agents' behaviours.

2. As in Rao et al. (1992) the definition of a social entity should be recursive. Therefore, what has been said with regard to the group as a whole applies to its subcomponents as well. In case z in turn is a multi-agent subcomponent, its will might be shared or not among its members. Its task (say, to legislate) might be accomplished in such a way that not all members share the same goals.

3. Utilitarian theorists would object that, *if* maintaining a MAS is useful for *all* its members, then the global utility will also break down into local utilities, at least in the long run. However, in such a case distributive rationality is only consequent to the collective rationality.

Chapter 7

1. Indeed, it is unreasonable to hypothesize that the decrease of normative behaviour is a linear function of the ratio between diminishing costs of transgression and increasing costs of obedience. As with the spreading of co-operation vs. defeat (cf. Glance & Huberman 1993), it is more plausible that, after some time interval in which the frequency of normative behaviours has been essentially steady, it falls dramatically. This hypothesis ought to be tested in repeated computer simulations of the phenomenon (cf. Ch. 11).

2. Norm obedience is to some extent costly: if the action is prescribed by a norm, it is probably unlikely that it will be done spontaneously (cf. Bicchieri 1990). As stated by Hart (1961; cf. Chapter 5, paragraph 2.1.2), indeed, a norm is characterized by its clashing with what the agents owing the duty wish to do. It does not correspond to what the agents would do on their own. Therefore, it implies some cost.

3. We take this principle exactly in the sense of classical equity theory. Unfortunately, for the time being, our model does not include a treatment of costs of actions. Therefore, we cannot provide a formal expression of this deduction.

4. We take this notion in the sense formally defined by Miceli & Castelfranchi (1989).

5. This is rather tricky. If one considers the alternative co-operation/defeat, a distributively rational outcome seems impossible, for what is rational for the agents at the individual level is irrational for them at the social level. However, game theorists hypothesize that what is rational at the individual level in one-shot games, is irrational in the long run. In the long run, therefore, the paradox seems to find a solution. Distributive rationality, at least in the game-theoretic sense, implies repeated interactions.

6. Within the game-theoretic perspective, instead, individual agents are *not* expected to be interested in the *maintenance* of the social group, nor in repeated games. Indeed, in games repeated a finite number of times, the last player is favoured since he can choose to play defeat without worrying about the consequences.

7. An example is "Haken's swimming pool" where people swim at random with

consequent frequent collisions, up to a point where agents find a conventional order (i.e. Hayek's spontaneous order, cf. Radnitzky 1993: 12) by chance, like swimming in a circular fashion.

8. Ethologists (Eibl-Eibesfeldt 1989; de Waal 1982) have shown that, to some extent, some precepts, like the *finders-keepers*, may be found even among our primate ancestors.

Chapter 10

1. Such an analysis, indeed, reformulates Tuomela & Miller's (1988) analysis of the *We-intentions*.
2. An analogous point is made by Searle (1990).
3. It is not clear how the philosophical notion of *I-intention* should be recast into a cognitive or AI formalism: as will be discussed in the following section of this chapter, an intention may be directed toward another social entity while remaining individual, at the same time. Now, whether the notion of *I-intention* can be extended to cover even the latter notion of individual *social* intention is not clear to us.

Chapter 11

1. As defined in the Introduction a resource is anything involved in the performance of an action. Social dependence may be derived from a resource dependence. *DEPNET* calculates also resource dependences, which for the sake of conciseness, we do not show here (but see Sichman et al. 1994a).

Appendix

1. Especially those derived from its treatment of time. In all the work of Cohen and Levesque, as well as in the present model, time is treated as a linear dimension, as an infinite succession of events. This feature has been shown to be responsible for a number of defects. *Inter alia*, it has led to what is usually known as the problem of *over-commitment*. Given the possible world semantics and the linear notion of time, what is implicit in someone's goals is *closed under consequence*: if x wants a hole in his tooth to be filled by a dentist, and the relevant dental care causes him some toothache, in the model presented here it follows that x wants to have toothache. This is what is usually known as the problem of over-commitment. In a branching time model, such as Rao & Georgeff's (1991), over-commitment is not allowed.

Bibliography

Agre, P. E. 1989. *The dynamic structure of everyday life*. Phd thesis, Department of Electrical Engineering and Computer Science, Massachusetts Institute of Technology.

Agre, P. E. & D. Chapman 1987. PENGI: An implementation of a theory of activity. *Proceedings of the 6th Conference of the American Association of Artificial Intelligence*, 268–73. Los Altos, California: Kaufmann.

Alexander, J. C., B. Giesen, R. Muench, N. J. Smelser (eds) 1987. *The micro–macro link*. Berkeley: University of California Press.

Alterman, R. 1988. Adaptive planning. *Cognitive Science* **12**, 393–421.

Axelrod, R. 1984. *The evolution of co-operation*. New York: Basic Books.

Axelrod, R. & D. Dion 1988. The further evolution of co-operation. *Nature* **242**, 1385–90.

Ayer, A. J. 1936. *Language, truth and logic*. London: Victor Gollancz.

Bell, J. 1993. Changing attitudes. In *Working Notes of AAAI Workshop on Reasoning about mental states: formal theories and applications*, 20–30. Stanford University, California.

Berger, P. L. & T. Luckmann 1966. *The social construction of reality*. New York: Doubleday.

Bicchieri, C. 1989. Self-refuting theories of strategic interaction: a paradox of common knowledge. *Erkenntnis* **30**, 68–95.

Bicchieri, C. 1990. Norms of co-operation. *Ethics* **100**, 838–861.

Bicchieri, C. & M. L. Dalla Chiara (eds) 1992. *Knowledge, belief, and strategic interaction*. Cambridge: Cambridge University Press.

Binmore, K. 1987. Modeling rational players I & II. *Economics and Philosophy* **3**, 9–55; **4**, 179–214.

Blau, P. M. 1964. *Exchange and power in social life*. New York: John Wiley.

Blumer, H. 1969. *Symbolic interactionism*. Englewood Cliffs, New Jersey: Prentice-Hall.

Bond, A. H. 1991. Commitments and projects. In *Proceedings of the AISB Conference 1991*, 115–21. London: Pitman.

Bond, A. H. & L. Gasser (eds) 1988. *Readings in Distributed Artificial Intelligence*. San Mateo, California: Kaufmann.

Bourgine, P. & F. J. Varela (eds) 1991. Towards a practice of autonomous systems. In *Proceedings of the 1st European Conference on Artificial Life*, I–XXX. Cambridge, Mass.: MIT Press.

Bouron, T. 1992. *Structures de communication et d'organisation pour la coopération dans un univers multi-agents.* These de Doctorat, LAFORIA, Université Paris.

Bragato, P. L. & V. Roberto 1993. *Communication among perceiving agents,* Technical Report (Department of Mathematics and Computer Science, University of Udine), 04.

Brooks, R. A. 1989. *A robot that walks. Emergent behaviours from a carefully evolved network.* Technical Report of Artificial Intelligence Laboratory. Cambridge, Mass.: MIT Press.

Castelfranchi, C. 1990. Social power: a missed point in DAI, MA and HCI. In *Decentralized AI.* Y. Demazeau & J. P. Mueller (eds), 49–62. Amsterdam: Elsevier.

Castelfranchi, C. 1991. Forse tu non pensavi che io loica fossi. *Sistemi Intelligenti.* 1, 141–159.

Castelfranchi, C. 1992. No more co-operation, please! In search of the social structure of verbal interaction. In *AI and Cognitive Science Perspectives on Communication,* A. Ortony, J. Slack, O. Stock (eds), 205–28. Berlin: Springer.

Castelfranchi, C. 1993a. Principles of bounded autonomy. Modelling autonomous agents in a multi-agent world. *Pre-proceedings of the 1st round-table discussion on Abstract Intelligent Agent – AIA '93.* Rome: ENEA.

Castelfranchi, C. 1993b. Commitments: from individual intentions to groups and organizations. In *Working Notes of AAAI '93 Workshop on AI and theory of groups and organizations: conceptual and empirical research,* 35–41. Washington D. C.

Castelfranchi, C. & R. Conte 1991. Problemi di rappresentazione mentale delle norme. In *Le norme. Mente e regolazione sociale,* R. Conte (ed.), 157–93. Rome: Editori Riuniti.

Castelfranchi, C. & R. Conte 1992. Functionality among intelligent systems in interaction: co-operation within and without minds. *AI & Society* 6, 78–93.

Castelfranchi, C. & D. Parisi 1984. Mente e scambio sociale. *Rassegna Italiana di Sociologia* 1, 45–72.

Castelfranchi, C., A. Cesta, R. Conte, M. Miceli 1989. Pragmatic knowledge for social interaction. In *Proceedings of the 1st Conference of the Italian Association of Artificial Intelligence,* 165–75. Genoa: Center International Books.

Castelfranchi, C., R. Conte, A. Cesta 1992a. The organization as a structure of negotiated and non negotiated binds. In *Human Computer Interaction: tasks and organization. Proceedings of the 6th European Conference on cognitive ergonomics (ECCE6),* G. C. van der Veer, M. J. Tauber, S. Bagnara, M. Antalovits (eds), 187–197. Hungary: EACE.

Castelfranchi, C., M. Miceli, A. Cesta 1992b. Dependence relations among autonomous agents. In *Decentralized AI – 3,* E. Werner, Y. Demazeau (eds), 215–31. Amsterdam: Elsevier.

Cesta, A. & M. Miceli 1993. In search of help: strategic social knowledge and plans. In *Proceedings of the 12th International Workshop of Distibuted Artificial Intelligence,* 35–49. Technical Report of Robotic Institute, Carnegie Mellon University, Hidden Valley, Pennsylvania.

Cohen, P. R. & H. J. Levesque 1987. *Persistence, intention, and commitment.* Technical Report 415 of SRI International, Menlo Park, California.

Cohen, P. R. & H. J. Levesque 1990a. Intention is choice with commitment. *Artificial Intelligence* 42(3), 213–61.

Cohen, P. R. & H. J. Levesque 1990b. Persistence, intention and commitment. In *Intentions in communication,* P. R Cohen, J. Morgan, M. Pollack (eds), 33–71.

Cambridge, Mass.: MIT Press.

Cohen, P. R. & H. J. Levesque 1990c. Rational interaction as the basis for communication. In *Intentions in communications*, P. R. Cohen, J. Morgan, M. A. Pollack (eds), 221–55. Cambridge, Mass.: MIT Press.

Cohen, P. R. & H. J. Levesque 1991. *Teamwork*. Technical Report 504 of SRI International, Menlo Park, California.

Cohen, P. R. & C. R. Perrault 1979. Elements of a plan-based theory of speech acts. *Cognitive Science* 3, 177–212.

Cohen, P. R., J. Morgan, M. Pollack (eds) 1990. *Intentions in communication*. Cambridge, Mass.: MIT Press.

Cole, M., J. Gay, J. A. Glick, D. W. Sharp 1971. *The cultural context of learning and thinking*. New York: Basic Books.

Cole, M., L. Hood, R. P. MacDermott 1978. *Ecological niche picking: ecological invalidity as an axiom of cognitive psychology*. Technical Report Laboratory of Comparative Human Cognition, University of California.

Conte, R. 1989. Institutions and intelligent systems. In *Operational research and the social sciences*, M. C. Jackson, P. Keys, S. A. Cropper (eds), 201–6. New York: Plenum.

Conte, R. 1994. Norme come prescrizioni: per un modello dell'agente autonomo normativo, *Sistemi Intelligenti* 6, 9–34.

Conte, R. (ed.) 1991. *La norma. Mente e regolazione sociale*. Rome: Editori Riuniti.

Conte, R. & C. Castelfranchi 1994. Mind is not enough. Precognitive bases of social action. In *Simulating societies: the computer simulation of social processes*, J. Doran & N. Gilbert (eds), 267–86. London: UCL Press.

Conte, R. & C. Castelfranci 1995. Understanding the functions of norms in social groups through simulation. In *Artificial societies: the computer simulation of social processes*, N. Gilbert & R. Conte (eds). London: UCL Press.

Conte, R. & C. Castelfranchi in press. Norms as mental objects. From normative beliefs to normative goals. In *Proceedings of the 5th European workshop on modelling autonomous agents in a multi-agent world*, J. P. Mueller, C. Castelfranchi (eds), Berlin: Springer.

Conte, R., M. Miceli, C. Castelfranchi 1991. Limits and levels of co-operation. Disentangling various types of prosocial interaction. In *Decentralized AI-2*, Y. Demazeau & J. P. Mueller (eds), 147–57. Amsterdam: Elsevier.

Covrigaru, A. A. & R. K. Lindsay 1991. Deterministic autonomous systems. *AI Magazine* Fall, 110–17.

Davies, R. & P. G. Smith 1983. Negotiation as metaphor for distributed problem-solving. *Artificial Intelligence* 20, 63–109.

Demazeau, Y. & J. P. Mueller (eds) 1990. *Decentralized AI*. Amsterdam: Elsevier.

Dennet, D. C. 1983. Intentional systems in cognitive ethology: the "Panglossian paradigm" defended. *The Behavioural and Brain Sciences* 6, 343–90.

Donaldson, L. 1985. *In defence of organisation theory. A reply to the critics*. Cambridge: Cambridge University Press.

Douglas, M. 1986. *How institutions think*. London: Routledge & Kegan Paul.

Durfee, E. H., V. R. Lesser, D. D. Corkill 1987a. Coherent co-operation among communicating problem-solvers, IEEE *Transactions in Computers* C–36, 1275–91.

Durfee, E. H., V. R. Lesser, D. D. Corkill 1987b. Co-operation through communication in a problem-solving network. In *Distributed Artificial Intelligence*, M. N.

Huhns (ed.), 29–58. San Mateo, California: Kaufmann.

Eibl-Eibesfeldt, I. 1989. *Human Ethology*. New York: Aldine de Gruyter.

Elster, J. 1985. *Sour grapes. Studies in the subversion of rationality*. Cambridge: Cambridge University Press.

Elster, J. 1987. *Rationality and social norms* University of Chicago, manuscript.

Ephrati, E. & J. Rosenschein in press. A framework for the interlearning of execution and planning for dynamic tasks by multi-agents. In *Proceedings of the 5th European workshop on modelling autonomous agents in a multi-agent world*, J. P. Mueller, C. Castelfranchi (eds), Berlin: Springer.

Fennell, R. D. & V. R. Lesser 1977. Parallelism in Artificial Intelligence problem solving: a case study of Hearsay–II. *IEEE Transactions on Computers* C–26, 98–111.

Fikes, R. E. 1982. A commitment-based framework for describing informal co-operative work. *Cognitive Science* 6, 331–47.

Fudenberg, D. & D. A. Kreps 1988. A theory of learning, experimentation, and equilibrium in games. Manuscript.

Galliers, J. R. 1988. A strategic framework for multi-agent co-operative dialogue. In *Proceedings of the 8th European Conference on Artificial Intelligence*, 415–20. London: Pitman.

Galliers, J. R. 1990. The positive role of conflict in co-operative multi-agent systems. In *Decentralized AI*, Y. Demazeau & J. P. Mueller (eds), 33–49. Amsterdam: Elsevier.

Galliers, J. R. 1991. Modelling autonomous belief revision in dialogue. In *Decentralized AI – 2*, Y. Demazeau & J. P. Mueller (eds), 231–45. Amsterdam:Elsevier.

Garfinkel, H. 1967. *Studies in ethnomethodology*. Englewood Cliffs, New Jersey: Prentice-Hall.

Gasser, L. 1988. Distribution and co-ordination of tasks among intelligent agents. In *Proceedings of the 1st Scandinavian Conference on Artificial Intelligence*, 177–92. Amsterdam: Elsevier.

Gasser, L. 1991a. Knowledge and action at social and organizational level. *Working Notes AAAI Fall Symposium*, Asilomar, California.

Gasser, L. 1991b. Social conceptions of knowledge and action: DAI foundations and open systems semantics. *Artificial Intelligence* 47, 107–38.

Gauthier, D. P. 1969. *The Logic of Leviathan*. Oxford: Oxford University Press.

Gibbard, A. 1990. *Wise choices, apt feelings. A theory of normative judgement*. Oxford: Clarendon Press.

Giddens, A. 1984. *The constitution of society*. Oxford: Polity.

Giesen, B. 1987. Beyond reductionism: four models relating micro- and macro-levels. In *The micro–macro link*, J. C. Alexander, B. Giesen, R. Muench, N. J. Smelser (eds), 337–55. Berkeley: University of California Press.

Gilbert, G. N. in press. "Emergence" in social simulation. In *Artificial societies: The computer simulation of social life*, G. N. Gilbert & R. Conte (eds), London: UCL Press.

Gilbert, G. N. & J. Doran (eds) 1994. *Simulating societies: The computer simulation of social phenomena*. London: UCL Press.

Glance, N. S. & B. A. Huberman 1993. The outbreak of co-operation. *Journal of Mathematical Sociology* 17, 281–302.

Goffman, E. 1959. *The presentation of self in everyday life*. New York: Doubleday.

Gouldner, A. Z. 1960. The norm of reciprocity: a preliminary statement. *American*

Sociological Review **25**, 161–74.

Greif, I. 1988. *Computer-supported co-operative work: a book of readings.* San Mateo, California: Kaufmann.

Grosz, B. J. & C. L. Sidner 1990. Plans for discourse. In *Intentions in communication*, P. R. Cohen, J. Morgan, M. E. Pollack (eds), 417–45. Cambridge, Mass.: MIT Press.

Halpern, J. Y. & Y. O. Moses 1985. A guide to the modal logics of knowledge and belief. *Proceedings of the 9th International Joint Conference on Artificial Intelligence*, 480–91. Los Altos, California: Kaufmann.

Hammond, K. J. 1986. CHEF: A model of case-based planning. *Proceedings of the 6th Conference of the American Association of Artificial Intelligence*, 267–72. Los Altos, California: Kaufmann.

Hare, R. M. 1952. *The language of morals.* Oxford: Oxford University Press.

Harsanyi, J. C. 1990. Advances in understanding rational behavior. In *Rationality in action. Contemporary approaches,* P. K. Moser (ed.), 271–93. New York: Cambridge University Press.

Hart, H. L. A. 1961. *The concept of law.* Oxford: Oxford University Press.

Hayek, F. A. 1948. *Individualism and economic order.* London: Routledge & Kegan Paul.

Hayek, F. A. 1976. *Law, legislation, and liberty, vol. II. The mirage of social justice.* London: Routledge & Kegan Paul.

Hayek, F. A. 1978. *New studies in philosophy, politics, economics, and the history of ideas.* London: Routledge & Kegan Paul.

Hewitt, C. 1991. Open information systems semantics for distributed artificial intelligence. *Artificial Intelligence* **47**, 79–106.

Hewitt, C. & P. de Jong 1983. Open systems. In *Perspectives on conceptual modeling*, M. L. Brodie, J. L. Mylopoulos, J. W. Schmidt (eds), 203–20, New York: Springer.

Hobbes, T. 1948. *Leviathan.* M. Oakeshott (ed.). Oxford: Oxford University Press.

Hobbs, J. R. 1990. Artificial Intelligence and collective intentionality: comments on Searle and on Grosz and Sidner. In *Intentions in communication,* P. R Cohen, J. Morgan, M. A. Pollack (eds), 445–59. Cambridge, Mass.: MIT Press.

Homans, G. C. 1959. *Social behavior: its elementary forms.* New York: Harcourt.

Jasay, A. de 1990. A stocktaking of perversities, *Critical review* **4**, 537–44.

Jennings, N. 1992. On being responsible. In *Decentralized AI – 3,* E. Werner & Y. Demazeau (eds), 93–103. Amsterdam: Elsevier.

Jennings, N. R. 1993. Commitments and conventions: the foundation of co-ordination in multi-agent systems. *The Knowledge Engineering Review* **3**, 223–50.

Jennings, N. R. & E. H. Mandami 1992. Using joint responsibility to co-ordinate collaborative problem solving in dynamic environments. In *Proceedings of the 10th National Conference on Artificial Intelligence*, 269–75. San Mateo, California: Kaufmann.

Jones, A. J. I. & I. Pörn 1986. Ought and Must, *Synthèse* **66**, 89–93.

Kelsen, H. 1934. *Reine Lechtslehre. Einleitung in die rechtswissenschaftliche Problematik.* Vienna: Deuticke Verlag.

Ketchpel, S. 1995. Coalition formation among autonomous agents. In *Proceedings of the 5th European workshop on modelling autonomous agents in a multi-agent world,* J. P. Mueller, C. Castelfranchi (eds), Berlin: Springer.

Knoke, D. 1990. *Political networks: the structural perspective,* Cambridge: Cambridge University Press.

Kreps, D., P. Milgrom, J. Roberts, R. Wilson 1982. Rational co-operation in the repeated Prisoners' Dilemma, *Journal of Economic Theory* **27**, 245–52.

Lesser, V. R & D. D. Corkill 1987. Distributed problem-solving. In *Encyclopaedia of Artificial Intelligence*, S. C. Shapiro (ed.), 245–51. New York: John Wiley.

Levesque, H. J., P. R. Cohen, J. H. T. Nunes 1990. On acting together. In *Proceedings of the 8th National Conference on Artificial Intelligence*, 94–100. San Mateo, California: Kaufmann..

Lewis, D. 1969. *Convention*. Cambridge, Mass.: Harvard University Press.

Lomborg, B. 1994. Game theory vs. multiple agents: The iterated Prisoners' Dilemma, in *Artificial social systems*, C. Castelfranchi & E. Werner (eds), Berlin: Springer.

Luce, R. D. & H. Raiffa. 1989. *Games and decisions*. New York: Dover (12–38); also appeared as: 1990. Utility theory. In *Rationality in action. Contemporary approaches*, P. K. Moser (ed.), 19–41. New York: Cambridge University Press.

McFarland, D. 1983. Intentions as goals, open commentary to D. C. Dennet, Intentional systems in cognitive ethology: the "Panglossian paradigm" defended. *The Behavioural and Brain Sciences* **6**, 343–90.

Magri, T. 1986. Teorie dell'azione e dilemmi della cooperazione. *Teoria Politica* **3**, 49–71.

Malone T. W. 1987. Modelling co-ordination in organizations and markets. *Management Science* **33**, 1317–32.

Malone, T. W. 1988. Organizing information-processing systems: parallels between human organizations and computer systems. In *Cognition, co-operation, and computation*, W. Zachary, S. Robertson, J. Black (eds), 78–90. Norwood, New Jersey: Ablex.

Manicas, P. 1987. *A history and philosophy of the social sciences*. Oxford: Basil Blackwell.

von Martial, F. 1990. Interactions among autonomous planning agents. In *Decentralized AI*, Y. Demazeau & J. P. Mueller (eds), 105–20. Amsterdam: Elsevier.

Maynard Smith, J. 1982. *Evolution and the theory of games* Cambridge: Cambridge University Press.

Mayr, E. 1982. Learning, development and culture. In *Essays in evolutionary epistemology*, H. C. Plotkin (ed.), 158–67. New York: John Wiley.

Mead, G. H. 1934. *Mind, self and society*. Chicago: University of Chicago Press.

Medeina-Mora, R., T. Winograd, F. Flores, R. Flores 1992. Work flow management technology: examples, implementations and new directions. *Proceedings of the 4th Computer Supported Co-operative Work Conference*. New York, ACM.

Miceli, M. & C. Castelfranchi 1989. A cognitive approach to values. *Journal for the Theory of Social Behaviour* **2**, 169–94.

Miceli, M. & A. Cesta 1993. Strategic social planning: looking for willingness in multi-agent domains. In *Proceedings of the 15th Annual Conference of the Cognitive Science Society*, 741–46. Hillsdale: Erlbaum.

Miller, G., E. Galanter, K. H. Pribram. 1960. *Plans and the structure of behavior*. New York: Holt, Rinehart & Winston.

Morgenbesser, S. 1967. Psychologism and methodological individualism. In *Philosophy of science today*, S. Morgenbesser (ed.), 150–59. New York: Basic Books.

Moses, Y. & M. Tennenholtz 1992. *On computational aspects of artificial social sys-*

tems. Technical Report CS91–01, Weizmann Institute.

Muench, R. & N. J. Smelser 1987. Relating the micro and the macro. In *The micro-macro link*, J. C. Alexander, B. Giesen, R. Muench, N. J. Smelser, (eds), 356–88. Berkeley: University of California Press.

von Neumann, J. & O. Morgenstern 1953. *Theory of games and economic behavior*. 3rd edn. Princeton: Princeton University Press.

van Parijs, P. 1982. Functionalist marxism rehabilited. A comment on Elster. *Theory and Society* **11**, 497–511.

Parunak, van Dyke H. 1987. Manufacturing experience with the contract net. In *Distributed Artificial Intelligence*, M. N. Huhns (ed.), 285–310. San Mateo, California: Kaufmann.

Parunak, van Dyke H. 1990. Distributed AI and manufacturing control: some issues and insights. In *Decentralized AI*, Y. Demazeau & J. P. Mueller (eds.), 81–101. Amsterdam: Elsevier.

Pearl, J. 1993. A calculus of pragmatic obligation. AAAI *Working Notes "Reasoning about mental states: formal theories and applications"*, 96–106. Stanford University, California.

Pears, D. 1984. *Motivated irrationality*. Oxford: Clarendon Press.

Pollack, M. A. 1990. Plans as complex mental attitudes. In *Intentions in Communication*, P. R Cohen, J. Morgan, M. Pollack (eds), 77–105. Cambridge, Mass.: MIT Press.

Power, R. 1984. Mutual intention. *Journal for the Theory of Social Behavior* **14**, 85–101.

Radnitzky, G. 1993. Knowledge, values and the social order in Hayek's oeuvre. *Journal of Social and Evolutionary Systems* **1**, 9–24.

Rao, A. S. & M. P. Georgeff 1991. Modelling rational agents within a BDI architecture. In *Proceedings of the International Conference on Principles of Knowledge Representation and Reasoning*, J. Allen, R. Fikes, E. Sandewall (eds), 473–85. San Mateo, California: Kaufmann.

Rao, A. S., M. P. Georgeff, E. A. Sonenmerg 1992. Social plans: a preliminary report. In *Decentralized AI – 3*, E. Werner & Y. Demazeau (eds), 57–77. Amsterdam: Elsevier.

Rasmusen, E. 1990. *Games and information: an introduction to game theory*. Oxford: Basil Blackwell.

Reddy, M. & G. M. P. O'Hare 1991. The blackboard model: a survey of its application. *Artificial Intelligence Review* **5**, 169–86.

Resnick, L. B., J. M. Levine, S. D. Teasley (eds) 1990. *Perspectives on socially shared cognition*. American Psychological Association, Washington D.C.

Riegel, K. F. & J. A. Meacham (eds) 1975. *The developing individual in a changing world: historical and cultural issues*. The Hague: Mouton.

Rizzo, P., A. Cesta, M. Miceli 1994. Basic ingredients for modeling help-giving in multi-agent systems. In *Draft Proceedings of the 2nd International Working Conference on Co-operative Knowledge Based Systems (CKBS94)*, Keele, England, 453–64.

Rosenblueth, A. & N. Wiener 1968. Purposeful and non-purposeful behavior. In *Modern systems research for the behavioral scientist*, W. Buckley, (ed.), 372–76. Chicago: Aldine.

Rosenblueth, A., N. Wiener, J. Bigelow 1968. Behavior, purpose, and teleology. In

Modern systems research for the behavioral scientist, W. Buckley, (ed.), 368–72. Chicago: Aldine.

Rosenschein, J. S. & M. R. Genesereth 1988. Deals among rational agents. In *The ecology of computation,* B. A. Huberman (ed.), 117–32. Amsterdam: Elsevier.

Ross, A. 1968. *Directives and norms.*London: Routledge & Kegan Paul.

Savage, L.J. 1990. Historical and critical comments on utility. In *Rationality in action: contemporary approaches.* P. K. Moser (ed.), 41–55. Cambridge: Cambridge University Press.

Schegloff, E. A. 1987. Between macro and micro: contexts and other connections. In *The micro–macro link,* J. C. Alexander, B. Giesen, R. Muench, N. J. Smelser (eds), 207–36. Berkeley: University of California Press.

Schelling, T. C. 1960. *The strategy of conflict.* Oxford: Oxford University Press.

Schotter, A. 1981. *The economic theory of social institutions.* Cambridge: Cambridge University Press.

Scribner, S. 1975. Situating the experiment in cross-cultural research. In *The developing individual in a changing world: historical and cultural issues,* K. F. Riegel & J. A. Meacham (eds), 316–21. The Hague: Mouton.

Searle, J. R. 1969. *Speech Acts.* Cambridge: Cambridge University Press.

Searle, J. R. 1990. Collective intentions and actions. In *Intentions in communication,* P. R. Cohen, J. Morgan, M. Pollack (eds), 401–15. Cambridge, Mass.: MIT Press.

Shechory, O. & S. Kraus in press. Coalition formation among autonomous agents: strategies and complexity. In *Proceedings of the 5th European workshop on modelling autonomous agents in a multi-agent world,* J. P. Mueller, C. Castelfranchi (eds), Berlin: Springer.

Shoham, Y. & M. Tennenholtz 1992a. On the synthesis of useful social laws in artificial societies. *Proceedings of the 10th National Conference on Artificial Intelligence,* 276–82. San Mateo, California: Kaufmann.

Shoham, Y. & M. Tennenholtz 1992b. Emergent conventions in multi-agent systems: Initial experimental results and observations. In *Proceedings of the International Conference on Principles of Knowledge Representation and Reasoning,* 225–32. San Mateo, California: Kaufmann.

Sichman, J., R. Conte, Y. Demazeau 1994a. Reasoning about others using dependence networks. *Atti del D-AI*IA '93, Incontro del Gruppo dell'Associazione Italiana di Intelligenza Artificiale di Interesse Speciale sull'Intelligenza Artificiale Distribuita,* 113–24. Rome: Fondazione Ugo Bordoni.

Sichman, J., R. Conte, C. Castelfranchi, Y. Demazeau 1994b. A social reasoning mechanism based on dependence networks. In *Proceedings of the 11th European Conference on Artificial Intelligence,* Amsterdam.

Sidgwick, H. 1962. *The methods of ethics.* London: Macmillan.

Steels, L. 1990. Co-operation between distributed agents through self-organisation. In *Decentralized* AI, Y. Demazeau & J. P. Muller (eds), 175–97. Amsterdam: Elsevier.

Stevenson, C. 1937. The emotive theory of ethical terms. *Mind* **46**, 14–31.

Suchman, L. A. 1987. *Plans and situated actions: the problem of human-machine communication.* Cambridge: Cambridge University Press.

Tuomela, R. 1989. Collective action, supervenience, and constitution. *Synthèse* **80**, 243–66.

Tuomela, R. 1991. We will do it: an analysis of group-intentions. *Philosophy and*

Phenomenological Research **11**, 249–77.

Tuomela, R. 1993. What are joint intentions? In *Philosophy and the cognitive sciences*, R. Casati & G. White (eds), 543–47, Vienna: Austrian Ludwig Wittgenstein Society.

Tuomela, R. 1994. *The importance of "us"*. Palo Alto, California: Stanford University Press.

Tuomela, R. & K. Miller 1988. We-intentions. *Philosophical Studies* **53**, 367–89.

Ullman-Margalit, E. 1977. *The emergence of norms*. Oxford: Clarendon Press.

Waal, F. de 1982. *Chimpanzee politics*. London: Jonathan Cape.

Watkins, W. J. N. 1952. The principle of methodological individualism. *British Journal for the Philosophy of Science* **3**, 186–9.

Werner, E. 1988. Social intentions. In *Proceedings of the 8th European Conference on Artificial Intelligence*, 719–23. London: Pitman.

Werner, E. 1989. Co-operating agents: a unified theory of communication and social structure. In *Distributed Artificial Intelligence*, vol. II, M. Huhns & L. Gasser (eds), 3–36. London: Kaufmann and Pitman.

Werner, E. 1990. What can agents do together? A semantics for reasoning about co-operative ability. In *Proceedings of the 9th European Conference on Artificial Intelligence*, 1–8. London: Pitman.

Wilensky, R. 1983. *Planning and understanding. A computational approach to human reasoning*, Reading, Mass.: Addison-Wesley.

Williams, G. C. 1978. *Adaptation and natural selection*. Princeton, New Jersey: Princeton University Press.

Winograd, T. & F. Flores 1986. *Understanding computers and cognition: a new foundation for design*. Norwood, New Jersey: Ablex.

von Wright, H. G. 1963. *Norm and action*. London: Routledge & Kegan Paul.

Zamparelli, R. 1993. Intentions are plans plus wishes (and more). *Working Notes of* AAAI *Workshop on "Reasoning about mental states: formal theories and applications"*, Stanford University, California.

Zlotkin, G. & J. S. Rosenschein 1991. Negotiation and goal-relaxation. In *Decentralized AI – 2*, Y. Demazeau & J. P. Mueller (eds), 273–86, Amsterdam: Elsevier.

Zlotkin, G. & J. S. Rosenschein in press. One, two, many: coalitions in multi-agent systems. In *Proceedings of the 5th European workshop on modelling autonomous agents in a multi-agent world*, J. P. Mueller, C. Castelfranchi (eds), Berlin: Springer.

Index